No Hard Feelings - A Dancer's Reflections

David Arthur Walters

Published by David Arthur Walters, 2021.

NO HARD FEELINGS - A DANCER'S REFLECTIONS

First edition. December 10, 2021.

ISBN: 979-8230823292

Written by David Arthur Walters.

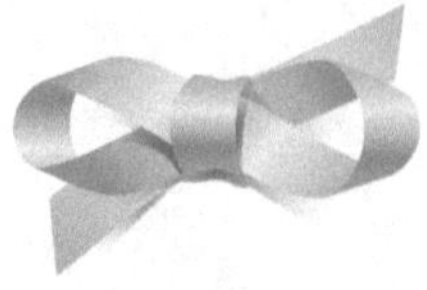

Introduction

I happened to hear an Amazonian author bawling that she had been writing a dozen hours a day for four years, and all she had to show for it was a one-star review and practically nil sales. She had tried her hand at other careers with dismal results. She is facing eviction since the federal coronavirus relief program is coming to an end. What should she do? Prostitution is out of the question at the moment. Should she use her coronavirus handouts from the government to design better book covers and hire someone to do search engine optimizations? Her book might be a bestseller. You can't tell a book by its cover, but the sorriest content goes for a premium nowadays.

What would I do? Since I am a square from the Midwest, I would find the proverbial "night job," or even better, a half-time day job with excellent pay, and when not working I would just write because that is what I do. I am a writer, and a compulsive one at that, so I do not have writers block. My worst critic called me a "writing machine." It did not occur to her that The Machine is actually writing most of the books nowadays.

I tried my hand at dancing, singing and acting, too, and that, without a job reduced me to turning in an alcoholic's beer bottles to buy subway tokens and pay for classes. That saved me from the terrifying suspicion I way dying on the vine and needed to recreate myself as immortal. I was thrown into a state of panic if I missed dance classes for a day. I needed an art to do, and dance is the foundation of the arts, as I explain in this book.

But I did not take up the performing arts as a career. I returned to writing, not as a career, but as an evasion of careers. I had always called myself a writer because I lost myself in books when I was a child in terrifying circumstances. Is that not what the arts are essentially for, the evasion of reality, the highest arts being metaphysical or useless, and is not writing an art? I stopped telling people that I wrote to educate myself and to free people, something I had heard successful authors say. Nonetheless, I have been afraid to confess what I have always known, that I write to avoid "reality," to avoid striving for success as usually defined. The failure to make a profession of art is a prescription for failure if it is defined as such.

When people at the foster home asked me what I was going to be when I grew up, I rebelliously said that I was going to be a "bum." I lied. I would sooner rob a bank or die than be a beggar. I learned thrift when living on the streets as a teenager. Spending money unnecessarily is more painful than excreting a concrete block to me. It was not easy to get off the streets with a sixth-grade education and lie oneself into better and better jobs. Being six-foot tall and an avid reader of Alexander Dumas and Victor Hugo helped a great deal. The goal? To survive reality by transcending it with "ideals."

There came a time, when on the verge of extraordinary wealth considering my background, that I threw my future as a successful winner away in order to become a successful loser living on a pittance for my art—call it cowardice if you will. It is what shrinks call the fear of success as they define it. I took up existentialism, embracing the notion that life is really meaningless in terms of goals except to live as a responsible individual, whatever that might be without an afterlife. I thought and wrote in that vein for several years. I might have been better off taking up Epicureanism, but I could not afford good taste on my savings.

That worked for quite a while as I wrote and wrote as a "self-publisher" for nothing except millions of "reads" and a few hundred reviews, and there was always the knowledge gained, hopefully approaching wisdom. I wrote for Nothing. I mean the kind of nothing that is pregnant with unlimited possibilities.

As I approach The End of my seemingly interminable ramblings, I have a sinking feeling that I have just wasted thirty years of my life for nothing at all except a deep depression or bottomless pit of regret. I am alone, without family or friends nearby, through my devotion to avoiding the common reality of what life is supposed to be all about.

Oh, how glorious was my goal, undefined as it was, so I wind up in a hole in the wall wishing I could go back to the good old days of rejection slips and compliments from editors, and the chance of a front cover if not a bestselling book. But I wanted to become a self-published author, one of the fools who thought we could all be famous without being sorted out by editors, and now we are sorted out by machines, and readers believe in and reinforce the results. Once a writer, always one, and now I am too late, too late for Amazon and pretty book covers and pictures and ranking algorithms. At least that poor Amazonian got a one-star review instead of nothing.

I was more than despondent after composing the anthology of articles included in this little book appertaining to my artistic endeavors. Was it all for nothing? Did I not enjoy the ride? Oh I liked the clicks. And now Amazon will not even tell me how many people "click" on this book unless I pay for advertising, and why should I do that when its Community members are telling me the book cover is terrible and the contents worthless ramblings that the algorithms will not expose to more than a handful of people?

I thought of all those dust covers I used to throw away right after I bought a book that had nary an image within; or maybe I would tear off the flaps about the book and author to paste in the book, using some of the rest as a bookmark. But the best books were the older ones with great contents and titles simply embossed on the hard covers. For example, I have *The Best of Coleridge,* published 1934 by Thomas Nelson and Sons of New York. "This Book Belongs to Lillian L. Rose" claims the pretty sticker inside, bearing the image of 'White Roses' by Vincent van Gogh.

I opened the book at random, and, with my eyes closed, put my finger somewhere on the page, then look to see where it has landed:

"Work without hope draws nectar in a sieve, And hope without an object cannot live."

So there I had it, the famous last two lines of Coleridge's 'Work Without Hope.'

My heart sank.

What did I do?

I walked over to my machine and wrote this Introduction.

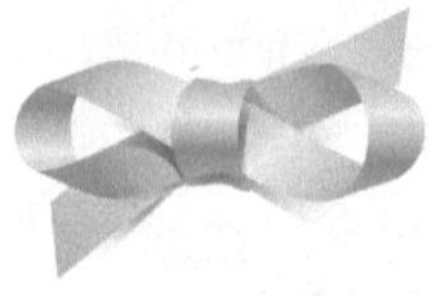

Dance Foundation of the Arts

I thank my lucky stars that I am a so-called dumb dancer, for I can state unequivocally, without presenting an elaborate argument to prove it, that dance is the foundation of all the arts.

It is with that in mind that I say any writer worth reading is a good dancer or at least a frustrated dancer whether he knows it or not. And a good singer is a dancer too, as well as an orator who can move the crowd. Likewise, the sculptor and the painter liberate us by virtue of their dance. As far as I'm concerned, the arts require little deliberation and a lot of practice. I do not mean to say that the good artist is stupid. Rather, I mean too much deliberation obstructs the expressions of the profound, primordial wisdom that inspires the creative arts. We tend to give far too much credit to man-made reason, and not enough to Reason as we find it.

It takes a lot of practice to form the disciplinary vessel required to liberate the flow of meaning. I inspire by this instant practice to let the words flow rather than force them into logical forms. I therefore fervently pray that I am able to get out of the way so that a being much wiser than I may speak through me. Perhaps later, when I find confirmation somewhere or another of what I have said, maybe in a musty old book, I shall have good cause to ponder on how I came to know something before I learned it.

Dancing all day makes for a good night's sleep. Before I fell asleep last night, I was reading Rousseau. He had a practice of modeling his political urgings into very concise forms, which he would then use as a vocabulary for choreographing many lovely combinations. I was dreaming accordingly. It was a simple dance. A very large company was on stage, a company that comprised many small groups performing diverse variations on a grand theme. The dancers within each group had their own unique characteristics. However, the differences between the groups and the individuals within them began to diminish as the dancers approached absolute unison. I could not distinguish one form from another. I felt a great tension, as if an enormous irruption was imminent. I heard an anxious choir singing, "The Union is dangerous, the Union is dangerous, the Union is dangerous!" The chanting somehow dissolved the tension. I arose pleased and refreshed, because the tension was apparently in me, and I felt my questions about the true nature of Rousseau's political philosophy had been danced for me in my dream.

Naturally there is a relation between the arts, and there exists special relations between each and every one of us. My special way of expressing myself might seem peculiar to you, so a little background on my dearest subject might help you to understand my way of becoming. Like so many dancers before me, I went to New York in 1986 shortly after I caught dance fever. I heard someone say that New York is the dance capital of the world, so I quit a very good job and made reservations with an image in mind, a vision that dancers were waiting for me with open arms to welcome me into their loving family.

Two religious acquaintances of mine said I'd fallen into Satan's clutches. A psychologist stated that only mentally disturbed people feel the need to dance, but comforted me with his diagnosis that actors are the most neurotic people of all. Nevertheless, off to the Big Apple I went.

As I learned to dance, I also took up my childhood love, writing, to write dance reviews and to pay for my dance classes with the proceeds. It all made a lot of sense at the time. There I was, the greatest dancer and author the world had yet to know, writing dance reviews as the means to become a so-called dumb dancer. It was a neat fit!

Little did I know that I would wind up being rejected by the critical world, or that I would be sleeping on living room floors and in closets, buying cheap vegetables and fruit with the returns on my alcoholic roommate's empty beer cans, using slugs to beat the subway fare, and eventually wind up homeless with seventeen dollars while my friends back home were almost ready for an early retirement. But I was doing what I loved to do.

And I did meet many wonderful dancers who were also wonderful people. For example, Delilah, with whom I often commiserated over a cold quart of beer and two cheap falafel-on-pita sandwiches: several dancers I knew enjoyed beer and falafel diets in those days. I'll never forget the story she told me, about how she found out she was a "black" girl when she was twelve years old in South America: someone gave her a whitening agent and explained the facts of discrimination to her.

Well, I eventually got tired of poverty. Some of us learn faster than others. It took me awhile to realize that, in order to survive for much longer, I would have to either start chanting Hare Krishna full time or get a day job. I was given an opportunity to write news summaries for a desktop publisher, but I turned it down because it paid next to nothing; it seems everyone is a writer if not an actor in New York, so the competition is very stiff. I stopped writing; an old friend of mine, a psychoanalyst, said not to worry, for most writers are writers just because they are unable to cope with reality.

Well, to make umpteen years quite short here, I got a great job and wound up making per month what the average writer makes in a year. The job was so great that it was also part-time, affording me the opportunity to keep dancing as well, which I did with zeal; I even performed at Lincoln Center. As for writing, I forgot all about it. That is, until I got fed up with Easy Street, quit my dream job, a job that would be the envy of any struggling artist, and took up my pen again.

Yes, I am terrified by the high failure rate of writers, and the chance that I might wind up eating dog food as an old man, or not even that, for dog food is very expensive. Nevertheless, here I go again, for I am still a so-called dumb dancer, and, as far as I am concerned, dance is the foundation of all the arts, so I may succeed at the art of writing if I never stop writing. I am 75 at this writing. I still do dance exercises and improvise routines at Crunch Fitness when I have access to the studio. I suppose I could have been a professional actor, dancer, and singer because I was what people called "talented" so had opportunities despite my late start. But I had no such expectations. I danced for my sanity. That is the foundation.

And then I wrote and wrote, without expectation except to learn something and share it with anyone interested in freedom from what they used to think. I converted Luigi's motto, Never Stop Moving, into a narrow Never Stop Writing. The danger there, besides tendinitis and arthritis from bad posture at the keyboard, is that thinking is a symbolic activity that can withdraw one from the real world of action. Indeed, such preoccupation may be the ultimate flight from reality when reality is not defined as ideal. Obviously there must be a balanced unity of mind and body. After all these years, I cannot help but ask, when reflecting on my activities, "Have I become a coward?" What is it that I am afraid of most of all?

Being pinned down, defined, and that is what commitment to a professional goal can do. I was afraid of success. I was afraid to admit that I am at heart really a ham, would love to be a famous dancer, actor, or singer, and a writer as well. People do call me a writer. In fact, I am pinned down to my computer, and my neck and hands hurt. I should dance otherwise at least three hours a day. When I do, I rejoice, so why do I tend to refrain from that now? Why not let dance be my foundation as a writer? Why not profess writing as my profession?

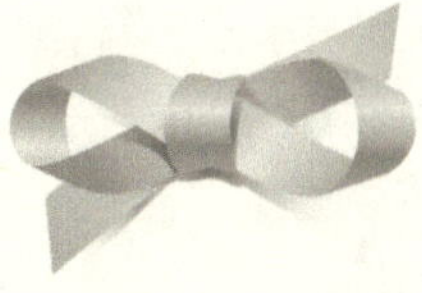

Minerva Bloom My Patron Saint

Minerva Bloom, a poet and author who met her husband, Dr. John Bloom of Ft. Lauderdale, in Guadalajara, passed away in 2018. She was a vivacious champion of artists, and devoted the last eight years of her life to Naval Air Station Ft. Lauderdale Museum. She showed me the possibility of becoming a professional writer instead of a literary slut. I knew her from Internet writing sites at the turn of the century, back when we thought the Internet would free us from established publishers and make us rich and/or famous. One day I received in Honolulu a box of food and clothes from her. Also inside that box were a few copies of a little chapbook entitled *Reflections in the Well,* within which were some articles by namely me, whom I guess she supposed to be a starving artist. Unbeknownst to me, she had taken the articles from the internet, designed and distributed the book personally to local bookstores, and had it also placed in some libraries.

"What? What right did she have to do that?' I asked myself. And then, "What's not to like? After all, I am a literary slut. She is a patroness of the arts, and she saw something in my work."

Bookstores have been selling copies of *Reflections in the Well* through Amazon for years. Maybe her heirs will revive the chapbook for printing. Come to think of it, why not compile my work and put my books up on Amazon where they will be available in one place, at least to my heirs? After all, I am ADA, Almost Dead Already, and Amazon is destined to be around for a very long time.

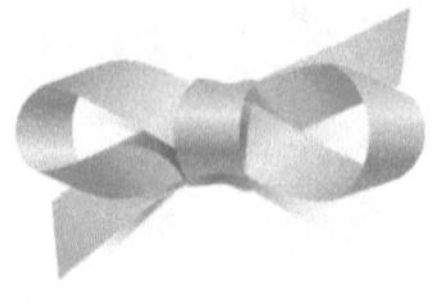

My Teachers

My dance teachers deserve much credit for my salvation from chaos, and it is customary for dancers to provide a pedigree. There were some I loved more than others, but here is the alphabetical order: Janie Brendel, Jill Crosby, Ruth Currier, Madame Darvash, Linda Diamond, Alan Danielson, Luigi Faccuito, Keiko Fujii, Deboral Hay, Amy Horowitz, Betty Jones, Joy Kellman, Elena Kunikova, Joe Lanteri, Evee Lynn, Francis Roach, Jeff Weinberg, and Serge, whose last name I cannot recall.

I am ashamed to say that I had forgotten the names of Serge and Evee Lynn although I remember them very well. A list I kept on a once "free" website along with much of my early writing is being held hostage by a company called Lycos unless I pay a monthly fee.

First of all, there was Serge, a black Haitian teacher of African dance. His father was a voodoo doctor, but he did not follow in those footsteps although he could appear to turn into a panther when he danced. I studied with him in the 80s. His love was a most beautiful, alabaster-white woman who taught and danced Afro-Caribbean dance. She was an excellent dancer in all respects, but I remember her most of all for her *port de bras* and double-jointed wrists. He taught at Joy of Movement on Lafayette where Dennis Wayne had his studio. He supplemented his income painting interiors into the late night hours. I shall never forget how I helped him haul cases of beer into Times Square for a New Year's Eve celebration, and had a great time with him and friends. African is danced for personal feeling, yet it can be performed for audiences, and he had a talent for choreography. He eventually was retained by a European ballet company, I think for Stuttgart Ballet. I find no reference to him on the Internet.

Linda Diamond identified the other dance master whose name I had forgotten, as Evee Lynn.

Evee Lynn

Evee Lynn was much beloved by many students, very strong athletic dancers all. She was from Austria, where she studied dance during the Nazi regime.

"If you didn't behave in your dance class when Hitler was in charge, you would be expelled and your career was over. You could not just run off and take class somewhere else, as is done here."

Madame Lynn gave the most severe, killer-ballet barre in New York. I recall she would not let any of her students drink more than two little sips of water after taking the barre because she was afraid they would faint.

I was fortunate because the open class system allowed me to do my best to try to keep up with them at my old age (for ballet). I tried and tried and did fairly well. Scouts who appeared from time to time took notice of me until my age betrayed me.

"David, you're too late for ballet," she observed one day, but she did not advise me to take the bus home and find something else to do, as I heard Finis Jhung say one day to a girl in the same studio as he stood at the window and motioned to the bus stop, probably doing her a favor at her young age.

Madame Lynn also liked to hit me with one end of the long scarf she always wore, and say, "Boy, how you're going to suffer today." Things like that gave some of us cause to call her, affectionately of course, "Evil Lynn."

I saw her running to catch a bus on Broadway and 79th Street one afternoon. She tripped, fell down and injured her leg. She would not let me take her to the hospital. She continued teaching with the injury, leaning on a crutch, and was permanently crippled when the bones set wrongly.

She had a Germanic protégé who was a rather well known, freelancing *primadonna*. She was also a *primadonna* in a psychological sense; she had a bad habit: if she made a mistake, she would storm off the floor and have a tantrum. She also had a bad habit of soliciting dancers in various classes. You would be doing your *tendus*, feel a little tap on the back, and she would hand you her card and whisper, "Come take my class, you will love it." She taught classes at Carnegie hall; I took two or three of them and she was quite good, but I preferred her Austrian friend, Evee Lynn. As Luigi once said, when he found I was taking classes way out in Brooklyn with one of his students, "Why go there when God is here?"

Now, then, Linda Diamond informed me that Evee Lynn has gone to teach class in the Great Beyond. She apparently died unheralded despite her good efforts on Earth. She is famous for often saying, "You must give and give and then give some more in your life, and then on your deathbed someone will say you did not give enough."

Well, Evee Lynn gave more than enough, more than some students could handle. Those who could suffer with a smile, something she always made us do, proudly list her as one of their teachers.

Oh, several of my teachers were far more famous than her. Google them. For example, beloved Luigi, who asked me, "Why didn't I get a Christmas card from you?" "I did not get one from you." "But David, I am famous!"

Well, Evee Lynn, I am devoting this little chapter to you. Dancers love to gossip. You may yet be famous. We may pick up your bones if they exist and can be found, and parade them down Broadway.

Reflections in the Well

The Author's Reflections on Postmodern Dance Pioneer Deborah Hay with Special Thanks to Minerva Bloom for designing, printing, publishing, and distributing the original little chapbook on foot.

• • ⁂ • •

RETURNING TO THE WELL

• • ⁂ • •

WHERE AND WHEN SHOULD I begin? Here and now shall do quite well. As far as I am concerned, anywhere and anytime is good enough to press ahead with this pressing business called life. Yet from my progress I am always returning to the well for yet another drink that I may proceed.

I would fly free beyond the arc between ashes and ashes and dust and dust, but my flight is rooted in the past. I fly backwards like the mythical Jayhawk. I don't give a damn where I am going and I only care about the where I've been. What else is really mine? What else can I know except the past as I realize it in the future? To that end my life is an essay or trial. I double back on what I have done along the way, pull myself together and carry on. I am constantly rewriting my life, but my life's essay I would never throw away.

The arc of my life is really an ark. The arc is the cradle of dimensional existence. Witness the Earth falling into the Sun, missing the Sun curving away from it. Thus the orbiting Earth falls while it recovers itself. Likewise I would never stop moving. But I know I will slow down soon enough. Long before the Earth stops moving, I shall achieve an absolute state of rest in Nothing, where everything gets done by doing nothing. I shall ride the arc until then and dance upon the globe. I do believe I am going somewhere as I circle back on myself. I am never quite satisfied with my present state when I return to where I once was, hence I dream of returning to the place from whence I returned.

Today I returned to the dustbin of my history, reached into it and pulled out an essay I wrote in 1985, entitled 'Reflections in the Well.' Therein I described Deborah Hay's (1) choral dance workshop at St. Mark's Church in Manhattan and her subsequent performances of 'The Well' and 'Leaving the House.' I knew nothing of Deborah at the time: I did not know that 'Leaving the House' was considered by critics to be a major feminist statement of the day.

Part of my essay was published in 1985 by arts enthusiast and feminist Effie Mihopoulus in her literary magazine, *Salome.* As I examined my manuscript, I felt a twinge of regret that the rest of my essay, my reviews of Deborah's performances, had not been published. Therefore I decided to edit the entire essay. Now I have not altered any of Deborah's statements nor have I made any fundamental changes to my views at that time: I have simply dusted off the work and polished it up a bit.

At first glance the reader might not suppose my subject would be of much interest to the non-dancer. But I believe it is, for I speak of the human spirit, bound by matter to dance on Earth. The dancer is a moving, conscious synthesis of spirit and matter. She needs no other machine or tool than her body to express the tragic joy of her Earth-bound existence, to convey to her audience the essence of humanity's gravity, dimensions and dynamics. For that expressive purpose I believe Modern Dance evolved.

Everyone is essentially a dancer; we can all experience the joy of dance movement. Modern dance pioneers such as Isadora Duncan and Rudolf Laban strove to bring the direct experience of that joy to everyone. Isadora wanted to bring America to its feet; unappreciated at home, she became a dance prophet in Europe. Laban, a native European dance prophet, worked to restore dance to its ancient and rightful place at the center of the community where all can come together to mutually celebrate life. He trained cadre leaders who in turn organized dance movement choirs for community participation. One massive pageant orchestrated by Laban in Germany had over 10,000 participants. But the Nazis did not appreciate the democratic aspect of Laban's dance choirs, wherein each person is autonomous although interdependent. The fascists preferred to march people around aimlessly yet in drilled order, using the elements of carefully choreographed pageantry to mesmerize the marchers into believing they were doing something grand besides being obedient. But Laban's dance choirs celebrated the individual's striving for spiritual harmony with the cosmos and not collective submission to the leadership principle. Goebbels disallowed Laban's choral movement entry (Of Warm Breeze and New Joy) for the 1936 Berlin Olympics. Laban fled to Paris. His work in Germany was thoroughly annihilated by the Nazis, but his ideas gained influence in Britain and America. It is with Laban's aspirations in mind that we may better understand Deborah Hay.

PEERING INTO THE WELL

"Flee then, be free then,
A clay pot bewinged be then,
In your saintly seriousness
Be then like those who weep for joy,
Speeding to the mark that is

But is not.

• • ~ • •

DEBORAH HAY, "THE JUNG of post-modern dance" (*Dance Magazine*), asked me what I thought of her workshop at Manhattan's St. Marks' Church.

"A cup of cold water in the desert," I responded, and returned to the serenity of a grand silence I had forgotten until Deborah had returned me by indirection to the profound source of inexhaustible nourishment. And still, until this very moment as I sit grasping this hard pen in my soft clerical hand, it is difficult to shatter that precious silence with an explanation. It is not that I have nothing at all to say: rather, I would say it all at once and once and for all, say everything that could possibly be said; but, alas, that is impossible.

"I moved from New York City to a commune in Northern Vermont," Deborah explained to us when the workshop began, "and I lived there for eight years. Moving to a small community, I was fresh, naive and frightened. In fact, I am attracted to states of insecurity. For me insecurity is AHA! Without an AHA! Two or three times a week, life is too painful for me. Unless you put yourself into this state of opening, of unknowing, there is no AHA!"

I was deeply moved by her soft-spoken introduction. Her honest words and sincere demeanor gave me cause to believe she had refreshed herself from the same Well I had fearfully abandoned some time ago, the Well referred to in the ancient *I CHING, the Chinese Book of Changes*, translated by Richard Wilhelm:

• • ~ • •

The Well. The town may be changed,
But the well cannot be changed.
It neither decreases nor increases.
They come and go and draw from the well.

If one gets down almost to the water
And the rope does not go all the way,
Or the jug breaks, it brings misfortune."

• • ❧ • •

AS I OPENED MY HEART in recognition and felt myself reflected in Deborah's being, I appreciated once more the value of what I had forsaken, what had now been inexplicably returned to me by fortuitous contingency, coincidentally unmasking my destiny yet again. "Coincidence or God?" Herman Melville once posed the question. A small coincidence can bear the stamp of the universal. I suppose we have all prayed for big things at one time or another. Other than my life, my god does not supply me with big things but rather communicates to me with seemingly insignificant signs, such as the eraser lost by a stranger and found by me just when I needed it, in lieu of the small fortune I had prayed for. I ask my god for the universe and I am given a tiny detail in time and space that simply says "I AM", then the mystical moment vanishes leaving a vague, soon forgotten impression of the divine detail. But every vanishing moment is a divine gift, is it not? I believe existence is a constantly changing changeling. I want the security of being permanent, but my presence here is all motion, I thought as I surveyed Deborah Hay's lithe figure before me. Yet the only thing I can take for granted is in itself Nothing that I know of. So here, once again, I stand again at Hecate's crossroads, at the crisis of being in existence, my heart suddenly thumping with a skip: AHA!

"The only constant is change," Deborah reminded the class, as if she had read my mind. "Our purpose here is to present change fully and visibly, and to create AHA! in dance, taking nothing for granted," she continued. "As a choreographer, I am least interested in choreography as choreography. I am most interested in the performance of movement. Of course, there are some little tricks, some of which I will demonstrated to you."

Aha! Tricks! I was eager to learn a few tricks. My eagerness was due in part to the suggestive emphasis she had placed on the word "performance" when she pronounced it, insinuating something wonderfully exciting and inscrutably sacred underneath its sound. A writhing serpentine shape came to mind, or was it a rope projected and enlivened by her maya? Obviously this subtle mistress of suggestion knew many tricks. I was already losing my objectivity. I felt as if I were leaning over the edge of the Well, peering into the depths, fascinated by my fortune.

CRAWLING INTO THE WELL

WE PROCEEDED WITH OUR warm-up exercise lying flat on our backs in a circle with our feet towards the center. Deborah Hay, our body-spirit guide into hitherto unknown, improvisational regions, began with firm suggestions to "open up" various areas such as the top of the head, the temples, the soles of the feet, the palms of the hands and so on. Her commands were punctuated every once in a while with a liberating "AHA!" Her opening-up suggestions induced physical relaxation without directly ordering it - as policemen and other authority figures know only too well, ordering an uptight person to relax can provoke a violent reaction. Eventually she advised us to pick a moment and to begin moving close to the floor as spontaneously as possible.

"Open your eyes. See change. Let your eyes see change constantly, ceaselessly changing," Deborah intoned, seemingly in harmony with some transcendental power. "Brighten your performance with seeing. Your eyes are excellent indicators of where you are." I saw I was wrapping myself around one of the church pillars as if I were an uninhibited python in paradise. In any event, we never stopped moving. We squirmed and crawled about the floor for a while, eventually sitting up or getting onto our thighs or knees while moving every part of the body still moveable.

"Use each other to recognize change. BE everything you are in your changing," we were instructed. Clueless and without a cue, we stood up, everyone moving, moving, moving, changing, changing, changing....

"Keep yourself free from path, create pathlessness...every cell is awake, open, stimulated...now move the spine...this dance is not your duty...this dance is the perception of the beauty and the perfection of your spine....your goal is single-mindedness.... AHA! Embrace the floor with your feet...feel the sense of vulnerability of a child embracing the floor with its feet...now let your eyes reflect that embrace...let your body follow where your eyes takes you...take your eyes, take your heart with you...now deliberately create changes in direction, be fully there, be there in the change...use your eyes to recognize one another changing....", Deborah incanted.

During this phase I stepped back to observe, listen and take notes for future reference - I fancied I was a writer in those days. And what a sight is was to behold, thirty people wending their way to mysterious destinations, turning and curving, winding and weaving, bending here and there, always changing wholeheartedly as individuals yet bound by the bodies of the other writhing occupants in the thriving community space....

Deborah suddenly interrupted and scolded us, insisting we were not seeing yet, not really SEEING, for she could see we were shielding our eyes as city people tend to do. Instead of shielding ourselves, we were asked to "invite people to see you, invite being seen, open your eyes, show a willingness to be seen. This is one of the tricks," she confided, "finding the balance between seeing and being seen. This is rarely achieved, but we must take this practice seriously, and if we do, we shall arrive at our goal with an AHA!"

The participants recommenced moving, now to the Zulu vocals of 'Manguzutho.' Deborah danced with the group. She was poetry in motion, an African dancer possessed to possess. Fleet-footed with winged feet, she flew about the church; which, despite its modern-dance reputation, had never before bore witness to such a wild liturgy. She encircled the participants with her dynamic charms; each person was in turn visibly energized: each charge was amplified, and all felt the shock of each.

Although I had withdrawn to the perimeter to record the occasion, I became enchanted by Deborah's African sorcery. I was tempted to hurl myself into the discombobulating frenzy. The others could not see what was going on in its entirety as I did from my assumed reportorial perspective. The sight of the incongruities her sympathetic manipulations had aroused in the crew caused me to crack up and cackle in a silly manner that had, nevertheless, as most good jokes have, the import of some profound truth.

That being done, we were in the mood for the lunch break, soon to be followed by some theory and practice to temper our indiscipline. As we enjoyed our drinks and snacks, Deborah casually remarked, "The older I get, the more I return. Returning to the moment, the principle of change, I can acknowledge change, being present in the change." I ruminated on her words as I chewed my buttered roll. The older we are, I opined, the more we return because there is more to return to. That is our pool of experience, I reflected, as I took a sip of water. We note how older people live in the past, I noted, thinking of my old friend Paul, who became so occupied remembering the glory days that he wound up sleeping in a Bowery shelter. We should admonish a young person who dwells on the past too much, I proposed to myself as a terrible memory of my childhood flashed in my mind—especially if the dwelling is negative.

It is impossible to live in the past anyway, I mused, then noticed that the guy at the deli had spread the butter on my roll much too thinly.

The thought of the past, or of a future derived from past information, I went on, occurs in the present and influences my behavior. Wait a minute, I paused: Where did I put my water? What was I thinking? I wondered, after finding the bottle slightly behind me. Oh, yes, I was thinking about thoughts. Maybe thoughts do not really matter unless we are superstitious about them. I swallowed the last of the bread, finished off the water, swept the crumbs into the corner to feed the insects and mice, then was moved to further ponder my personal situation.

I cling to the past by returning to the places I have been, so here I am again in New York hoping for a repetition of the glorious Sixties I ran away from. Back and forth I oscillate in a vicious curve carved by jet flights between Hawaii and New York. That vice can only end virtuously in the present moment, when I am fully aware of the fact that everything is in flux and that, by the time I get to where I am going to recover my past, that place has changed and so have I. Only in the present world before me may I perform fully as a person. Perform: to thoroughly complete. Is not that the joy of living to a happy ending? Then we may not adjudge a man happy until his completion in death, hence the ultimate question is not how to live well but how to die well. As I try to tear myself away from the community I cannot do without and to which I must always return to refresh myself, I may be just another imagined personal mask projected by the social mirror. Still, imagined or real, the show must go on. I must not falter in mid-stage, slump and slink away, hoping I am somehow rendered invisible. I must finish well. I must die well. I must perform fully across the stage, from wing to wing, and plunge into the wings as if I know exactly where I am going. Yes, to die well, that is.....

"O.K., break's over, let's go," Deborah announced to the workshop participants, halting my ponderous reverie—and I was gladdened by her voice, for I had not the slightest idea of where I was going on that old black freight train.

• • ❦ • •

WELL MADE TRICKS

• • ❦ • •

AFTER OUR LUNCH BREAK, Deborah Hay introduced us to a sequence of images taken from her choreography 'Leaving the House', which she was scheduled to present as a solo performance at the Roulette performance space over the weekend. She called the images "fronts for being aware", or "references that assist us in returning to the moment to fully perform conscious movement." She meant by "consciousness" a more contemplative, expansive state of mind than a concentrated, contracted state of mind. She gave us a little demonstration or movement hint of each image as she described it, then we experimented with each dynamic image.

• • ❦ • •

LEAVING THE HOUSE

• • ❦ • •

"DO A SLOW, WELL-PACED run, leaving everything behind you, with a clean slate before you," Deborah instructed, and we tried doing just that. Someone, not understanding what he saw or heard, asked what she meant by a "slow well-paced run." She watched his effort for a moment, then advised, "Not too much down in order to go forward, just find the place where you are always travelling forward." That did the trick for him, and he proceeded with an AHA!

'Leaving the House' had a surrealistic appearance. We did our best to imitate what we had seen, but because of the state of consciousness recommended for the action, the subject imitated was not an entirely objective model. And if the motion itself were imitated without consciousness of the motive, the performance did not come off well. As for running without a memory of the past, and with a clean slate: if everything were completely forgotten, we would be in an infantile state, rendering the act of running impossible; but Deborah's suggestion was helpful to the extent thought and self-awareness did not hamper full expression of the movement. For a moment, however, being the sort of person I am, the idea of a clean slate or Nothing before me provoked me to think rather than act, inasmuch as it brought to mind the silent whistle of that ol' black freight train to nowhere—thinking is my favorite stalling activity. But then we moved onto the next image.

THE WAVE

THE GUIDED IMAGERY of 'The Wave' is that, while running, the runner encounters a big wave breaking his forward motion, to which he reacts with a strong wavering motion in harmony with the wave. Deborah's personal wave was uncannily realistic. I had often tried to abstract 'waving' while living on the North Shore, but I did not have much success, therefore Deborah won my respect. It is difficult for a dancer to successfully represent a wave or any other object with the human body so effectively that an audience will immediately recognize it. Yet when the objective is made known before it is performed, we certainly know which dancer is most faithful to it.

• • ❧ • •

BUBBLING OR REFLECTING BROOK

• • ❧ • •

THE WAVE ENDS IN A bubbling brook. The dancers' feet become that bubbling brook with little side-steps in line and stamping indicative of a shallow brook gurgling over stones on its bed. The body above reflects and magnifies the movement below: arms wave, head rolls, torso twists and so on and so forth.

• • ❧ • •

STILL SUMMER HILL

• • ❧ • •

THE DANCER BECOMES a still summer hill, holding whatever pose she may strike for the expression: each person strikes a different interpretative pose. Again, the observer usually does not know precisely what object is being represented unless he is informed of the performer's intent; then, AHA! However, if the motive of the dancer is strong enough, sometimes the still summer hill is intuitively recognized by the uninformed observer, or by the mind reader.

• • ❧ • •

DISSOLVING

• • ❧ • •

NOW THE STILL SUMMER hill dissolves or melts away. Deborah was asked for tips about how to dissolve. She said the face dissolves before the rest of the body, that dissolving starts with the eyes, and the mouth relaxes and rounds. This continues throughout the body. Taking this as their cue, everyone in the group melted differently, as if they were snowmen of various sizes and shapes under different temperatures. Eventually everyone became a puddle on the floor.

• • ❧ • •

SHORT FAT JUMPS

• • ❧ • •

EACH IN THEIR OWN WAY, the dancers started jerking some part of their bodies off the floor, eventually arising to jump up and down in a squat. Short fat jumps backward and forward. Plop! Plop! Short fat jumps from side to side. Plop! Plop! Short fat jumps around and around. Plop! Plop! Plop! Short fat jumps turning in the air. Plump! Plump! Deborah told us to "feel the weight."

• • ❧ • •

UNIVERSAL/PARTICULAR LOVE

• • ❧ • •

WITHOUT PROMPTING FROM anyone, the dancers wound up their short fat jumps facing the same direction, ready for the next image: Universal Love, a moving image resembling a victorious god or goddess with face lifted to the heavens, one palm lifted up and forward to receive blessings, who, with long, slow strides, leads everyone who cares to follow. Particular love is a contraction of universal love in mid-stride, a moment in the path where the extended palm returns to the body, bringing in universal love to the particular person. As the dancers repeated the movements across the floor, I envisioned dark lines flashing in the background, black neon signs forming two hexagrams from the I CHING. I looked the hexagrams up later:

'Universal Love' evoked the 20th hexagram for me: 'Contemplation' or 'Kuan'. 'Kuan' means both contemplating and being seen as an example. It refers to the deepest inner concentration, between Libation and the Offering, during the sacrificial ceremony: "The ablution has been made," states the I CHING, "but not the offering. Full of trust they look up to him." Richard Wilhelm explains: "If piety is sincere and expressive of real faith, the contemplation of it has a transforming and awe-inspiring effect on those who witness it. Thus also in nature a holy seriousness is to be seen in the fact that natural occurrences are uniformly subject to law. Contemplation of the divine meaning underlying the workings of the universe gives to the man who is called upon to influence others the means of producing like effects."

'Particular Love' evoked the 61st hexagram, 'Inner Truth', or 'Chung Fu.' The humble heart is open to receive truth from outside, while being strong in inner truth. For example, when deciding tough cases, a judge should be free of prejudice and willing to hear the truth given by others, yet at the same time he should remain true to his insight. In this truthing process, we are brought into an interdependent relation with each other, as trustworthy members of the cosmos, thus resolving at once our alienation from the natural world without and the supernatural realm within.

Man's alienation from the cosmos and his self proceeded with self-conscious thinking, the division of thinking subject from its objects, including other thinking subjects. Thus divided, homeless thinkers have yearned to return home again from their homeless state. No doubt 'primitive' people felt at home in the foundation of all the arts, dance, wherein they communed with God and Nature. But the formal development of thinking eventually led to the death of god and nature, aggravating man's homelessness. The industrial-scientific revolution embedded the logical process in machines, and now the information age is gradually rendering many of us rather redundant by means of thinking machines. We are gradually being reduced to the performance of meaningless tasks for the production and consumption of vanities.

The modern dance movement recognized the modern, industrial form of alienation and sought to resolve it by casting off meaningless, impersonal routines. Modern dance made a heroic effort to re-establish the primordial harmony of man the microcosm in community with the cosmic macrocosm. For that redemption he has his human energy. He needs no other tool to apply than his human spirit. He needs no other matter to mold than his own body. Barefooted modern dancers protested ballet's pretty lies about man's Fall, defied ballet's illusory defiance of gravity and grave. In other words, although the modern dancer might be striving for heaven, she dances her heavenly redemption on Earth.

Modern dance recognized that man's recovery is from the fall to nature, and that his destiny here is to fall and recover again and again in living motion. Thus modern dance focused on the moving principle of life above dead forms, just as the Hindu goddess Sakti, in her Kali form, dances on her dead husband, Siva. Modern dance recognized and even emulated the efficient machine of the modern age, yet its dancer turned the wheel and was not crushed beneath it. Most of all, the spirit of modern dance rebelled against perfunctory dance movements which alienated the dancer from the meaning of her performance.

However, modern dance evolved into various technical cults. Before long modern dancers were taking ballet classes and 'doing technique' instead of dancing. But that was contrary to the leading principle of modern dance. Enter post-modern dance pioneers such as Deborah Hay to protest the stultification of dance and the alienation of the dancer. The post-modern dancer seeks unity not in formal choreography but in naturally moving awareness, when mind and body are at home with each other and at home with spirit and matter in cosmic unity. Of course that is nothing new although it is revolutionary and radical in the sense of returning to the roots of dance. There is nothing new under the Sun. All rebels are spoiled by the authorities they rebel against, and in their protest they harken back to a previous protest, ultimately to that first point and instant which is the principle of their line at any position in space and moment in time.

I think if philosophy is to know thyself, then at its best modern dance is the energetic philosophy of being thyself in motion moving through forms in contrast to striking permanent classical poses. But what do I know? In the final analysis: nothing. My philosophy shall always fail pending my end. My particular freedom is my failure to achieve the universal ideal wherein no further movement is warranted. So, again, I think the modern dancer, feeling the fire between the poles, never stops moving between and through all possible forms, which are, as Deborah Hay might say, "fronts for awareness."

Be that as it may, during the enactment of 'Universal Love' and 'Particular Love' by our workshop, each dancer had a different manner of bringing in universal love to herself. Deborah, for example, seemed to deflect or reject Universal Love with her hand before it reached her, hence I longed to see her bring her palm boldly over her heart so the heart she shared so ardently with others could be returned to her. Sometimes she looked drawn and emptied by her giving. Perhaps she was suffering from jet lag and was now in fact exhausted as the workshop drew to a close. Be that as it may, her performance of the dynamic images of love reminded me of how I had turned away from the well a few years prior, my jug broken.

We had completed our experiments. Someone asked a final question about the images:

"Do the images really take us to the place we want to go to? Can we have, in this world, what we imagine? That is, by examining the object, can we obtain it?

"I am not hooked on imagery" Deborah replied. "The process is a very long one. Sometimes the movement itself takes me to the place."

Sadly, our workshop with Deborah Hay at St. Marks Church in Manhattan was drawing to a rapid close. I made sure I had the flyer, announcing her performance for the coming weekend, in my dance bag.

"I appreciate your willingness to play, "Deborah said in closing, "Your willingness to play is visible. It can be seen. But do not forget, always remember that choreography is not to be seen. What is to be seen is performance, the consciousness, the light. What is to be seen is all of the person, not just the dance, not just part of the person, but all of the person. Thank you."

QUESTIONING THE WELL

YES, THE BEATLES WERE certainly right, it is "a long and winding road," I mused as I rode the subway home. As the hours passed, I plunged into reverie to a depth where my thoughts took on a life of their own. Submarine monsters, bearing no resemblance whatsoever to any creature I had seen before, glided in the deep, occasionally illuminated by shafts of light from above, then, AHA! Without bidding from me, certain recognizable features from my past emerged, animated images, long since submerged and embedded in sandy bottoms, were now reincarnated and swept through my mind in a flood of nostalgia.

"The older I get, the more I return," Deborah's recent remark recurred to me as memories from the past long gone proceeded. Now willing to cooperate, I dug into my unpacked suitcase - my home was a temporary space on an old friend's floor - and brought out phonograph records I had been lugging around unplayed for several years; I could not afford to purchase a record player while on my long and winding road. I gazed at the album covers advertising music played by the courtly, mystical gamelan, the lyres of ancient Egypt, and the long flutes of the East. Deborah had broken the cryptic seal, and now, despite my necessary concern with present exigencies, I had become the archaeologist of my own existence.

"Belay the past! Set aside the irrevocable reality of the past in brackets!" I ordered myself and withdrew abruptly from my excavation. This is the present, this is my now, I am what I am here and now, nothing more nor less, hence the past avails me not for it is forever gone and better forgotten lest it interfere with my pressing task.

Still, I could not put Deborah aside. She is an uncanny woman, I conjectured, someone who has sipped the sacred spring from the occluded well by which the dragon sleeps. As time proceeds, her suggestions will take root and grow in those of us who attended her workshop. Unbeknownst to us, her commands shall have enlightening effects above as the subliminal stalks draw sustenance from the mud below.

"I must see her perform at the Roulette this weekend!" I enthusiastically proclaimed to my alter ego, putting my records back in their rightful place under the trousers at the bottom of the beat-up suitcase doubling as my portable bureau. "But take care," I warned myself, "and know whom you really adore. In her you see yourself mirrored, the self you actually love, and, if your self is false, so shall be your love. Hopelessly infatuated romantic do not be, then, for a romantic's great expectations causes him always to fall short of his mark with a broken heart and, in the end, to exclaim, 'Twas not love but mere foolishness!'"

As I traveled along the long and winding subway tracks next Friday evening to the performance space downtown, I wondered if Deborah Hay would realize her visions in public performance or if she would fall short. I determined to approach her work from a more critical, "objective" perspective. That would require the consideration of objects other than my subjective projections onto her personal screen.

Deborah had called her images "fronts for being aware." Aware of what? What is behind the image if the image is just a front? She had also said, "I am not hooked on imagery. It's a long process. Sometimes the movement itself takes me to the place." And what place might that be? An invisible spiritual home? Does she dream the old dancer's dream of reconciliation with the Object in order to BE the subjective within the objective, which is not its image or front but its spirit? Would she be one with the Universe or its Law or Energy by moving through its representative forms? Perhaps her images or fronts for awareness are fetiches. Maybe she makes an image to make a connection with the ultimate Power. Maybe she uses the image as a tool to realize the Supernatural beyond the Natural. Yet the spirit within is always unseen although it might be felt, hence any image without is incompetent to adequately express it. It would seem that, as a postmodern dancer, the images would be inconsequential to her true intent. If any particular order is irrelevant, then choreography is futile.

Well, if the indefinite spirit within cannot be seen as a sight or scene, why bother to perform before an audience? The performance might feel good to the performer, but feelings can be had anywhere. And if whatever is behind the image could be communicated to others by parapsychic means, no performance would be required.

I think postmodern dancers want to break through the traditional images and dispense with the imagination itself in order to spontaneously obtain the concrete realization of ideas; as if ideas were beings divorced from the imagination, with its relative and continuous motion of time through definite spatial boundaries perceived as forms. No matter how much we might object that our "beings" or ideas represent or are the real principle of the natural rather than the contrived supernatural, our intention is still transcendental; that is, we really want to escape. But concrete realization of the supernatural on Earth presents a paradox, for escape velocity is only achieved in death, and, although Nothing exists, Nothing cannot be portrayed or imagined in any shape or form. The danse macabre in itself is futile as a means of communicating the reality of death behind maya's imaginary front.

Well, then, we might as well return to the pretty balletic illusion that gravity does not exist instead of bemoaning gravity and somehow trying to find our existence in the mass or in the grave. Of course modern dance would demonstrate the tragic synthesis of matter and spirit in the human being. Despite our transcendental aspirations, redemption is only had on Earth; with modern dance we can have joy in our complaints and communicate the same in sublime forms appreciable to a broad audience. But what can postmodern dance do in its protest of the modern? Where can postmodern dance go except to eventually return to the very images it protests, to return to the sophistries of classical and modern dance rhetoric in order to coherently communicate its protest?

I think we want to get behind or beyond the imagination by means of ideation, yet we are the prisoners of imagination. Our very ideas are grounded in and arise from the imagination. And I speak not only of the optical imagination, upon which most of us are too dependent, but of the imagination of the blind man as well, whose other senses are sharpened to compensate for what the seeing take for granted.

With those reflections in mind as I hurtle along the winding subterranean rails to witness Deborah Hay's solos at Roulette, I cannot help but think my trip is unwarranted given the postmodernist rejection of objective standards. I might as well be blind to them; someday I will ask a blind man what it is like to attend a dance concert. Will he say the spiritual ambience of the postmodern audience feels better than that of the modern or classical?

I had already seen postmodern dance performed once before. I described Pooh Kaye's choreography in my review 'Punkmodern Object Relations.' Her company's performance had its sensational merits in gut feelings, but its chaotic flip-flopping around was not very handsome or pretty, nor did it communicate anything in particular; rather, it seemed to simulate a hysterical, narcissistic return to the womb. It seemed as if the rebellious dancers, feeling homeless in their alienated individuation, were struggling to leave the house forever, unaware that the process of rebellion was returning them to the house they were rebelling against. Indeed, rebels, like snails, carry that house around on their backs, but they think it is a new house, a house of freedom, when they withdraw into it at another location. But the good they flee to has its origin in the evil avoided. Their attempts to leave the orderly house behind collapses into hysterical antics. Finally, In order to overcome the dread of incest implied by the mission, the individual human is bound to return to the horrible scene of the alienating crime, where he fell into time and space as an individual.

Well, now, it is 1985 and Deborah is about to perform 'Leaving the House' in Manhattan. I recall she said her movement takes her "there" (wherever that might be) more than the image. But again, whoever we might be, are we not prisoners of our images? Is not a man's epitaph an image of his work upon which is inscribed 'He Tried To Break Free.' And do we not as rebels against the traditional wisdom throw off our shells to travel the long and winding road to freedom, and, if we survive the circuitous road, find ourselves embracing the very concepts we rebelled against? Moreover, are we not all snails who have, besides our individual personalities housing our guilt, the same cosmic house on our backs? We would shed our skins, cast off our shells, dispense with the standards and become function itself, but function has it being through forms. Function has an objective, meaning a communicable use, and has no end in itself.

Which forms shall Deborah Hay use and to what end? What sort of solo per-formance or "through to completion" shall she present at the Roulette? That remains to be seen. Some of us might want it to be a "sight" or vision fixed to permanent reality, preferably planned out well in advance to please us with recognizable forms we are safe and sound at home with in a neat, tidy house. Others, more bold, or perhaps more foolish, want no choreography at all and would rather be thrilled by the challenge and homelessness of improvisation; they would view a continuous operation, experience every house as a never-ending house with stuff thrown all over the place to trip over. Indeed, seeing is continuous motion of the eye; nevertheless there exists, relative to the motion, the immovable sight.

Finally! The subway train is pulling into the station. I am climbing the stairs. I shall see.

REFLECTIONS IN THE WELL

THAT WE MAY BETTER understand the gravity of Deborah's performance, we should remember that dance is the foundation of the arts. Despite Cicero's statement that sober Romans did not dance, common sense informs us that life itself is a dance no matter how seriously we take it. No matter how silly dancers might appear to sober sages, life will never stop moving. As we settle into our seats we may rest assured that Deborah Hay is a significant example of a science and art requiring no other tool for discovery and expression than the dancer's original triunal gift of body, mind, and spirit. After all, she is one of the founders of the "radical", "revolutionary" and "explosive" Judson Dance Theatre. Since we heard her say that, the older she gets, the more she returns, we may expect a stunning show this evening as she approaches her radical roots.

Existentialists claim existence is prior to being no matter what the definition of being may be. Therefore we might assume that the return to existence explodes traditional conventions. However that may be, I feel guilty for the past because I believe it could have been different if only I would have taken that other path, but I could not know then what I know now, so things could not have been different then or, alas, for that matter, now.... All I can envision is the past because that is all there is therefore I am revisioning and not changing. My supposed freedom alienates me. I want freedom from freedom, freedom from guilt, freedom from thinking that it could have been otherwise than it was, freedom from my revisioning.... There is always some thing, person or god to blame for the inevitable, but I do not want to give up this freedom that irks me.... Maybe the past could have been different after all, maybe it can be different now.... I shall return to the primitive dance and start all over again.... Where are my explosive plastics?

Cram a woman in a box and she might seem rather small and pathetic until she is atomized and explodes—then all hell breaks loose. Deborah's 'Leaving the House' has been critically acclaimed as a leading feminist statement of her time. I have asked her what that means. Did some man beat the hell out of her in the traditional manner? Did she have to summon all her courage to leave the house that was supposed to be her security but was actually a hell hole? I don't know. In an attempt to dispel the "myth" that we must know something about art to appreciate art, the show bill quotes her as saying:

"When we are confronted with art, we usually think there is something we should know before we see it, but what I am dancing is what you see...whatever you see."

So, Deborah brought us to the Roulette to spin our own answers with the aid of her visual images. Fortunately, she did not leave us with only the visual aids, but with hearing aids as well. The celebrated postmodern composer, Pauline Oliveros, armed with her glistening 120-bass accordion, personally accompanied Deborah, in 'The Well.' And, for 'Leaving the House,' Deborah used Pauline's composition, 'The Wheel of Time', recorded by the Kronos String Quartet, Now Pauline has this to say about her music, which supports the proposition that knowing something about art does in fact aid our appreciation of it:

"As a musician, I am interested in the sensual nature of sound, its power of synchronization, coordination, release and change. Hearing represents the primary sense organ - hearing happens involuntarily. Listening is a voluntary process that through training and experience produces culture. All cultures develop through ways of listening. Deep Listening is listening in every possible way to everything possible to hear no matter what you are doing. Such intense listening includes the sounds of daily life, of nature, or one's own thoughts as well as musical sounds. Deep Listening represents a heightened state of awareness and connects to all that there is. As a composer I make my music through Deep Listening." (Pauline Oliveros, www.deeplistening.org[1])

The Roulette performance space, an apartment converted into a dingy and dirty, poorly lit avant-garde studio, certainly required a heightened state of aesthetic awareness in 1985. But the audience was oblivious to the dust and grime; New Yorkers are inured to dismal scenery; besides, the dreary conditions gave the theatre an air of postmodern authenticity. On second thought, no better house

1. http://www.deeplistening.org/

could have been contrived for 'Leaving the House.' When Deborah entered the crummy lighting, her right side appeared dark, old and lame, and her left side was bright, young and spry, lending her the appearance of a person split between despair and hope. She entered anxiously, seemingly frightened at first, then exhausted, drawn, unbalanced, clumsy, grieved, possessed, quite mad. I recalled what she had said at the workshop the day before the performance:

"What is to be seen is performance, the consciousness, the light. What is to be seen is all of the person, not just the dancer, not just part of the person."

As Deborah staggered around, I was initially disappointed by my high expectations for her, expectations due to my previous admiration for her in her teaching role. Now all eyes were on her, and, true to her word, she made no attempt whatsoever to hide her weaknesses. I suppose I was subconsciously expecting a pretty ballerina to tombe pas de bourree glissade jete into heaven; or an equally lovely but modern Persephone to pull up a narcissus and sublimely descend in a wonderfully choreographed struggle with the underworld lord. Therefore I was saddened and embarrassed by the reality before me.

This is meaningless, I thought, as if the meaning of life must be all peaches and cream and bowls of cherries. She plunges into the abyss of despair and chaos under our noses to fathom Nothing. Still, I felt hope for her redemption welling up in my aggrieved heart. Maybe she will emerge from her grave depression, ecstatic in her dance. Perhaps in dance, in the seemingly illogical, mad unity of life and death, of spirit and matter, she will break the common mold with an uncommon revelation, obliterate the world with creative destruction, and by her portrayal of the essential madness of human life, momentarily resolve the paradox of human existence, so on and so forth. Therefore, whatever she brings back from chaos, I am now ready to receive it, to experience it vicariously, or, in other words, speaking words of wisdom: "Let it be."

AHA! Now that I was open to her revelation, Deborah's candor amazed me. Her performance was marvelous in the Now that I was seeing as she was seeing. Regardless of the physical tension demonstrating the images she calls "fronts for awareness," I perceived she was inwardly open and relaxed. Her expressions communicated something fantastic, but never mind, for the intuitive experience itself was beyond any imaginable fantasy: it was....

Reality?

I don't pretend to know. I can only describe what I saw and felt. The images I had not seen before had a greater effect on me than the ones Deborah had previously demonstrated at the workshop. I was curious. I was both stunned and inexplicably moved. Soon Deborah was crawling across the floor with her face under her body. She uttered something unintelligible to the rational mind but profoundly affective to the heart, a cry of emotive unity: fearful yet defiant; angry but loving; begging while giving, joyous in sorrow, beastly and human. She was a baby. Normally a crying baby is unappreciated at public performances, resulting in the removal of the bawling artist from the scene - provided the parents are civilized - but this baby had our deepest sympathies. I felt like picking her up. Is not that what we all cry for, since our alienating fall into the world, for our mothers and fathers to pick us up and hold us?

Deborah convulsed. Although wracked by contradictory movements, there was still method to her madness, an awesome harmony in her disheveled disorder. What her intention was, if there was any intention, remains a mystery to me. Maybe she set out to emulate chaos, or to somehow deliberately express the inchoate, but I received the impression she was ultimately seized by some higher order superseding her contradictions. Mystified by these proceedings, we paused for an intermission.

I gazed into the amazed faces of the audience during the interlude. The conversations were hesitant and subdued. I saw the dead ancestors in the living faces. We are the dead alive, I thought. I am returning. I am looking behind me now for my future meaning. I see a grave. I would rob it, and...

And it was time for the final performance of the evening: 'The Well.' Pauline Oliveros played her accordion as Deborah danced. The accordion sparkled in the light, its bellows pumping life into the song of the....

What? Music from my past! I was seven-years old when a huge 120-bass Noble accordion was bestowed on me in pursuant to the acculturation movement of the Fifties. Every child was gifted in those days; every gifted child just had to play a musical instrument for their own good. My foster brother Jim got a violin: he hated it with all his heart and soul. But I loved my accordion, heavy though it was. Since there were no accordion teachers in Muskogee, Jim's violin teacher tried to teach me to play the accordion. Fortunately for the discriminating ear, I graduated to an accordion school when I moved to Topeka. I vividly remember dragging my instrument several blocks to that school, occasionally encountering black people marching along the avenue singing "We Shall Overcome." I was in an accordion band. I received Third Prize at the Heart of America Accordion Festival, where I also danced a Strauss waltz. When I took my seat on stage to play my solo, 'Malagueña', I was paralyzed with fear; my teacher loudly whispered the name of the beginning chord from the wings; somehow I got through the performance; to this day I cannot remember a bit of it. Shortly thereafter I played the accordion for the military school dance band - the colonel saddled me with a tuba for the marching band. I continued playing the accordion after military school - I was particularly fond of the kind of classical music Isadora Duncan liked to dance to. But I needed money when I got married, so I hocked my accordion: that was the end of my accordioneering career. I regret I stopped playing. We must never stop dancing our favorite pastimes.

And now Pauline Oliveros is playing her accordion at the Roulette: I am all ears. Her music comprised delicate, simple tones of various durations, gentle discordants here and there, multiple rhythms, even and uneven. It did not distract from the dance but augmented it, or rather it was the golden thread by which Deborah found her way to the Well of Inexhaustible Nourishment. When I saw Deborah enter with a bolt of cloth draped over her head, I remembered the peculiar dream dreamed for me a few nights before, of three women approaching the village well; one of them asked, "What is the difference between a Christian and a Jew?" Another responded, "It is the taste in your mouth," and she began drawing water from the well.

As Pauline spun the fateful musical thread, Deborah, eyes covered by the cloth, paced about calmly. The burial cloth slowly slid off her head. She wrapped it around her torso, a dress of life, and proceeded with her dance. I was being drawn into a trance. I saw an Egyptian priestess, maybe Isis. I heard high-pitched screams, then very low, hollow, round, open groans. That is all I can remember until the end, when she knelt, cupped her hands and drank....

"A cup of cold water in the desert."

• • ☙ • •

NOTES:

• • ☙ • •

(1) *The I Ching*, The Richard Wilhelm Translation, Transl English, Cary F. Baynes, Princeton: University Press, 1972

• • ☙ • •

OFFICIAL WEB SITE BIOGRAPHY of Deborah Hay (*deborahhay.com*[2])

• • ❧ • •

DEBORAH HAY "IS A PHENOMENON capable of expanding and diversifying the language of movement in the most striking and unexpected ways." Dance Australia. Her choreography, from exquisitely meditative solos to the dances she makes for large groups of untrained and trained dancers, explores the nature of experience, perception, and attention in dance.

Born in Brooklyn in 1941, Deborah grew up making annual pilgrimages into Manhattan with her mother, to see the Rockettes at Radio City Music Hall and the New York City Ballet at City Center. She was a founding member of the Judson Dance Theater, one of the most radical and explosive art movements in this century. In 1964 she danced with the Merce Cunningham Dance Company. In 1965 she abandoned all dance training. By 1967 she was choreographing exclusively for untrained dancers thus removing herself from the performing arena.

Hay left New York in 1970 to live in a community in northern Vermont. Her daughter Savannah was born one year later. It was here that she began to follow a rigorous daily movement practice which, to this day, continues to inform her as a student, teacher, and performer. She created a series of Ten Circle Dances, which did not have public performance as a goal. Her book, *Moving through the Universe in Bare Feet*, Swallow Press, 1975, is a collection of these simple dances.

In 1976 she moved to Austin, Texas, and began performing as a solo artist for the first time. Since 1980 she has conducted fifteen annual large group workshops, each lasts four months and culminates in public performances. The group dances become the

2. *https://www.blogger.com/blog/post/edit/5752168/866635134407665129l#*

fabric for her solo performance repertory. Her book Lamb at the Altar: The Story of a Dance, Duke University Press, 1994, documents this unique creative process.

Deborah received a 1983 Guggenheim Fellowship in Choreography and was awarded numerous National Endowment for the Arts Choreography Fellowships. She was awarded the prestigious McKnight National Fellowship from the Minnesota Dance Alliance to conduct an extensive performance residency in 1996 in Minneapolis. She is also the recipient of a 1996 Rockefeller Foundation Bellagio Fellowship in collaboration with the Austin sculptor, TreArenz.

She tours extensively as a solo performer and teacher. Her writings appear in The Drama Review, Contact Quarterly, Movement Research Journal, and the Performing Arts Journal. She was just awarded a National Dance Project Touring Grant from the New England Foundation for the Arts which will help subsidize her tour My Body, The Buddhist, on Tour from January through May 2001, will be available from Wesleyan University Press, Fall 2000.

Since 1980 she has collaborated with composer/musicians Pauline Oliveros, Richard Landry, Terry Riley, Ellen Fullman, with poet/percussionist Bill Jeffers, visual artist Tina Girouard, and TreArenz, and theater directors Saskia Hekt and Johannes Birringer.

No Hard Feelings

I ran away from a hellish home in Kansas to the streets of Chicago two weeks after my thirteenth birthday. I hitched a ride in a stolen car driven by a man on his way to the Windy City, and along the way I heard the radio announcement about the crash in Iowa of the plane carrying the Buddy Holly, Rudy Valee, the Big Bopper, and their pilot, Roger Peterson, on 3 February 1959. It was bitter cold in Chicago. I had no coat. The man gave me fifty cents. I took the elevated train to the Loop. My first love in Chicago was a 17-year-old stripper in Calumet City, hence my love for dance and beer.

Thus began a rather colorful and unusual life on my own, grist for a series of novels if the tales be told as once suggested by my daughter. Long story short, I eventually wound up on the Big Island of Hawaii, regrettably divorced from my beautiful, second wife, from whose bad moods, some of them justifiable, I had run away. I rented a two-bedroom, one loft, two bathroom condo on Keahou Bay. I was standing on my lanai there one day, watching the whales blow by, when it struck me that my life was almost over, that I was wasting what was left of it in Paradise. I panicked, took my personal belongings but for a suitcase of clothes, to the dump, got rid of my Ford and Lincoln Continental, and bailed out of Hawaii with what cash I had left from liquidation of assets held with my former wife.

I flew up to Anchorage to manage a business owned by a friend of mine who had suffered a heart attack. While there in midwinter, I took jazz dance classes with Jill Crosby at the community college. I needed the exercise, and had never liked excise for its own sake. I noticed that I only felt secure when he was dancing, so much so that, whenever I missed a class, I became exceedingly anxious. Therefore, when my management contract came to an end, I decided I would fly to New York City and become a dancer.

So 'No Hard Feelings' is unfinished story about the adventures of a man in his forties, namely me, whom I named Paul Bowman, who, while living a luxurious life on a modest income in a South Pacific paradise, thought his life was being wasted, decided to get rid of his possessions, move to New York City, and, of all occupations, to become a dancer. He has been ridiculed ever since, except by the dance community.

I was about 50 years old when I landed. My savings would run out. I was left standing on the street, homeless, with only $50 to my name.

My comeback was nothing short of amazing, at least according to my friend, Bob, a Freudian psychoanalyst whom I had met at pot parties after running away from Chicago to the Big Apple with $150 on me in the late 60s. I was now making good money working as a part-time controller of a small business. That afforded me with the time and means to dance, sing and act. I was definitely a latecomer, but I was good performer of all three, and might have had some success if I had persisted.

I chose the day job instead of the arts, accepting an offer to manage an offshore enterprise funded by tax-avoiding professionals. The offer included a month's vacation anywhere in the world, pilot's training and access to a small airplane, and association with wealthy people who would appreciate my unusual skills. No doubt I would be a multimillionaire at age 60.

As for the arts, well, they had saved my life, but, considering my past, I could not pass up this opportunity of a lifetime. My personal possessions were on the steamer, my bags were packed, and, out of the clear blue, I received a call from the past, from my father, whom I thought must be dead. I had had no contact with him or other family members for decades.

My bags were packed, but I was not me. I was someone else, on the verge of success. Remembering who I was gave me cause for panic. I turned over my plane tickets to the company that engaged me and I ran away. I had, in effect, murdered myself, and the night after I broke my engagement with the offshore company, I had a terrible dream, of a fire breathing dragon, deep in a cavern, and Paul Bowman was incinerated, leaving me to be, at best, a successful loser. That is not to say that I may not be, as myself, a late bloomer. There is nowhere to run away to now except nothingness.

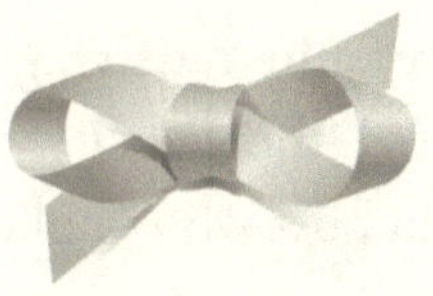

I. Senior

"Why did you send me that stuff? It's not worth a shit! I read the first five articles, and let me tell you, they're a pile of shit! You wasted an hour of my precious time!" vehemently exclaimed John Wilson, Sr., affectionately known as "Senior", from his bar stool at the Peculier Pub in Greenwich Village. There he was known to enthrone himself in the midst of his motley court of companions for hours on end, buying his more attentive subjects round after round of oddly assorted drinks. Of course, Senior preferred to call the shots for his company, which grew in direct proportion to his generosity, and he found comfort in the fact that all who really counted were drinking the same potion at the same time and at his expense.

Senior's candid exclamations on this particular occasion were directed at Paul Bowman, the heretofore relatively unknown aspiring author who had conceived of his premature midlife crisis as a wonderful opportunity to drop everything and journey to the Big Apple with foolishness as his biggest asset, to make his fame and fortune as the greatest author the world will ever or never know. Paul had recently mailed Senior, who happened to be a wealthy industrialist, a few of what he thought were his best articles, hoping that Senior would sponsor him.

Paul Bowman had met Senior and his son, John Wilson, Jr., sometimes derisively referred to as "Junior", a few weeks before at this very pub. It was an establishment frequented by college students and an otherwise fascinating gathering of villagers including a few alcoholic poets who would, from time to time, recite something incoherent and therefore quite satisfying to the inebriated ear. In fact, Paul had discovered the Peculier Pub as the result of a commotion over a certain poet who publicly identified himself, just as several other local poets were wont to do, as "the Greenwich Village Poet."

II. The Greenwich Village Poet

Paul Bowman had noticed a commotion on the other side Bleeker Street, then rushed across it to join a small crowd surrounding the cynosure of its attention. There stood a long-haired, white-bearded man, naked in the winter except for his red socks and green swimming trunks. With an empty cup in his hand and ringing a bell like a Salvation Army Santa Claus, the man was declaiming as follows:

"I am the Greenwich Village poet. Whatever you put in here," he declared, holding up the cup, "you will get back a thousand fold. So step right up, folks, and invest in a thousand happy returns!"

Paul vied with the others to deposit his investment first. His eagerness was in part due to something he and St. Francis had read in the Bible, although he suspected that a thousand-fold return was an exaggerated multiple. Nevertheless, he multiplied it against the quarter he faithfully deposited in the poet's cup,

"Ah, good, very good," said the poet after all deposits had been made. "Gather round me now, my dear children, gather round and take ahold of each other's pinkies and form the mystic magic circle. Go ahead, now, link your pinkies together. Good. I shall now bestow upon you the blessing of the Greenwich Village poet."

As Paul and the others stood around the poet with pinkies reverently linked, Paul did not feel even slightly ridiculous. Quite to the contrary, he was a firm believer in the power of confidence to make even absurd claims come true. His anticipation was so great in this case that he felt his spine tingle and his knees slightly buckle.

"Harken, harken to me," the poet commanded, "be free like me, be free of the dreaded beast who steals the feast! Have no fears for two years, my dearly beloved children, of the most dreadfully dreaded disease, herpes!"

Almost everyone present snickered disdainfully. A few were severely disappointed, having been let down from great expectations, yet they still looked forward to the thousand-fold return. The chaste felt cheated. And Paul felt like having a beer to take the edge off. After the crowd broke up, he observed the poet don an overcoat and slippers he had retrieved from a trash bin down the street. Paul followed him for a few blocks and, when the poet slipped into the Peculier Pub, Paul saw that as a sign of the right place to slake his own thirst. After a suitable pause, he went in behind the poet. And there he met by fateful coincidence, Senior and his good son Junior.

III. Paul's Brass Balls

The Peculier Pub is famous for its hundreds of brands of beer. When Paul Bowman entered the pub, there sat Senior and Junior guzzling Weissebier, frequently chased with shots of Sambuci, for which Kamikazes were soon substituted. Senior immediately befriended Paul, to the drunken extent that Paul counted his lucky stars the next painful day for getting home to Brooklyn alive in a cab that seemed to be careening like a toboggan on wheels, spiraling around an endless section of sewer pipe to nowhere.

When Paul met Senior, who was obviously a wealthy man, he had a weird hunch that he had encountered by chance or by the deliberate machinations of Providence the patron and mentor who would recognize his talents and skills, who would see him as the national treasure he was, and who would free him to work in the most artistic of fashions. Paul had that same feeling he sometimes had when he heard the right song playing just before he turned on a radio.

"Tell me about yourself, "Senior ordered, "Where do you come from and what do you do?"

"I'm from a small town out West. I was a business executive there, but quit my job and came to New York to write and to dance. I've been writing to amuse myself for a long time, but I've just begun to dance and I really like it."

"Hey, I like you. You've got brass balls! Say, meet my son, here. He's an award-winning film maker," Senior stated matter-of-factly, then tossed back another shot. Junior had been staring at his beer glass; he looked up with a countenance that said, "Here we go again, Dad's hooked another one," and offered Paul a limp hand to shake.

"Like I said, you've got brass balls to come here out of the blue like that. Well, at least you came to the right place. What are you working on now?" Senior asked.

"I've just completed a series of articles about dance in New York City."

"Where is your work? I want to see it now," Senior leaned over and leered at Paul. "You give it to me and I'll tell you what, if I like it I'll back you up."

"I don't have a copies with me," Paul said, as if that were the end of it. He felt like he was on the verge of winning a jackpot, yet he did not want to blow it by seeming too eager. But he had no reason for reticence. "Look, look here, look, uh, what did you say your name was?" Senior was well into his cups by now, his head lolling about, but he managed to stay in command.

"Paul. Paul Bowman."

"Look here, Paul Bowman," Senior ordered, now staring at Paul's face, "if your stuff is as good as you seem to be, I'm going to back you up. Understand?"

"Yes," Paul felt his heart thumping at the prospects.

"You send your stuff to John Wilson, Senior, Pittsburgh, Pennsylvania, zip code, zip code, oh what the hell, just send it along to me. Everybody knows me."

"What street is that?"

"Never mind that. Here, better yet, I'll be at this steel company when I get back from Nashville," Senior declared, handing Paul a card he had extracted from his jacket pocket. "You just send it there, and send my boy a copy too. Son, give, uh, Paul here your address. My boy's an art critic you know, and if he says your stuff is good, you're in like flint. Say, where do you live?"

"Brooklyn."

"Brooklyn!" shouted Senior incredulously. "What in hell's name are you doing there?"

"A lot of talent has come from Brooklyn," Paul offered defensively.

"Yeah, sure, FROM Brooklyn. All bad roads lead TO Brooklyn, or to New Jersey. You're an oddball with brass balls and, I tell you, you should be living in the Village. I'll tell you what, you ready for another beer?"

"Sure."

"Give the man a beer, and shots all around here." Senior ordered again. "What was I saying? Yes, whether I like your stuff or not, and don't you send me any shit, if you want to live in the Village, I'll put you up in the Village. That's the least I can do."

Paul's heart joyfully skipped a beat at Senior's offer, for he had been hoping that by some stroke of good fortune in the throes of his poverty that he would be removed to the Village for good. That is where he took his dance classes for several hours each day, and where he was making so many warm-hearted friends like Senior.

Yes, Paul mused over his seventh beer, Yes, while living in the Village, I will write and dance with my head and my feet in harmony, my spirit unhampered by dismal rides to the transit system's worst stop, a nauseating cavern where unprepossessing vagrants slumber in the reeking scent of urine at one foot of the fabulous Village.

To live in the Village had been Paul's fondest dream ever since he read stories in his youth about the famous writers there, the jazz, the Communists, the Beatniks, and all the rest that lives and has its being in such exotic places. But the monthly rent for an apartment there exceeded his entire budget for six months. As far as Paul knew, at the end of that budget stood, if he failed, penniless poverty on the Bowery, or chanting Hare Krishna in the park, or a leap off the Brooklyn Bridge—he had ruled out the Empire State Building on the grounds someone else might get hurt.

"But he's drunk," Paul said to himself sometime later, after he had bade Senior farewell and hailed a cab to Brooklyn, having decided to splurge on cab fare given his high hopes and besotted spirits. "I know better than to believe in bar talk anyway. I'm no kid!"

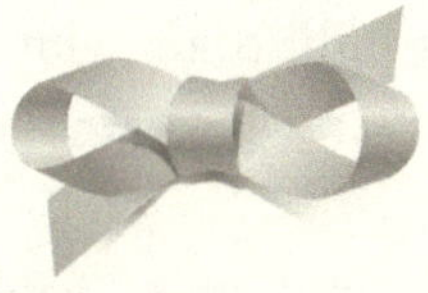

IV. Paul Goes Postal

Paul Bowman is the sort of person who honors his word regardless of when and where given. In this case, the night before, in a drunken stupor at the Peculier Pub in Greenwich Village. Despite his sober reservations about Senior's drunken offer to read his manuscripts and to sponsor him if he liked what he had read, Paul, suffering from a fierce hangover, dutifully walked over to the post office the next morning with his manuscripts sealed in an envelope neatly addressed to Senior at his Pittsburgh steel company. While standing in line to buy stamps, Paul uneasily reflected on the conversation he'd had at the pub with Senior's son, Junior, after Senior had headed toward the restroom - it was difficult to carry on an extended conversation with anyone except Senior when Senior was around buying rounds, as he tended to dominate all conversations at once.

While Senior was relieving himself outside of earshot, Junior had introduced himself to Paul. Junior seemed to be an intelligent, sensitive young man. Paul had already gotten the impression that he was a browbeaten son, one who knows better than to interrupt or to disagree with his father over matters of peripheral interest. Junior told Paul that he was a graduate student and was working as a psychiatric orderly at Bellevue. Paul then wondered how Junior's father could be as rich and powerful as he appeared to be with his expensive suits and jewelry and wallet stuffed with hundred-dollar bills and gold and platinum credit cards. Junior said his father was a self-made man who did not get much of a formal education but had still managed to pull himself up by his bootstraps and become a powerful Pennsylvania industrialist. Junior said his father didn't care for fancy talk at all, then wondered out loud whether he would appreciate Paul's writings.

"Well, he might like my style," Paul responded. "I got my education in the school of hard knocks, in the tradition of America's greatest writers. And I think most people will love my work if they get a chance to read it. The articles I'm sending along to your father are about dance performances...."

"Dance performances? That doesn't sound like hard knocks," Junior remarked.\"It can be a tough life, you know - poverty, hard work, smoking and drinking too - not as rude as the circus life, though. Anyway, I wrote the articles from the perspective of a member of the audience rather than that of a professional critic. I think your dad will understand the reviews whether he likes dance or not."

"Well," Junior grinned with anticipation, "I can just see the expression on dad's face now. Okay, then, I suppose your dance audience will like your articles because you don't try to dictate taste to them like an expert, you just aim to please, right?"

"No, I don't cater to the audience either. I believe they'll like me even more for that."

"Whatever for?" asked Junior with raised eyebrows, "Because New Yorkers like abuse?"

"Because I'm not one of those unscrupulous writers who orient themselves to the whims of the public."

"Right, Screw the audience! Who needs 'em anyway?" Junior exclaimed after downing a shot of Sambucci.

"The public quickly tires of hacks who write to please and who therefore become deadly bores," Paul continued, momentarily encouraged by Junior's enthusiasm. "There is nothing more uninspiring than someone who caters to the public. I refuse to compliment the public with its own thinking. I would.... "

"Who cares what other people thinks?" Junior licked his liquor-sweetened lips and guffawed.

"I would rather die of starvation in a garret," Paul sincerely declared, "or jump to my death from its only window than to worry about what other people think. I must honestly record my own experiences and consult only with my muse."

"How amusing."

"I must say whatever comes mind, regardless of whether or not someone might be offended by what or how I think. After all, who cares..."

"Nobody," Junior interrupted Paul's fervent declaration of independence, reaching for his beer mug.

"Huh?"

"I said nobody cares. You'll never become a five-star writer with that approach, pal, I mean, Paul. You'll rub too many people the wrong way."

"Look, Junior, sorry, what can I call..."

"That's fine, call me Junior."

"OK, then, no problem. If everyone found me agreeable and agreed with me, I'm sure the world would be in big trouble." Paul was hurt by the retort but did not want Junior to know it.

"Why? Would you take over the police and the military?" Junior jested, and wiped the beer foam off his lips with his sleeve.

"Maybe, if I could do no wrong. But I can do wrong, yes I can. I seldom agree with myself on the subjects I write about, and to push a particular point of view would make a liar out of me. I am not pleased with any work of mine until I have contradicted myself several times. Anything of importance has three or more sides, and running around a polygon is not pleasant work for opinionated people, so I'm bound to upset them."

I thought you said people would love your shhh, uh, work." Junior had grown impatient - he looked around for Senior, who had stopped to chat with someone at a table on his way back to the bar.

"Sure they will, but some people will read it because they love to hate it. As long as they look at it and have a strong opinion, that's good enough for me. As for being a five-star or a ten-star writer. No matter how many stars there are in the rating system, I'll be content with two stars as long as I am true to myself."

"Like you said, maybe dad might go for your stuff," Junior offered wanly. "As for me, I'm looking to make another film soon."

"A documentary?"

"No. I've thought about doing another documentary, but art films are my thing."

"Cool. I recall something on cable the other night, an art film showing flies buzzing around cow paddies."

"Did you see that? That was mine!"

"Get out of here! No kidding?"

"No kidding!"

"It was excellent, I was really impressed. Say, how would you like to do an artistic documentary about Legs Ballone, the choreographer I told your father about?"

"Sounds good, but without any legs, the guy's name should be 'Legless.'" "He can still dance. Dance is the mother of all arts, you know, the most sacred of arts...."

Paul's recollection of his conversation with Junior was suddenly interrupted by the shouts of a frustrated New Yorker from the corner of the post office: "I've had it up to here with you nitwits!" a disheveled man barked out for the whole world to hear, as New Yorkers are sometimes wont to do. "You sent me over here for stamps, but there are no stamps! No money returned! Paleeeze, somebody get off their rear and come over here and fill up the damned machines!"

Paul had by then worked himself up to sixth in a line of nearly fifty people in a city where the most important thing in the world is one's place in line. The postal clerk at the head of the line next to Paul's line was saying to a customer, mincing his words with pent-up fury, "There's no stamps at this window. Please read the sign. It says, 'No stamps.' That means there are no stamps at this window. Please read the sign. You can get in the line over there or get stamps from the machines." Now the clerk servicing Paul's line was chewing gum and was conversing with yet another clerk who was sitting behind her almost out of sight, eating a candy bar. From what Paul could glean, they were talking about their union newsletter and their kids. Meanwhile, the irate customer at the stamp machine, one of several who had been turned away from the stampless window and directed to the stamp machine, continued with his tantrum - nobody paid him any mind. An elderly woman, supported by her walker, entered the post office and stopped directly in front of the enraged man, thinking he was speaking to her.

"What? What?" the woman, hard of hearing, asked

"There's no stamps and no change, lady, so you might as well go home!" he bellowed, turned and ran out the door. The lady slowly navigated a U-turn with her walker and followed him out. Paul was struck by the ludicrous situation and laughed. Now, third in line, he returned to his recollection and his hopes of having his literary dreams financed by John Wilson, Senior, Pittsburgh steel tycoon, as improbable as that eventuality might seem to any reader in his right mind.

V. Droppings from Heaven

There is nothing like having your face rubbed in your own waste when you are the greatest writer the world will ever know, especially when you believe your droppings are from heaven. And having your illustrious face so distastefully smeared by the very Pittsburgh industrialist you expected to be your patron can only compound your dismay. Therefore we can imagine how Paul Bowman felt that night at the Peculiar Pub, after Senior, who was four sheets to the wind as usual, told him over and over and over again that the articles Paul had sent him were "shit."

\While that was hitting the fan, Paul felt like punching Senior in the face, but he did not do so for several good reasons. One, he was built like a brick shit-house. He was one of those self-made men who comes down out of his office from time to time to show everyone he can still do the grunt work in his plant, such as loading steel bars onto railroad cars. Two, besides his bulging muscles, Senior was surrounded that night by his usual sycophants at the bar, and they would take none too kindly to their patron being punched in the nose. Three, Senior was not only loaded with booze, he was otherwise fully loaded with what most poor people want; and the prospect, no matter how dim, of getting a substantial stipend to support his artistic endeavors, kept Paul too submissive to throw punches at Senior or to even hurl a few obscenities. Four, although Paul was no fool, as we can see from the first three reasons, he also happened to be a so-called dumb dancer: dancers seldom pull punches, although many have been heard cursing themselves for bad performances.

Paul was not a moron, yet, if someone told him that his back yard was a field of diamonds, he would tour the world impoverished without a map or shovel, seeking hidden treasure, wondering all the while what the secret meaning of the message back home had been. Even when he recognized the obvious value of something in front of his face, he pursued something else, something second-rate, or rather obscure, as if he were afraid of fame and fortune. Unfortunately, despite their graceful antics, very few dumb dancers like Paul wind up with either fame or fortune. More than a few have retired to Jersey City where they can be found in dingy apartments littered with photo albums and dog-eared scrapbooks.

After Senior's castigations at the pub, to which Paul submitted like a willing flagellant, Paul did get a glimpse of the secrets of success, not through the cigarette and cigar smoke, but through the pangs of his hurt feelings. After dampening his disappointment with the shot of tequila Senior had bought him earlier, Paul mused, "Senior is obviously an aggressive man of the world who makes no bones about letting people know what he wants and then taking it. I should be more like him, then I would have the means to do what I want to do." But that thought was fleeting: it scurried away, not to recur to Paul during the next fifteen years of dancing around what's best for Number One.\Yes, Paul was weak in the asking and taking departments. He had helped other people get millions, but he had served himself rather poorly, taking only a little cut for himself. Because of his small interest in possessing things, the distance between him and destitution grew narrower as the years dwindled. Ironically, his greatest fear of all was of winding up on a park bench. Confounded, he often wondered why such a common source of distress as the fear of poverty was not the major concern of all mental-health experts. He simply could not get his wits about him long enough to realize that it was in fact their main concern, and that that is why experts make good money.

Paul had always been a dumb dancer, metaphorically speaking - mind you, not all dancers are dumb; besides, he had not always been a dancer. In fact, he fancied himself as a writer. But after many years of rejection - about a year before he met Senior and his crowd in Manhattan's West Village - he figured writing was futile, so he went north to Alaska to make his fortune or to drink and smoke himself to death, whichever might come first.

Paul came down with cabin fever one frigid night in Alaska. His neighbor Harry, a biker from California, had succumbed to it the day before: Harry shot up his own apartment, then wrapped himself around his TV - the cops had a terrible time prying him loose and getting the straight jacket on him.

As for Paul, he was saved by Madonna: he was washing dishes that night when he realized he was a dying man going nowhere, a man destined to cheat himself out of his dreams. He saw a knife in the sink and was about to slash his wrists then and there, when he heard Madonna singing *Borderline* on the radio - little did he know he was to be in the same studio with her in New York a year later. Paul started dancing with his dishrag. The sight was not too pretty, as he had had no training; however, feeling incredibly beautiful instead of alienated and depressed, he was hooked on dance. When Madonna stopped singing, he sat down breathless and thought: "Success is a real bitch! To hell with goals. I must dance! That's IT! I must dance! "

Paul enrolled in Madame Crosby's jazz dance class the very next day. He privately wept when he squeezed on his first pair of dance shoes, and not because they were two sizes too small. But he did not give up writing altogether, at least not yet. He thought he could kill two birds with one stone by writing about dance. And that is why we find him stewing sullenly in his juices at the Peculiar Pub in Greenwich Village, stunned by Senior's criticism to the effect that his writing was a pile of "shit" because it was on the subject of Paul's love and salvation, Dance.

Borderline feels like I'm going to lose my mind. You just keep on pushing my love over the borderline.

VI. I'm No Critic!

Paul Bowman, the greatest author the world will ever know, awoke at eleven o'clock Saturday morning in Flatbush in a pessimistic mood, thinking he might be the greatest author the world will <u>never</u> know instead of the greatest author the world would <u>ever</u> know. He had been able to sleep in late because his roommate, Billy O'Malley, who was usually up drinking rum and cokes by eleven on Saturdays before heading to the pub, was still in the hospital.\The bathroom ceiling had collapsed on Billy while he was sitting on the toilet late Thursday evening. Alarmed by the extraordinary rumbling and groaning, Paul rushed into the bathroom, found Billy bleeding in the rubble, and called an ambulance. Billy, eyes glazed but still conscious, did not know what had hit him; he still had his usual "I Love New York No Matter What Happens" attitude; he did his best under the circumstances to calm Paul down with a barely audible "No problem, Paul, I'm fine, just call 911." You see, when Billy was twelve years of age, the doctors told him he would not live to see twenty, so he had been living it up now, until his fortieth year - a mere concussion was not going to depress Billy O'Malley, no way!

Sleeping in was not much of a luxury for Paul on this particular Saturday morning; in fact, his sleep had been exceedingly anxious. He was not worried about his roommate's injuries, for Billy was being well taken care of: Carla Williams, a working girl from the Bronx, Billy's true love for over twenty years, had taken time off to watch over him at the hospital - her apprentice, Jasmine, was covering for her, taking care of her regular clients. No, what had turned Paul's rest into silent turmoil was John Wilson Senior's repeated references the night before to Paul's writings about dance as "shit", and to dancers as "a bunch of pansies prancing around in tights, peons nobody is really interested in."

Senior's initial offer to sponsor Paul if he liked his writing had thus turned into a nightmare. Paul had decided he must be his own man, so to hell with Senior, he told himself; no matter how filthy rich the Pittsburgh industrialist might be, a jerk is a jerk. Still, Paul had a sneaking suspicion that Senior might be right. Paul had tossed and turned all night long, Senior's parting remarks at the Peculier Pub rolling around and around in his groggy head. Senior had poked him in the ribs at the bar, and confided:

"Look here, buddy, I don't mean to hurt your feelings, but I said to my son, after reading your shit, 'Junior, don't talk to that guy again. He's crazy, wasting his talent on dance like that.' That's what I told him, but look here (Senior demanded Paul's undivided attention, staring bleary-eyed into Paul's eyes, moistened by his hurt feelings), so you like to dance. But you're a talented writer. I could see that when you mentioned the hamburgers and hotdogs in one of your articles, and when you got mad at something a critic said..."

"I'm no damned critic, I hate those prejudiced bastards!" Paul interjected - Paul was normally mild-mannered when he wanted something, but he could not tolerate being called a critic.

"Now you're talking, son! But you write like a critic."

"I'm not a critic!"

"Hey, relax, son, let me tell you something." Senior's face was now six inches from Paul's). "You can put stuff together, and I could see some style coming through." Paul leaned away from Senior, disgusted by the smell of garlic combined with the scent of Sambuci and beer, mentally noting how drunks repeatedly push points. "But that stuff you sent me was shit! I'm telling you here and now, forget dance! Write! Don't mix dancing and writing! Just write, son, just write!"

With that memory churning his mind Saturday morning, Paul wrenched himself out of his Brooklyn bed of discontent, took a leak, staggered into the kitchen, and gazed into the icebox. There was nothing within but a quarter of butter, a half-empty litre and four full litres of Diet Coke Billy used to mix with the three or four fifths of rum he loved to drink on weekends. Funny, Paul thought, nobody would know of Billy's love of intoxicants during the week. Billy arose unfailingly at six on Monday mornings, apparently without a hangover, and did not touch another drop of booze until the next Thursday evening at McGowan's - even after that abstinence it took eight rum and Cokes to prime his pump for another fun weekend in the Big Apple. Sometimes another kind of coke kept him running in high gear, and he was known to have acid in his batteries for special occasions. Paul took the butter out of the icebox, made himself four slices of buttered toast, and downed some coffee. The coffee, along with Senior's command, "Write!" motivated him to start writing. But Paul was a slow learner: despite Senior's good advice not to mix dancing and writing, he started writing about dance. Nevertheless, he did strive to put some meat and anger into his effort. He seized his pen and scrawled out a heading on his college-ruled notebook paper:

I'm No Critic!

VII. Tubby Bias & Kurt Jooss' Green Table

Now, then, Paul Bowman, either the greatest writer the world will ever or never know, sat at the kitchen table in Flatbush and furious wrote the following:

"The stupidity of professional dance critics is nauseating. Take that ravenous bird-brain, Tubby Bias of *Dance World.* She was the first one to belly up to the buffet table at the reception following the Oakland Ballet presentation of Kurt Jooss' *The Green Table',* an anti-war danse macabre about the universal death and destruction provoked by greedy gentlemen who cannot agree. The Nazis did not take kindly to his choreography: he and his company escaped 18 hours before they were to be sent to a concentration camp.

"Tubby was gorging herself on baloney," Paul scribbled on. "I approached her, thinking I should get to know a few professional critics who would, because of my love of dance, I supposed, welcome me into their inner circle as their natural ally. To start a conversation, I thought I would ask her if she believed dance criticism served to improve the quality of choreography and dancing.

"She was chewing on her sandwich, and before I could ask my question, she blurted out with a mouth full of bread and cold cuts, "Bad ballet makes me awfully hungry."

"But it was modern dance," I observed.

"No, it was bad ballet," she insisted.

"I was shocked at her bad taste as she continued, a complete stranger to me, with crumbs falling from her mouth, to bad-mouth not only the 'ballet', which, as a professional critic, she had viewed for nothing, but the free food she was chewing as well. He calmly retorted that, at least in his opinion, *The Green Table* was primarily modern dance, although some of the logic and discipline of ballet was apparent in the choreography.

"As you know," I said, "Kurt Jooss was a pioneer of the synthesis of ballet and modern dance. He radically reformed ballet's dogmatic posturing and rid it the supernatural illusion that gravity does not exist, bringing dance down to Earth where man actually exists in his essential human predicament, his dance unto death. Kurt Jooss sought economy of expression," I continued pedantically as Tubby Bias piled three cheeses on her paper plate, "to rid ballet of its archaic ornaments and to invigorate it with the dynamic principles of modern dance."

"Are you a critic?"

"No, I'm not!" I exclaimed, then caught myself, and softly reiterated, "No, ma'am, I'm not a critic, just a dance lover."

"Modern? Egad!' Tubby Bias exclaimed incredulously, then said imperiously, "*that's* not *modern* dance!'"

“How arrogant this hussy is," I had said to myself as Tubby heaped mayonnaise onto her second sandwich. “I was trying to impress her with my knowledge of her favorite subject, hoping she would accept me, and she wants to pick bones and split hairs wit. Not modern dance? Jooss is known in Germany as the father of modern dance! Modernity is not a complete divorce from the past, the ancient ballet, for crying out loud, but she won't admit the modern. She's been gorging herself on perfect *passes* too long. She doesn't want to dance! She wants to do technique! Maybe she'd better learn to chew with her mouth closed..."

Paul was ramping up to one of his outrageous, extenuated rants, which inevitably wound up in the trash basket, and he knew it, hence he pulled himself up short and took time to pour himself another cup of coffee, thinking he had better change the subject for the time being, come back later, edit and conclude his criticism of Tubby Bias in politer vein. That being decided, he put down his coffee mug and scrawled on about another critic, but in the same bad temper.

"And take that frilly-mouthed Banana Kissoff of *The Monotonous Times*. She had the gall to call the artistic devices used by Valery Panov in his interpretation of Chekov's *Three Sisters* corny. Yes, she said 'corny.' What a fool!

"There is nothing more outrageous to Kissoffs ill-humored, critical ilk than a ballet performance exalting the audience instead of putting it to sleep. So she calls the ballet "a can of corn" because everyone else likes it. Well, there is nothing cornier to a cynical New York critic than romance!

"Banana Kissoff really thinks she knows something about dance. I'll bet she did a few *pirouettes* herself before falling flat on her face, then took up imitating the hackneyed phrases of the critical magpies because of her own technical shortcomings. Can of corn, indeed! Her hypocrisy is revealed by her corny style. She really loves the mechanics of dance, the machine. Why, she's a card-carrying member of the Balanchine cult. Fine, Balanchine was great but he's gone. We love his museum, but not the cult's maudlin mausoleum. We have Panov now. He's from the same school as Balanchine, and Panov is alive. Yet Ms. Kissoff wants a legend. How preposterous! I certainly am glad I am not a critic!

"And how about Hack Neanderson, also of *The Monotonous Times?* He called Panov's macho manner of manhandling willing women - in the *pas de deux* during *War and Peace* - "vulgar' and 'hammy." Hack has obviously never felt the brutally desperate will that drives us to perpetuate our species in the face of death, an urge tempered of course by the conventional niceties of peaceful love.... The only things Hack has the nerve to appreciate are bare conventions, dance phrases like *tombee pas de bourree glissade jete*.

"When Panov passionately, violently renders the ballet vocabulary invisible, Hack is arrogant and supercilious. He does not like Panov, the romantic *refusnik* who would not comply with Soviet reasoning, who got out of Russia with his glorious wife Galina, whose partner on the Brooklyn stage she now trusts to swing her head within an inch of bashing her brains out on the stage. To compound his absurd hypocrisy, Hack says he likes narrative ballets with a story line, but when he sees an excellent romantic ballet he bad-mouths it, like his fellow-critic Banana Kissoff, and why? Because the audience loved it.

"Where the hell do these critics get off?" Paul rapidly penned the question on the next page, winding himself up to launch a most bitter and venomous tirade against the critical race at large. But suddenly his conscience halted his writing hand."

This is no way to behave, he observed as he eyed his furious scribbling. Maybe Senior was right about critics, he reconsidered, and maybe the greatest writer the world will ever or never know, namely me, wants to be a critic, and is now venting his jealous rage over the competition. A good man does not harbor resentment against the competition.

"Successful people who do resent competition usually have the good sense to praise it or at least to keep their hostility to themselves," he said out loud picked up the several pages of his rough draft, tore them into shreds, and tossed the morning's production into the waste can. Having unburdened himself and cleared his conscience, he felt quite relieved. Then he remembered how the bathroom ceiling had collapsed on Billy while Billy was taking a dump, and decided to visit him in the hospital after all.

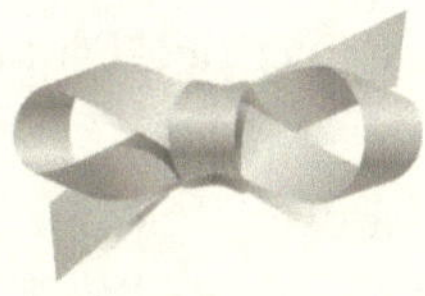

VIII. Something to Write About

Paul Bowman, the greatest aspiring author the world will ever or never know, recalled how he had mailed his articles to Senior, the wealthy Pittsburg industrialist who said he would sponsor Paul if he liked his work. Senior had told Paul to meet him in two weeks back at the Peculiar Pub in Greenwich Village where Senior regularly held court with his son Junior and his motley court of drunkards. So Paul entered the pub with a fluttering heart to receive Senior's verdict. Sure enough, there sat Senior, and, as luck would have it, there was an empty stool next to him upon which Paul sat down. Senior noticed him immediately, turning to greet him with beer stein in hand.

"That stuff you sent isn't worth a shit! It's nothing but shit!" Senior exclaimed to a stunned Paul. "I'm being honest, pal, it's nothing but shit! Tell me, who would produce or publish such shit?"

Paul wiped the flecks of Senior's spittle from his face, and replied, "I intended to write a few dance reviews...."

"But who would produce such shit? I don't understand! You're trying to be a critic...."

"I already told you before, I'm no critic," Paul interjected, visibly affronted by the term. "I just wrote a series of articles about dance, my favorite subject, not as a professional expert, but from the broader perspective of an innocent member of the audience who...."

"That's what I mean, you're trying to be a critic. Darlene (he called to the bartender) set us up with tequila here and you have one yourself, sweetie. So you're trying to be a critic...."

"Look here, sir, I am not a critic!" Paul was getting hot under the collar. "I hate critics!"

"Relax, pal, and have a drink," Senior commanded, then tossed down a shot of tequila. "You sound like a critic. I read the first five articles you wrote about dancing, and I wondered what you were doing wasting your time writing about a bunch of peons and pansies. I'm just your average Joe, and I could care less about going to see people prancing around in pink tights, let alone reading what some nitwit thought about them. Take a look around the bar here, and you tell me, who gives a shit about what you think about dancing?"

"I know the market is narrow," answered Paul with a sunken heart. "But, but I believe I could expand it. I mean, well, you know there are lots of people who read about dance, so I...."

"Hold on there," Senior interrupted, glaring at Paul. "Did you send that shit anywhere else?"

"Yes, I sent each review to the papers and the magazines."

"Did you get a reply? Well, did you?" Senior challenged.

"No. But one editor wrote on the rejection slip that I...."

"There 'ya go! Forget that! How much would you make on a best seller?"

"I don't know, maybe fifty-thousand."

"You stupid idiot! Try a half-million bucks for size!"

"Oh."

"Yeah, oh. So, why are you screwing yourself short with that shit? Nobody wants to read about that sissy stuff. You've got to write about the right stuff to make it big. Hey, Junior (he called down the bar to his son) ain't this guy's writings shit?" Junior nodded his assent compliantly.

"As I said, I wanted to write about something..."

"Something? Something? What do you want, ten bucks?"

"Well, no," Paul answered wanly.

"That's what it looks like!" Senior concluded and turned to talk to his son, thus leaving Paul, the greatest aspiring writer the world will ever or never know, to his reflections and a full shot of tequila.

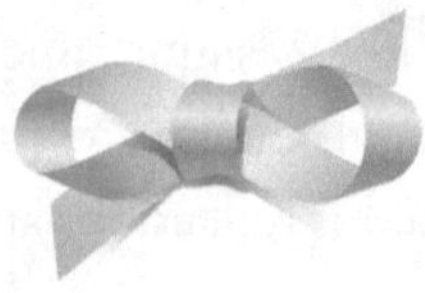

IX. Legs Ballone

It was a muggy morning in Flatbush. The greatest author the world will ever or never know heard his roommate, Billy O'Malley, get up at five o'clock sharp. Billy had returned home from the hospital two weeks before; he was almost fully recovered from the injuries he had suffered as the result of the bathroom ceiling collapsing on him as he sat on the toilet. Billy was an air-conditioning mechanic - business was brisk this stifling summer. Paul heard him getting ready for work: water running, toilet flushing, rattling in the kitchen, keys jangling, the fiddling with five locks, the front door slamming with a boom resounding in the carpetless hall - a dog yelped in response.

Paul had the spare bedroom. It was more like a storage space, bare of furniture, stacked up with boxes. The walls were stained brown with leaks from the bathroom above. Paul had just enough space for his suitcase, which he practically lived out of, and to stretch out on the floor on top of two blankets - he hoped to find a discarded mattress soon. Now that Billy was gone, Paul got up, sweaty and stiff, paddled his bare feet across the living room and flopped down on the couch under the window fan, after turning it on to 'HI' - despite Billy's profession, there was not an A/C in the apartment, and Billy did not like to run the fan at night because he said it was a waste of good electricity since nights are usually cooler than the days.

Paul enjoyed the air rushing over his naked and unusually hairy body. He soon dozed off to the whirring of the fan, and began to dream. The dream had a window looking out upon a gruesome ritual. Three obese priests were cutting open their bellies and pulling their bloody intestines out, cutting off pieces and dumping them into a basket. Then a black snake with a shark's head arose from its own coil in the basket; it was covered with scales that looked like human teeth; it writhed wretchedly to a Blue's tune one of the men was playing on a harmonica. Another priest was ringing a bell while the third priest, who had taken up a cigar, blew smoke rings into the air.

The phone was ringing. Paul woke up with a start, shook his head, and stared at the phone. It kept ringing and ringing - he got up and strode across the room to answer it.

"Hello."

"Paul, my boy, is that you?" The voice sound odd, somehow misplaced.

"Yeah. Who's this?"

"John, John Wilson, Senior."

"Oh, you sound strange, like in a tunnel or something, sir."

"Don't sir me, son. I'm on the speaker phone. Junior's here with me."

"Hey, Paul, it's me. Good Morning." Junior's voice was muffled.

"Good Morning," Paul said back, frantically trying to collect his thoughts. "Hold on just a minute," he asked, stalling, put the receiver down, grabbed one of Billy's KOOLs from the pack in the fruit bowl on the kitchen table and lit it. This is the call he had been waiting for, or so he thought: Senior would be his patron, sponsor his writing, maybe put him in a nice crib in the Village, like he said he would if he liked his work. But wait, Senior had read his dance reviews and said over and over that it was "shit", "shit", and "shit", that he didn't like it. So why is he calling? Paul, perplexed, picked up the receiver, and said, "Hi, I'm back, had to turn off the stove."

"Junior and I were just talking about that shit you sent me to read, right Junior?" said Senior.

"Right", came the muffled voice from the background.

"We were saying that stuff was really a load of crap, a lot of shit, if you don't mind us saying so."

Paul's heart sank then rose in anger. He'd heard all this before several times and was not going to put up with it again. Senior, he was convinced, was a jerk, some sort of wealthy and jealous masochist who likes to go around encouraging artists with hints of funding, then calling their work shit, rubbing their faces in it over and over.

"Senior, if you don't mind *my* saying so, *you*, and your son, are a couple of ....."

"I was saying to Junior," Senior interjected, "this kid would be a great author if only he'd take my advice and write about eating out of the dumpster and finding half-eaten hamburgers and hot dogs, and crummy nude photos of Madonna in there, jacking off on them, throwing them away not knowing they are worth a fortune. Or about the dancers on the beer diet, and those weirdos, like the guy, the guy, or that whore you mentioned, the one with the rubbers - who was that?"

"Oh, you're referring to the prostitute who had been receiving semen-filled condoms in the mail from a retarded pervert who started paying her child support because she wrote and told him she got pregnant and had his kid."

"Yeah, hot damn, that's it!" exclaimed Senior. "Write something with popular appeal, a novel with stuff like that in it, something real people can enjoy instead of that pansy-assed dance-review shit, that shit you sent me. I mean, why did you send me that shit, anyway? Never mind, forget about that shit."

"Dad, he might write about that choreographer with no legs," Junior suggested.

"Yeah, what about that successful guy you mentioned? Write about him."

Senior was referring to Legs Ballone, well known in esoteric dance quarters as the father of the Lyrico Technique. Legs Ballone had been a brilliant dancer at a young age, but he got his legs crossed practicing a dance routine on the subway platform while waiting for a train at Times Square. He fell off the platform, in front of the No. 2 Flatbush train, and lost his legs as a consequence. Yet he triumphed over that enormous disadvantage. He went on to dance legless, on his arms, swinging his trunk around, astonishing his students with the grotesque, surreal beauty of his dance - on rare occasions he performs at the *Gothic Village Dance Theatre*. And, by means of a special contraption he invented, his choreographic prosthesis, he trained some of the world's foremost performers and choreographers. Although an article or two appears about him from time to time, he is relatively unknown except in the closely knit dance family, where his Technique had cult status. The Lyrico Technique is based on the disciplined coordination of mechanical and spiritual principles. The dancer learns to move fluidly through the various lines of the Platonic solids, through the 'Universal Poses.' He never "strikes a pose" as such, but strives to "never stop moving", and to "feel the fire of the forms between the poles." Once the dynamic is mastered, so that the student is no longer "doing technique", but is "really dancing," once the execution of the movements has "educated" or "drawn out" the "cosmic inner state", the intense feelings expressed by the "Per Former" allegedly have an extraordinary, subtle influence on members of the audience, rendering them slightly susceptible to suggestion.

"Write about him," reiterated Senior. "Yeah, that's right, write about that legless dance master you talked about. Write me a good success story, I want to meet that guy, by the way. Write it out and leave it with Doreen at the bar. And have a few drinks on me while you're there, and one of the burgers too. Tell her I said to put it on my tab. Me and Junior will look it over, and I tell you what, if it's as good as I think it's going to be, you won't be sorry."

"I was going to do a story about him in the first place," Paul responded into the mouthpiece, "but I decided against it."

"Why?"

"I wanted a fresh angle on him."

"Success is always a good angle, fresh or not" Junior remarked.

"But everybody in dance knows about the terrible accident, how he overcame it, the people he's trained. I wanted a fresh angle. And there might be hard feelings."

"What the hell for? What is this shit? Are you going to bring me a good story or not?"

"Yes, I mean, I want to. I don't know about the accident thing," Paul mused over the phone. "I think he would have been a great dancer without the accident. Three of his students got the wrong idea and were hurt badly—one got killed."

"Killed?"

"Killed. It was horrible. The Lyrico Studio was scandalized. The whole thing about how Legs overcame his injury made some of his students think the injury had made him great. Three of them jumped in front of the No. 2 Flatbush train together. One was killed. The other two didn't lose their legs - one is in a coma and the other is a paraplegic."

"Damn! What a story, son. Dancers must really be dumb," said Senior.

"Paul, tell dad about the IBM dancing machine," Junior requested.

"You mean the ICM."

"What's that, again? I don't remember what you said about it," Senior remarked.

"It's the *Isocohedronic Choreographic Machine*. It's a cube inside a sphere. Legs straps himself into it with a remote control and navigates. The computer records the motions. Legs edits the information and uses it to produce ballets in the form of computer graphics and Labanotation print outs. He can also use the machine to teach on the spot."

"Why not just use a computer in the first place?" asked Junior.

"It can't be done by computer alone. The Master Pilot must strap himself in and actually feel the motion. Anybody will not do. An experienced and intuitive artist, a pilot, is essential. Only Legs has mastered the Machine, or so he says, but he's training his protégé, Senor San Francisco, to master it, and thousands have been educated in the subsidiary application, the Lyrico Technique."

"Is the Machine patented?" asked Junior.

"No, there's only one, not patented, and he keeps it close to home, well secured. Legs is afraid it will fall into the hands of the government and be used for political purposes. The Soviet ballet company, the Kirov, offered to buy or rent it some time ago, then the CIA showed up."

"CIA? Why would the CIA give a shit about pansies prancing around in tights with their crotches bulging?" queried Senior.

"According to Legs, the KGB put the Kirov director up to it, and the CIA picked up the scent. They caught onto him after he choreographed that piece for William Starret, the one where Bill rolled across the Russian stage on a skateboard. It's like I said, the Lyrico Technique itself makes an audience vulnerable to suggestion, but the influence is slight, so they figured they would use the Machine to choreograph ballets to be performed while radioing subliminal commands to the audience, which would supposedly be most effective in conjunction with baroque music, especially some of the *adages*. The CIA code name was *Project Adagio*."

"Dad, I told you, this is a good story!"

"Boy, I think you're right, by golly! Paul, write that up, bring it down to the Village tomorrow or the next day at the latest, give it to Doreen. You wanna bring a date, go ahead, it's on my tab, but make sure you leave the story, you hear?"

Paul covered up the mouthpiece on his phone, held the phone out, and shouted "Yeah!" But his scruples suddenly gave him pause again, and he said to Senior, "I'm afraid if I write about Legs, there will be hard feelings."

"Hard feelings?" said Senior.

"Hard feelings?" echoed Junior.

"Hard feelings. I can't write unless I tell the whole truth, and publication of the truth about the humongous master, I mean the great master might hurt his feelings, and I happen to love the guy."

"What the hell are you talking about? You mean there's more? Great, then tell it. Do you want to be a brilliant author or a dumb dancer? Then screw him! Tell it all. Hey, what did you say, that you love him? Were you screwing this guy? That's even better."

"No, no, not that, but he's gay."

"Gay?"

"Well, he was an idol with the women until the accident, and after that only men would love him, so he turned gay."

"People don't turn," Junior's muffled voice was heard. "They come out of the closet. It's like you said about wanting a fresh angle. Legs would have been a great dancer without the accident. People are what they are. Character counts. If you are evicted from your house and wind up on the street, you will become a drunk or a monk according to your character."

"That's right," affirmed Senior, "take me for example, I'm a drunk and I worked my ass off, and I deserve every million I got because this is how I am, doing what I want to do. Now let's stop yacking on the damned phone like women. This guy Legs sounds like a tough man, and there will be no hard feelings. We'll get him to sign off on it, anyway, so he doesn't sue, and get some pictures, promote his thing too. But it's gotta be good. Write it up good and don't be pussy footing around about it. Give me the meat, the hamburgers and hotdogs, stuff people like. Hang up Junior. Good bye!"

The phone went dead, just like that, leaving Paul hanging on to the other end, dumbfounded.

X. Never Stop Stretching

Paul Bowman had given a great deal of thought to Senior's offer to sponsor his writing provided that he write about the great jazz-dance maestro, Legs Ballone. And the more he considered the proposition, the more deeply he found himself mired in ethical dilemmas. Indeed, if it were not for Paul's tendency to agonize over relative ethical positions in hopes of finding a universal standard for his conduct, he would have secured his fame and fortune long ago.

For instance, the day after the wealthy Pittsburg industrialist asked him to bring a story about Legs down to the Peculiar Pub, Paul resolved to present his story as fiction in order to protect himself from any hard feelings Legs might have. His relief over this solution, however, was as momentary as his sigh, for, on second thought, it led to another moral question: Should he lie to protect the guilty? And was Legs really guilty of some mortal sin? Paul felt that he might be, but was not so sure now. Should he not tell the truth to protect the society? And, even if Legs was not guilty of some mortal sin, at least kids should not get the wrong idea, and jump in front of subway trains in order to become great masters through overcoming their disabilities - three kids had already done that! As Paul entertained one possibility after another for good and evil, it did not occur to him that, fiction or nonfiction, everyone who knew Legs would connect the dots and know who the story was about.

Instead of scribbling out and delivering a manuscript to the barmaid as Senior had demanded, Paul stalled - he called Senior's son in the Village and asked him to let Senior know that he would need a few weeks to write the story.

"All right," Junior said, "but dad doesn't like to wait. I'll tell him, but you'd better hurry it up or he'll write you off. He just fired his plant superintendent for being late to a meeting."

Wherefore Paul's mental conflict continued apace for two weeks, and, fortunately for the little bit of sanity he was clinging to, it was interrupted by six hours of dance classes every day, plus rehearsals for one of Linda Diamond's controversial modern dance productions. Yet the strenuous rituals on the dance floor had not tired him sufficiently to forget the invisible impediment to his writing career, the "writer's block", or rather his scruples, or rather his lack of them and his obsession with having a few of them, standing in the way of the greatest author the world will ever or never know. Nor did his physical exertions tire him enough to sleep restfully; no, the more he extended and contracted his muscles during the day, the less he slept at night: his slumbers were fitful affairs between his aching legs and anguished mind.

Besides his literary difficulties, Paul had problems with dancing. Dancing is not all it is cut out to be: it too can place a tremendous burden on the mind in several respects, some of them directly corresponding to the limitations of the body. For instance, Paul had short hamstrings, and months of stretching them had been for nought. A ballet master Uptown recommended that he have a surgeon slice into his hamstrings at intervals along their lengths, but Paul had not the money for that, and he considered such an operation to be unnatural, and, of course, immoral, maybe.... It was just as well, for a young fellow who did have the operation will never dance again. Another dancer, Dino, had a mechanical contraption he used for stretching his legs; it was too bulky to take on tours, so Dino tried stretching his legs while sleeping; he had a fellow dancer, his lover, tie his split legs to bedposts or to furniture before he went to sleep: he wound up in the hospital in Chicago - he is no longer dancing.

Now Paul had stretched and stretched just as he was told by his teachers, to no avail; he began to hate stretching with a passion, and was wont to exclaim ever so often, "I hate stretching, but I love contractions!"

No matter how much one might love dancing, if he hates stretching, he is going to have problems, especially in Graham classes where there is a lot of floor work. Some dancers are adept in all zones of dancing - low, middle, and high - but each dancer usually has his favorite zone: Paul loved to dance in the middle zone, with only his head in the ozone, because he could not do a split on the floor or, of course, in the air during the course of a leap - not only is the split in the air beautiful, it gives the illusion of additional height. Well, two days after his telephone interview with Senior and Junior, Paul was kicked out of the Graham class. After about twenty minutes of routines down on the floor, Paul interrupted the proceeds with this remark: "This kind of dancing is popular because women had to get down and clean the floors all the time. It's about time we let the mops clean the floor, and get up and do some real dancing." In response to which Madame Olson yelled, "Out! Get out, Paul, and don't come back!"

Not only did the eviction distress him. Madame Olson was a very popular teacher all over town, so he was greeted with sneers from her students at every major studio he frequented; or, even worse, they just ignored him, as if he were a painting on the wall. Fortunately for the dance world, Legs Ballone comforted him later that day, or he would have given up dance altogether. Legs, not having legs and therefore no longer able to do splits on the floor or in the air, still choreographed the low and high zones for his students and producers, but he personally preferred elegant, upright dancing in the middle zone. Legs knew something was up with Paul that day when Paul did not laugh at one of his off-color jokes in the dressing room as he helped him into his wheelchair.

"What's wrong, Paul?" Legs inquired. Paul told him what had happened at the Graham class, and how miserable he was about his short hamstrings.

"Never stop stretching, Paul, but don't expect too much. I've seen dancers start late like you, who could hardly touch their ankles let alone the floor, but in a few months they could put both palms on the floor then put their head between their legs and almost kiss their ass. I don't think you've got the length, Paul, and you've got narrow hips too, but keep what you've got stretched out. Don't worry about it, you're not a woman and aren't going to have a baby any time soon. When I was a boy, only the black men did the splits - white boys didn't do the splits! Everybody has advantages and disadvantages - hell, look at me! So use what you've got or lose it. And never stop stretching."

"Legs, you're the greatest master around," Paul said, and meant it.

"You should take three of my morning classes every week in addition to the one o'clocks, and you will improve much more quickly."

"I want to do some modern dancing too. I liked the Graham contractions. I just hated the floor work, the stretching."

"Then take Limon classes. They don't spend so much time on the floor, and they dance more elegantly than Graham, like me. But don't say the word 'contraction' in a Limon class, it's a dirty word to them. Jose had short hamstrings, you know."

"Really?"

"Of course he did. During a performance of, I think, of the 'Moor' or 'Moors' of something or the other, he overdid a *grande battement*, and the kick sent him backwards, smack down on his back. Ask Betty Jones about that, she was his partner. Okay, I'm on my way, Paul, give me a kiss."

"Yuck! I'm straight!"

"Ha, ha, you're so funny, Paul, you know we Italians like a peck on the cheek."

"It's the pecker I'm not interested in, at least not somebody else's."

"That's nature, Paul, even ducks are gay. You've got to come out in the country and check out my pond."

"Love to. See ya!!"

Paul felt much better about dance as he rode the No. 2 back to Flatbush. But his conflict over whether to write fiction about Legs, or to write the truth and nothing about the truth, and the hard feelings that might ensue as a result, resumed with a vengeance, for obvious reasons. He should have brought the subject up in the dressing room, but for some strange reason he could not bear to do so.

When Paul got home he drank a quart of beer and smoked a black Russian cigarette, his allotment for the day, went into his room, spread out a blanket on the floor between the cardboard boxes, laid down and drifted off to sleep.

Paul had a peaceful dream, that he was stretching his legs, bringing each foot in turn over his head, his legs against his ears. If felt wonderful. As he awoke, he thought the dream was a good omen for what was to come, but he fully awoke with terrible cramps in both legs. He stood up gingerly from the bed, then yelled out in pain—he had somehow sprained his back during the night as he twisted and turned with the blanket around him. He collapsed to the floor, tried to relax. The pain was awful. He painfully noted the difference between dreams and reality.

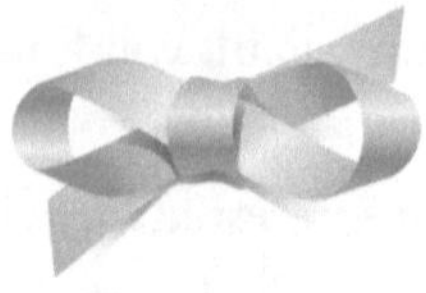

XI. Doctor Sagwell

As we have previously noted during our meandering tale of failure and success, the path of Paul Bowman, the greatest author the world will ever or never know, was obstructed by his scruples, or rather his want of them, and his perverse obsession with having a few. Instead of mounting a gift horse after looking it in the mouth, and riding it into the town of fame and fortune, Paul would agonized at length over which side of the horse to climb up on, then wonder why it had wandered off while he was wondering what was the right thing to do.

Senior's offer to sponsor his literary endeavors - providing that he expose the details of the life of his beloved dance master, the great maestro, Legs Ballone, to public scrutiny, which might cause hard feelings between them and inspire dance students to throw themselves in front of subway trains in order to become great masters - left Paul totally confused as to what course of action to take. Therefore he considered taking a course in ethics at Cooper Union, thinking that he might learn something that would enable him to resolve his dilemmas without regrets. However, since the time of course offered at Cooper Union conflicted with his African dance-class schedule, he consulted the *I Ching* instead, and was advised by the venerable oracle to maintain his center in the midst of shocking events, to follow his better instincts, and to withdraw at the appropriate moment. This reading left him even more perplexed, and somewhat shocked to boot, so he instinctively called his old friend, Robert Sagwell - a Freudian analyst by trade, famed for his founding of Old Friends Network. Paul was invited over for cocktails that evening.

Paul loved to visit Bob at his lofty and spacious rent-controlled apartment on Riverside Drive, overlooking the park and the Hudson River. Doctor Sagwell was paying six-hundred a month for the grand old flat, much to the chagrin of the condominium converters who valued it at nearly a million - if only they could put it on the market. He had refused to buy the unit. He believed a collapse of the real estate market was imminent, soon to be followed by the fall of the civilization he felt was rapidly declining with his advancing age. Besides, at sixty-something, he had no heirs he wanted to speak of, least of all in a will. He had been born into a wealthy family, and was well-taken of, but he was unloved or loved coldly, hence his familial relations where chilly at best.

Despite his frigid familial relations, Doctor Sagwell was a sociable bachelor who did not neglect his own life nor the lives of the many friends whom he loved. He went to considerable current expense remodeling his apartment - Paul helped paint it - and to generously entertain his guests therein.

The remodeling expenditures were partially offset by the savings Doctor Sagwell realized after he vacated his rented office next to the school playground a few blocks away, on West End. The shouts of children playing there had disturbed his sessions with patients, but the deciding factor was the fecal matter burglars had left behind in the toilet while he was in the Bahamas for two-weeks vacation one hot summer - Manhattan's stifling, humid weather was unfavorably compared that year to the Amazon jungle's climate. He was shocked by the smell and the appearance of the anal development after he entered his office upon his return - the police ascertained from the color of the unflushed evidence that at least two burglars had violated his rented domain. The tenant said he would never forget the unbearable stench polluting his desecrated office, and he packed his things for his exodus - his forfeited rent deposit took care of the subsequent fumigation of the demised premises.

After Doctor Sagwell evacuated his West End office, one room of his expansive flat on Riverside Drive served as his professional office. Upon one wall, he mounted a self-portrait that he had painted while dabbling in the psychology of aesthetics. A young woman was depicted sitting in a chair, behind and over which Doctor Sagwell towered, with his hands on her shoulders. She was an old flame of his, yet appeared, by virtue of the features painted by the doctor, to be closely related to him. The "experimental" painting eventually embarrassed him - someone asked him if the subject was his twin sister - he removed it from the wall, and will not say what he did with it.

The good doctor had otherwise equipped the office with a firm but comfortable couch for the analysands to recline on during their forty-five minute sessions. During off hours, he was fond of sitting on it himself, rubbing shoulders with a friend or two, casting off his official authoritarian role to chat freely and munch snacks as an equal to all.

Nearby the couch was a small desk and typewriter, an unabridged dictionary looking quite formidable on its own slender pedestal, and a peculiar chair upon which he perched during his psychoanalytic sessions. The "OrthoAnalysis Chair" had no back. The analyst had to wrap his legs around two of the three legs of this peculiar chair, which, of course, came with postural instructions to the effect that, if the instructions were followed to a 'T', then mind and body would be in the harmony best attuned for psycho-analysis and -therapy.\

By the way, the reader might not be surprised to hear that Doctor Sagwell was into the Alexander Technique. But the same reader might deem the doctor's occasional interest in crystal therapy rather odd - his Freudianism was unorthodox, extending far beyond the Jungian heresy, to the very frontiers of the 'Uncs'.

In any case, Dr. Sagwell's practice was in accord with the demand of his patients, all bourgeois neurotics. He referred the few seriously mentally ill people who came his way to competent specialists. Although his fortune was already assured, he did not mind if his clients added to it. From time to time, he generously provided accelerated therapy *pro bono* to humble members of the homosexual community, whom he occasionally met behind the boarded windows of the Black Saddle Club on Amsterdam Avenue - he believed homosexuality to be perverse but not immoral, and he had developed a therapeutic technique designed to help anxious gay men "adjust."

Now Paul Bowman had known Doctor Sagwell for many years, commencing some time before the doctor was a doctor; that is, when he was just "Bob", during the Sixties, when he smoked pot, became confused, visited a psychoanalyst, a direct descendant of the great Freud, and was so impressed on the couch that he decided to become an analyst himself. Paul looked up to Bob for many reasons. Paul allowed Doctor Sagwell, during his student days, to practice hypnotism on him, which only added to the doctor's aura of authority. Yet Paul had kept the awful ethical dilemmas that confronted him a carefully guarded secret, or so he thought. Something the doctor must have suggested to him during one of the séances had haunted him for years: *Remember, you will be a big success at almost anything if you set your mind to it.* It was the "almost" that worried Paul to no end.

XII. What's Your Issue?

"I'm going to have an extra-dry martini," Dr. Sagwell said.

"I thought bourbon and soda was your one and only," Paul remarked. "Do you have any beer?"

"Sure, in the frig. I like martinis when I'm feeling week, like after talking to my mother. Why doesn't she get it over with and die instead of tormenting me? Now she's agonizing about her will, who's going to get her millions. Well, I've got my own fortune.... Ah, just right!" Dr. Sagwell smacked his lips after taking a sip of his martini. "Now, then, Paul, come, let's move into the study, and you tell me about the problem - I mean issue - that you mentioned.

Paul followed his old friend into the study and sat down next to him on the couch. "Bob, the problem is this - I'm disturbed by a report that says linquists have long tongues."

"So do German Shepherds, my boy, so tell me, what's the problem? I mean, what's your issue?" You sounded worried, and mentioned someone, a senior, a senior...."

"John Wilson, Senior. He's the guy I met in the Village. He says he will sponsor me if I write about Legs Ballone."

"So? That doesn't sound like a problem, it sounds like the solution. You're a writer, so write for God's sake."

"I can't. I mean, I don't know if I should. There might be hard feelings if I tell the truth."

"I thought Legs was on the up and up, a great master, I think you said. Is there a scandal?" Dr. Sagwell loved to analyze scandals.

"Well, no, but there's something, quite a lot of stuff, if people find out, I think he'll be angry, and the accident thing, those kids who jumped in front of the train at Times Square in order to have a disability to overcome, and people might come after the Isocohedronic machine, but I don't know, I don't want people to look down on him, and I can't ask him, it's just that...."

"Paul, Paul, hey, hold on there," Dr. Sagwell interrupted. "The important thing is that you don't get hurt. If you're worried about hurting his feelings or exposing his secrets, why don't you just use some of your experiences with Legs as an occasion, as a point of departure for a novel? Why bother with biography?"

"That's what I was thinking of doing. Senior's keen on the story about Legs, but he also says a novel might be worth a half-million. So I started to outline the whole thing. Senior wants a short story on it right away, like a treatment for a movie. He has money and knows people. But as I was twisting the truth this way and that, I just couldn't go on with it. It's about a real person, and lying about Legs is just awful - I was feeling awful. I'm afraid he and some of the characters will be identified anyway, no matter how much I mix them up and recombine them, prevaricate and exaggerate. I just couldn't go on, I felt so constipated with writer's blocks," Paul said, wringing his hands pathetically, "and I haven't got anything ready for Senior. I've had to stall, and this is my big break."

"So what if they are identified?" asked Dr. Sagwell, putting his glass down while trying not to crack a smile. "You had no problems reviewing those dance performances. There might have been goodness, truth and beauty in the performances, but they were fictional forms. There is more lying in true stories, especially in people's *memoirs*, than under oath in court, and there is more truth in fiction than anywhere else in public."

"But artists distort the truth."

"No, Paul, they cut through the lies and reveal the truth. The poet who reveals the truth is called a maker, but he does not make the truth, he makes the poem, and even though it might not fully correspond to the truth about his subject, it has its own truth, and has its lies too, for it is necessarily a fabrication influenced by the artist's unique perspective - no two things in the universe are identical - that perspective of course is a unique coincidence of universals, if you know what I mean - I mean adjectives applicable to numerous nouns, or predicates possible of several subjects, therefore it is reasonable to assume if not presume...."

"Bob, please, you're confusing me. I don't know, I mean, it's like, well, I just want to be an honest author, not create illusions that lead people astray, but if I am honest, there will be hard feelings, I think, and if I am dishonest about Legs, people might not want to buy the story because, like Senior says, they want to read about the hotdogs and hamburgers and used condoms, so I don't know what I should do at this point, it's really bothering me."

"Condoms?" Now Dr. Sagwell's interest was piqued.

"Never mind. I hope you understand my predicament here, I am at a loss as to what to do."

"Hmmm, hmmm, I see," Dr. Sagwell said, frowned cogitatively and cupped his chin in his right hand. He was amused by Paul's confusion, and annoyed at the same time, that his work day analyzing people's problems never seemed to end because he could not help helping his friends instead of drawing the line between work and leisure. His eyes suddenly lit up, and he said, with an expectant expression, "Paul, excuse me, but I have a funny feeling that our civilization is going to pot, or that I've just smoked a joint."

"Sorry, Bob, my dealer was busted two months ago and I haven't had but a nickel bag since."

"Maybe it's the martini," said Dr. Sagwell, disappointed.

"Bob, I am thinking, here's the tragedy. We want to know about the ugliness of real people but we're all ugly in a way, so we don't want to be personally identified. Fiction protects us because we're all guilty and don't want to come out of the closet with it. Why don't people fornicate in the streets? Why are they ashamed to do publicly what they all do privately? And why be ashamed of the fact that wherever some good exists, evil can be found too? This whole thing has me in a quandary. Should I write...."

Geez!" Dr. Sagwell almost shouted as he raised one hand in the air imperiously. He was in truth getting sick and tired of the conversation and wanted to talk about himself for a change. "You're talking foolishly, Paul! Personalities are fictions in self-defense. They are masks. So change the name, the hair color, the habits and manners, the predicates and adjectives, all the universal trivial fictions. People lie to seem good and even be good. Almost all public conduct is a lie, people know it and don't really give a damn, so why all this agonizing on your part, what's your prob.... what's your issue, anyway? You tell me."

"It's just that what's inside or under the mask is indicated, and I don't want to give people the wrong idea."

"Paul, there is nothing under the mask, there is nothing inside once you take all the adjectives away."

"But that French psychiatrist Lacan said that elephant turds proves there is something inside. And I believe that might stink to high heaven."

"So what? Women in Africa have stood in elephant excrement all day long because they thought the power of the inside of an elephant would make them fertile. So if you find some slime under the mask, don't worry, tell the story, make some money. At the bottom of it all is nothing, so make something of it. Paul, I think it's yourself that you are afraid of, you don't want to identify your identify, not someone else's, and you are afraid because you don't know who you are. So make something of yourself."

"What? Bob, what should I do?"

"I want you to do what I tell you to do. If you're not going to do it, I don't want to tell you."

"Okay, I'll do it."

Dr. Sagwell leaned towards Paul, put his hand on Paul's knee, and looked him squarely in the eye.

"You will write a best-selling novel," Dr. Sagwell commanded, "and one of its characters will be Legs Ballone."

XIII. Epilogue to No Hard Feelings in New York

Senior became the subject of a federal indictment with the bankruptcy of his Pittsburgh business. Paul Bowman never heard from him or his son again. He continued with his dancing while working part-time in Midtown, at a salary that allowed him to save considerable money since he lived cheaply in a little studio he illegally sub-rented from an opera singer, who, fearing his career might go on the rocks, was afraid to give it up. Paul, after performing at Lincoln with a modern dance company—that being the culmination of his career as a dancer—returned to paradise with his savings to take up writing in peace and quiet.

Paul's Last Stand

The author's suicide essay may be his very best

Paul Bowman, the greatest author the world will ever or never know, takes pride in the enormous inventory of unpublished essays he has written since he quit his perfect job and moved to Paradise to devote himself to his writing career. His rose soon grew thorns. He thought his savings would be sufficient for him to ramp up to fame and fortune; alas, he has now fallen pathetically short of his imagined fame and fortune: he has sold only two of his brilliant essays over the last five years, both to a Catholic journal. It is not that Paul's work is worthless; he is just not cut out to be in any sales department, let alone be his own marketing staff of one.

Needless to say, Paul is a rather bookish man. Albeit he lives in Paradise, he is often in the library, his Heaven on Earth. He calls his library "the Ark of Civilization", and claims that it is a shame that only two or three people besides vagrant wayfarers are on board on any given day. But never mind, for who has time to rub shoulders with the locals when one has the intimate company of the greatest minds that ever thought?

Mind you that Paul, despite being a bookworm when not writing, is not really standoffish: he is in fact gregarious when not engaged in literary pursuits; but his gregariousness has little social support. You see, Paul is a member of a race even more despised over the centuries than the Jewish and the black race; to wit: he belongs to the intellectual race, which can be Jewish or black. He is fond of 'vulgar' people as people, as well as the intellectual elite as people, but the feeling is far from mutual. Many people get a college degree not for the liberty of a liberal education but to get a better paying office job. Paul takes his liberty too literally. Arrogant anti-intellectuals have no interest in his merely 'academic' liberty, thus his discourse sails over their heads. He cares little for sports. Although he enjoys sex, he doesn't care to discuss the most popular topic, 'pussy.' To make hanging out with the guys even worse, he does not get racist jokes, hence they think he is a stupid intellectual.

Since there is little love lost among the violently clashing wits of his own kind, the library is actually the ideal place for Paul - his vision of a stately throne is a private author's desk at New York Public Library. The library in Paradise is a cool and empty place to be on muggy days. The books love to be read and to have notes taken from their pages. Once in a while a new security guard, seeing Paul around so often and wondering if he should be discriminated against, asks him if he is homeless, to which he replies, with a smile, "So what if I am?" He gets no answer, except, "Never mind." The librarians are quite nice; the only thing he likes about the current U.S. president is that he had the good taste to marry a librarian.

No, Paul is not homeless, at least not yet. But homelessness is looming ever more near as the days pass. Again, Paul's sales are not ramping up to his production schedule. He is the greatest author the world will ever or never know, but he is not a salesman. Therefore he has been seeking work lately, as a keeper of books, of course. He has fine credentials, including glowing letters of recommendation concerning his proven abilities as a controller, accountant, and bookkeeper.

Paul applied for part-time or temporary work at first so that he could keep up his furious research and writing pace. Since no such engagements were forthcoming, he applied for 412 full-time jobs. He managed to get five interviews and one job offer, for $10 an hour, which he declined because he thought he could do better than twenty-percent of his last pay rate. He has had occasion to regret turning down that job, for now he is on the verge of eviction and is willing to take up anything for any income. Times are especially bad for unemployed liberal writers since the Republicans took over; for instance, car thefts in Paradise are up forty-five percent this year. Nonetheless, with his excellent references, what is Paul's problem? He doesn't know for a fact. On the one hand, he thinks he is having a bad run of luck. On the other hand, he supposes the hypothesis of cause and effect might provide a commonsensical explanation, hence he has speculated on the possible causes of his help being so unwanted. For one thing, that he is an off-color stranger in Paradise, and there is not much Paradise to be shared with those who are far from flush. And that he is over fifty but not eligible for Social Security; thus he falls into a sort of limbo pending his warehousing for death. His age-bracket, a bracket that in traditional cultures is associated with experience and wisdom, is a bracket young managers and executives have small interest in. After all, after leaving home and getting a job with the corporation, who wants to hire someone who reminds them of their dads? Anyway, he has had his chance and he is not a top executive or retired to Palm Springs already, so there must be something terribly wrong with him.

Fast-paced companies today are looking for career-minded people who have three to five years of experience and who must have pushed the latest sequence of buttons many times. These detail-oriented, highly motivated people must be able to independently follow instructions in order to meet deadlines under pressure while making sacrifices. During his second interview, Paul was asked what sacrifices he would be willing to make if he were asked to work overtime. He said, "I would be willing to sacrifice at least one chicken. I would sacrifice a wife, but I don't have one at present." The interviewer, one of the many thousands of under-paid women in Human Resources, grimaced; end of interview: a sense of humor was definitely not wanted by that firm, a rather large one whose operating attitude reminds one of the United States Army.

But Paul is not giving up. This very morning he is sending out more resumes, and he will make calls until he is blue in the face and his ears are sore - he does not have a speaker-phone. Then he will write late into the night until he is exhausted. Then he will go to bed for a couple of hours. He can barely sleep at night because he is tormented by the looming prospect of houselessness. Just before he went to bed last evening, he witnessed an absurd scene on his 13" television:

A woman of thirty or so had found her husband sleeping with another woman; there are no kids; she got the house and alimony. Now she enters her abode. She misses her husband, looks at his photo, and is obviously depressed. Maybe she made a bad mistake, and now she is all alone. Tears stream down her face as she walks through the luxuriously furnished rooms of her home, and finally throws herself onto her huge bed. She takes up the fetal position and moans. Fade out.

Woe is me, thought Paul. What numbskulls these people are!

In the good old days, homelessness was not a curse but was a virtue to wise men. In those days, Confucius himself would sleep in the dirt with the crook of his arm as a pillow rather than work for the wrong prince. Some of the Greek wise men would not work for any prince or price, for they in Truth were already wealthy, powerful and free citizens of the Cosmos. As far as they were concerned, poverty consists in desiring things, in wanting fools' gold instead of wisdom. And if poverty is a lack of temporal things, then, at least for Franciscans, Poverty is a Lady to be loved. Indeed, how can someone who is busy chasing after the things of the world become wise? Worldly people did not despise such wise men very much providing they did not get in the way. People even felt obligated to give them alms in India. But never mind: nowadays homelessness, or rather houselessness, is considered the worst of all curses, and homeless people are despised and feared as if they were Dr. Frankenstein's monsters.

In any event, Paul Bowman is no young man today; and this is not the Sixties where bohemians took some pride in vagrancy; nor is it the Great Depression where hoboes had the comfort of numbers even though the bulls beat some of them to death for loitering. There is plenty of food and shelter to go around, but this is the day when everyone has the duty to work, even at the production of junk, trash and garbage, just to get something to eat and shelter from the elements and the spite of people who fear homeless people.

Paul once wondered why people in This Great Nation of Ours, Leader of World Civilization, have a duty to work but no right to work. He asked the president, "Why?" But of course, since Paul is still a nobody, not yet the greatest author in the world, he got no reply. He thought, if the almighty president himself cannot provide me even with a meaningless, wage-slavery job, why should I care about the president and his damaged Pentagon? Or, for that matter, the commercial system it protects? After all, it is a system that intentionally makes things scarce in order for the few to make enormous profits. But never mind that, Paul told himself, for I am willing to cooperate, even though the culo with the great job on television says six-percent unemployment is just right.

Paul is not lazy. As a matter of fact, he works up to 70 hours per week without pay. He wants to belong to society, even if that means holding down a meaningless job so he can do his meaningful work in his spare hours. Just as Ssu-ma suffered castration to complete his history, Paul is willing to kowtow to become the greatest author the world will ever know. Alas that he gave up his job for the American dream. Now alas that nobody presently wants his mind or body in any form, either at the drill press or adding machine, or at his writing desk. Yet again, he has not given up. He rejects homelessness as an alternative. He understands why another man in similar circumstances is planning suicide on Thanksgiving Day. And why not suicide instead of a slow death on the streets? Where the false Christianity causing the problem wants to deprive people of their real opium? As Seneca said, "Do you like to be wretched? Live. Do you like it or not? It is in your power to return from whence you come."

A man's individual life is his last private refuge, Paul thought, and the state that makes suicide a crime commits the ultimate invasion of the liberty of privacy. How absurd it is that those who would kill each other in war would not allow a man to kill himself! Paul does not blame others or himself for his bad luck; he is not disposed to go on a killing spree at a useless employment office. But he loves his freedom and he does not want to be a despised houseless man without means even to continue with his beloved work. Therefore Paul, a true libertarian, has a marketing plan for his Last Day, the day the marshals are to evict him, if it comes to that.

Paul lives on a high floor from which he plans to take his last stand, and to jump to his death if push comes to shove. He has mounted a camera in order to broadcast his leap, live over the Internet, and also to record it elsewhere for posterity. He has composed another one of his brilliant essays to memorialize the tragic loss of the greatest author the world will ever or never know. The essay encourages talented artists to risk everything, even their lives, to live an artistic life. As has been noted, Paul detests marketing, perhaps because he unconsciously fears failure, yet now he is so convinced of the value of his work that he believes the filming of his death-defying leap, together with his last brilliant essay and his accumulated inventory, will be the very promotional scheme that will make him the greatest author the world has ever known to date.

The Changing Room

A room changes with the emotions of those who occupy and move about within it, carving its space into dynamic images indicative of their moods. Even after the vault empties, somehow unbeknownst to us the moods linger on, haunting echoes, invisible reflections of what happened there, memories of events that spring from the unknown, innermost chamber where feelings live and are given their being. More often than not those motives seem to have a will of their own. In spite of their misery, even the most miserable members of our lot live on in awe of that nearly indefatigable, indefinable freedom within

There are, of course, exceptions to the will to live. I recently dreamed of Art, my late best friend who died by his own hand. In my dream, and although I was dreaming in Hawaii, I called Art from a pay phone in Manhattan. As we conversed, I knew he was alive and well. However, much to my frustration, it was impossible for me to find his address so I could visit him in person.

Art's voice in my dream was real. Our conversation was genuine. How could that be? And, since he was really alive, how could he then be an exception to the will to live? Ghosts seem to have a will of their own.

Is a ghost, an apparition, a virtual image unreal? No, for, if that were the case, none of us could appreciate Art. Or, for that matter, a rainbow that exists for the pot of gold at one end or another. Or any other of the so-called illusions of life.

We may trace the content of a 'mere' dream back to its source in waking life, yet we cannot know why or how one source was selected over another. Although its essence is inscrutable, we know the will is no random exercise. If anything, it is magic. Yes, indeed, somehow the moods linger on of their own accord in the changing room, where even illusion and delusion is part and parcel of reality, where death is a mirage, and where life is a pretense.

A pretense? Then why do we go on creeping in our petty paces if life is a prevarication? By the magical operation of the will of which I speak, I am that entity scrawling symbols across the pages of my life. Between how I be this way or not be at all is an ineluctable mystery despite the prevarications and allegations of the pseudo-sciences to the contrary. Please rest assured, however, that I have invented good reasons for beating around the bush and being, at first glance from the perimeter, vague and nebulous. I do take the optional excursions within this great detour called life on Earth. Yet, on the fundamental plane of existence, when I answer for myself I answer for You. For I am a collection of yous in a form common to our nature. You may consider me to be an imposter or an imitator, but our differences are frauds. We are one. No one is dead. We are all here and now forever.

I could stop here but I will not, for I want to ramble on as to why I do not do away with myself forthwith. Because I love to dance. Dance is my reason. Dance is the foundation of all the arts, of which writing is my favorite. One must reason to write, and some say there is a big difference between reason and will, or reason and passion. Well, reason is my passion, writing is my dance. Stuff comes out and my job is to make it smell good. I like to dance with my head, so to speak. I like to polish the movement of apparitions. I like to translate feelings into living concepts. For me, writing is an adventure, a quest for some understanding of the unknown causes from which thoughts themselves spring. It is an Odyssey for its own sake: the end is an excuse. I'm like the Rom, the "Gypsy" who goes outside and sits in his car in the driveway when he feels restless but is unable to take a real trip at the moment. I'll drive with any subject, take on any passenger in my craft. I don't care what my article is "about", whether it has a point or gets anywhere besides where the muse takes me. I fly from Love to Love for Love's sake.

My dance begins and ends in a changing room on Oahu in the midst of the Pacific Ocean in stormy weather. My mood is the consequence of the turbulent passion of the surf. My alternative is to swim out in the ocean to the edge of the world. Who understands me? Who understands why I must keep moving just like the comedian who tried to get happy free-basing, accidentally caught himself on fire, then ran burning down the street for his life? So I seek to express that inexpressible frantic urge for life. That is the reason for my being: to give full vent to the qualities of a beloved I will never completely know. And most fortunate is my fatal ignorance, for Love does not abhor a secret.

Even as I speak, Poseidon smiles as I dance confidently on land, beckoning me with his trident to enter his watery realm. His call is appealing: is not my body mostly water? As I skim along the surface, I am unaware of the submarine expeditions of his surreal amphibian monster, who leaps occasionally from the sea to bring rain to Paradise. Never mind that. I'm not a trained diver therefore, Poseidon, hear my slight plea for a favorable wind to blow me wherever I am bound to be. Accept this plea as my offering to your dignity. If honors follow, they shall be my tribute to your power to stir up the best in me.

What? A breeze? Yes, a breeze. A gentle tropical breeze now takes me to a dance concert at the Jones-Ludin Dance Center in Hawaii. "Coincidence or God?" Hence here I am in a changing room, a dance studio. The program for the evening is entitled 'Changing Room'. Enter modern dancer Karen Miyake to perform a charming, tragic dance caress called 'Broken Flight'.

Karen kept her dance very close to the black vinyl floor she skillfully used to accentuate and complete her designs. Even her slightest movements conveyed a larger-than-life sense of a flight broken and a grand pathetic struggle to recover. No technical artifice was noticeable, just the natural movement of an animated creature whose flight is broken, not all at once but ever so gradually and painstakingly. Yes, it's the little things that are important, the little touches that make the heart leap for joy, and with sorrow.

I was transported by Karen's dance magic; she rendered the invisible truth visible. In the sorrow of the broken flight I was ecstatic in the sublime truth of its expression. How does one elicit such an apparent emotional contradiction in an audience by means of the same motion? Yes, we must know the context. The same word can have different meanings, but opposite ones? And here we speak of emotions, a much smaller vocabulary to draw upon. Another modern dancer, Isadora Duncan, addressed the question as beautifully as she danced, when she said:

"Only twice comes that cry of the mother which one hears as without one's self: at birth and at death. For when I felt in mine those little cold hands that would never press mine in return, I heard my cries: the same cries I heard at their births. Why the same? Since one is the cry of supreme joy and the other of sorrow, I do not know why, but I know they are the same. Is it not that in all the Universe there is but one great cry containing Sorrow, Joy, Ecstasy, Agony, the Mother Cry of Creation?"

Indeed. And 'Broken Flight' had that Unity of Motivation which does not merely interest the curious: it fascinates them and brings them into the "other" world where there is no changing room: nothing changes "there". Because our perceptions and conceptions require differences, and because belief is the gradual perfection of knowledge, we might believe the other world is nothing at all. But our appearances as ghosts as well as our ability to will something from nothing belie that notion to death.

I felt another breeze in my face this morning as I walked along the beach on the North Shore. I saw a bird gliding very low over the surf. Suddenly, the bird was transformed, into Karen, into Karen dancing, dancing in her changing room.

My Black Swan

Money and not morals is what counts most of all in the United States. If you do not have it you are nobody of note, no matter what you do, and if you have enough of it you may become President of the United States, whatever you happen to do. Yet, no matter who you are, your days on this earth are numbered, and your number may come up as quite a surprise to you although the statisticians have taken your demise into account when devising their mortality and accidental death tables for the insurance industry. And there is a chance you might win the $500 million lottery.

Enjoy the day the best you can because, as a matter of fact, you may be gone tomorrow as a result of some random, unexpected event, say, a bridge collapsing on your head, a plane crash, or perchance a terrorist attack. And on a larger scale, there are natural disasters, and do not rule out a pre-emptive nuclear attack. The planet itself is not perfectly secure since it might be encountered by a comet. I think it was Voltaire who remarked that this planet of ours might be a speck of dust in the road to be unexpectedly flattened by the hoof of a passing horse. So a lot of good your money will do you then.

Yes, there are some events even statisticians may not predict no matter their theories and how much historical data they may have. Every schoolboy knows that the mathematician and scientist Charles Sanders Peirce thought that nothing was determined for certain despite the habitual behavior we observe as laws. Chance events beyond the scope of those natural laws might irregularly occur. That is, there is such a thing a chance operating in the universe, the theory for which is dubbed 'Tychism,' after Tyche, the Greek goddess of luck, who was known to the Romans as Fortuna. Peirce, needless to say, was not a conventional man, though he was a great logician. His advanced scientific perspective aroused the jealousy of colleagues. He made some unfortunate choices including an unrewarding investment. Although he was helped out by relatives and his great friend William James, the successful philosopher who marketed his Pragmatism brand of philosophy, he fell upon hard times before he died destitute.

More recently, a nerdish Lebanese immigrant and Wharton School grad by the name of Nassim Nicholas Taleb, who said he made enough "f*** you" money as a quant and securities trader to say "f*** you" to people, enlarged his small fortune by writing his best-selling book, *The Black Swan*. A so-called black swan or unexpected event, because almost all swans are white, had come out of nowhere to embroil Lebanon in war.

The same sort of swan might be to blame for financial crashes, the budding probability theorist proposed as he developed his Black Swan or reverse-probability theory into a nice day job for himself because he discovered that everyone including himself was incompetent when it came to predicting future market prices. An investor might as well hire a monkey to throw darts at a list of securities than trust his money to experts, but without those experts there would not be a secondary securities market.

I like Taleb. He preferred to study instead of pursuing an infinite number of dollars. Indeed, he said he was ashamed when he engaged in the pursuit of wealth. The "inelegant, dull, pompous, greedy, unintellectual, selfish, and boring" business world literally disgusted him. Journalists "cluster" around the same subjects. Everyone consumes the same "news," the last thing one should do to know what is really going on; the more news consumed the less the cookie-cutter society knows about things except for things of "dubious value." The "achievers" in suits who do not read books and who become more sycophantic the higher their income are even more ignorant than cab drivers because cab drivers know they are ignorant.

He was so ashamed of his business that he did not want to tell people what he did for a living:

"When people at cocktail parties asked me what I did for a living, I was tempted to answer, 'I am a skeptical empiricist and a *flâneur* reader, someone committed to getting very deep into an idea,' but I made things simple by saying I was a limousine driver."

A *flâneur* was mythical 18th century artistic character or literary type who wandered Paris incognito without purpose, a random walker absorbed by the crowd although detached and somewhat cynical while experiencing the urban environment. He becomes blasé and disappears as the city is transformed into a modern capitalist hub and he into an insatiable shopper hypnotized by window displays. The whole of France may be said to heading in that direction as it is losing its distinct character to the European Union, much to the horror of Virginie in Nord France and millions of other French people. Contrary to Taleb's simile, the *flâneur* would never delve deeply into anything, because that would distract him from his detached observation of the surfaces. He was a suspicious person hanging around the arcades not to buy but to look, and perchance reflect at length on the scene. But the individual *flâneur* was absorbed by the masses along with the producer and consumer. The consumer skims the illusory surfaces of production, the superficiality of things, unaware of the modes of production. She may purchase, for example, milk without have even seen a farm let alone a cow. He is an ordinary shopper, a consumer whose consumption is determined not by what he really wants but by whatever happens to be advertised or on display. Both consumer and producer react to and are driven by the market. When he gets bored, he goes shopping and may wander for hours at the shopping center without buying anything. As a stock market gambler he would be technician unconcerned with the fundamentals of the companies whose securities he buys and sells, believing that patterns of price movements repeat themselves regardless of the changing historical circumstances. This while the crowd on the whole lives in a phantasmagoria of fake advertising including fake news manipulated by the power elite and media moguls. The Internet's virtual world perfects the alienation of the individuals who surf the superficialities created for them, all the while believing their demand for things causes them to be produced when in fact they are being force fed.

I was an anachronistic *flâneur* some years ago, randomly walking the streets of New York City as its distinct neighborhoods were gradually being absorbed by big stores. In fact, my life has been a random walk. I knew people were supposed to have goals in order to succeed, and success was determined by wealth, by the things and people one owned, but even as a young boy I rebelled against "being somebody" in that bodily sense.

No way was I going to have goals and plans. When I was a little boy I was angered when people asked me "what" I was going to be when I grew up. Why should be other than "who" I am? I ran away from home for good two weeks after I turned thirteen years of age, and proceeded to wander the streets of Chicago. I was lucky that I was a tall boy who loved to read and seemed intelligent to others as I eventually lied my way off the mean streets into steady employment, falling, by chance, into office jobs, and, ultimately, into accounting, where I, ironically, used some common sense I had picked up as a kid in Kansas and my Chicago street smarts to help my employers devise plans to achieve goals.

I might have done very well if I had taken my own advice, but I was not interested in success, except perhaps to be the greatest author the world would ever or never know. As it is, I am what one might call a successful loser, an idler who loves to think about what others do and to write about it in my own way. I guess I am, like Taleb, a *flâneur*. I was on a random walk. I ventured to New York City from Chicago and took a liking to it because the drinking age was 18 back then. Turned down for a job on Wall Street because they found out I lied about my formal education, I randomly walked around, and chanced by the construction site for the World Trade Center. I was angry that my application was rejected, so I cursed the pit upon which the twin towers would be set. I knew I would have performed as well as the college grads if I had been given a chance to analyze businesses and pick the best securities to invest in. I did not know at the time that the market was on a random walk, and that a monkey with darts could do as well as the average expert.

If I had been hired that day, I would have enough "f*** you" money to write a Black Swan book! As it were, I crunched numbers, was luckily paid well for that, and otherwise applied myself to reading and the theatre arts, i.e. dancing, singing, and acting, dance being my favorite because it allowed the animal to express itself, without a goal in mind. My studies were as always at random. It appeared to me that everything was connected, that one could start with any detail within the book of life and tell quite a tale no matter how pointless it might be to sharpened pencil heads. Theoretically, dancers who actually dance instead of just doing technique make good writers because they are exhibitionists, and writing is thinking out loud.

Now the problem with the exercise of my aimless avocation in the city was that it was difficult to explain and seemingly absurd to everyone with plans and goals. Even after I ventured to Hawaii to marry and lead a straight life, my wife had difficulty explaining what I did for a living although I did well enough financially thanks to a German wheeler-dealer whom I helped make millions in real estate.

"What do you do for a living?" had required a short answer in Manhattan, especially when asked by beautiful Jewish American Princesses on the West Side, and I, like Taleb, preferred not to identify myself with money grubbing! I was, after all, a *flâneur*, if you please.

"Once, on a transatlantic flight," wrote Taleb, "I found myself upgraded to first class next to an expensively dressed, high-powered lady dripping with gold and jewelry who continuously ate nuts (low-carb diet, perhaps), insisted on drinking only Evian, all the while reading the European edition of The Wall Street Journal. She kept trying to start a conversation in broken French, since she saw me reading a book (in French) by the sociologist-philosopher Pierre Bourdieu—which naturally dealt with the marks of social distinction. I informed her (in English) that I was a limousine driver, proudly insisting that I drove 'very upper-ended' cars. An icy silence followed, and, although I could feel the tension, it allowed me to read in peace."

That particular paragraph convinced me that Taleb is a kindred spirit. I would rather study than work, and study on my own at that. I do not write for money, I write to live, to avoid the end. I do not begrudge people their wealth, their escapes into matter no matter how professional. I feel sorry for them if they are miserable and are not having fun and contributing to the general good. Whether I like it or not, man is a goal-seeking animal, and the goal of life is to avoid the goal fated for all things, with the possible exception of fundamentalist Christians.

I am too engaged in writing to market my work, and that does not matter. People ask me what I do for a living, and I just say I am retired, because if I say I am an author, they want to know right away if I have been published by major publishers. If not, I am immediately demoted, albeit politely, and find myself treated disrespectfully. Whatever happened to the importance of Being over Doing?

The woman on the plane who wanted to know what Taleb did for a living may have just been curious, or perhaps she just wanted to pass the time in conversation, which is most likely. He did not say how many rings she had on her fingers. According to my favorite songstress, Alicia Keys, a "Real Man will know A Woman's Worth" and lay some diamonds on her.

Look, I took courses on the street in the school of hard knocks. I am not one to go around calling women prostitutes for renting their bodies when men are engaged in renting out their souls as well. People naturally want power, status has power, and wealth today buys the highest status in the minds of many competitors.

I lived on the Upper West Side, where I habituated a popular restaurant and bar on West 79th Street called Wilsons, and I cannot remember how many times a women asked me "What do you do?" and did not get around to asking my name after I answered. Clubs like Wilsons were called "meat markets" by guys who cruised meat markets to meet women.

The ladies were on the hunt as well, and usually for something more permanent than a handsome hunk of meat. A qualified man should have a substantial income, therefore, "What do you do?" No matter how smart or helpful a man might be, his "character" is determined by his wealth and how "generous" he is with it. I actually saw many women take the tips their dates had left on the bar as they departed, the gentleman leading the way, of course.

I did not like to be pegged down. I experimentally lied to assess the reactions, and discovered that if I loudly said, "I am a surgeon," almost every girl at the bar took inordinate interest. If I wanted to be left alone, perhaps because I did not like the girl I encountered, I would just say, "I am a file clerk," and she would turn her back on me to talk to someone else.

Now there was a jazz lounge on Upper Broadway, in the Nineties, called J's or Judy's, I think, where some great musicians appeared. It was not a meat market, far from it, so I was surprised when a woman I was chatting with asked:

"What do you do?"

"I'm a file clerk."

"Did you say a file clerk?"

"Yes."

"Oh."

"Not only do I file things, I retrieve them as well."

"You are just what I have been looking for, in my business," she said, handing me her business card. "Would you mind coming to my office on Fifth Avenue tomorrow?"

I may relate what happened afterwards in a novel, where personal truths are always better told as fiction. Yet another version of Swan Lake might do.

Taleb is probably right about the Black Swan. Dark matter is invisible so its effects seem to come out of nowhere. He relates that people were walking about shocked and dazed by the unexpected "Black Monday" stock market crash on 19 October 1987 when the average of the index decreased 29.2%, a virtually impossible event according to the Efficient Market Hypothesis; the odds against that happening at the time were 1 in 10 followed by 45 zeros. I noticed something strange about the mood on the sidewalk when I came out of the Fisk Building near Columbus Circle. I stopped by a bar and asked what was going on. The stock market had crashed! Thirty-three years after I observed the foundations being laid for the World Trade Center, the twin towers had tumbled down! Who would have imagined such a disaster was forthcoming?

We can never make ourselves completely secure from the untoward events fostered by the Black Swan. She is supernatural. We find no instrument between her as cause and her effects. Note that the Black Swan can be a male even though males like to characterize the opposite sex as hysterical.

The Black Swan is within so may not be walled out. Taleb arrived with the virtue of an immigrant after he became an ascetic rebel in a luxurious Lebanese setting "with a vastly sophisticated lifestyle, a prosperous economy, and temperate weather just like California, with snow-covered mountains jutting above the Mediterranean. It attracted a collection of spies (both Soviet and Western), prostitutes (blondes), writers, pimps, drug dealers, adventurers, compulsive gamblers, tennis players, après-skiers, and merchants—all professions that complement each other...."

And then.... "The Lebanese 'paradise' suddenly evaporated.... A Black Swan, coming out of nowhere, transformed the place from heaven to hell."

The only exception I might take at some length to Taleb's classical thesis is the association of catastrophes with color and gender. Some lucky people think success is entirely their own doing, while others confess that luck played a large part. Lady Fortuna has been called a bitch because she is faithful to no man or woman regardless of race, color, or creed. She can bring incredible luck as well as misfortune. Besides, the Goddess of Night conceals not only criminals but lovers.

Is the *The Black Swan*, the "dark side" or alter ego of the American ego, its death instinct, soon to be its suicidal undoing? Will the "Platonic" boxes people think in come tumbling down? Is the American 'paradise' about to suddenly evaporate?

The subtitle of *The Black Swan* is 'The Impact of the Highly Improbable." The highly improbable is still probable. The problem is too complex for the computers to figure out. We might enjoy the day before meeting our maker. We might remove the motive for hate with love and stop looking on people as numbers to be manipulated. The Black Swan might then become our Black Stallion.

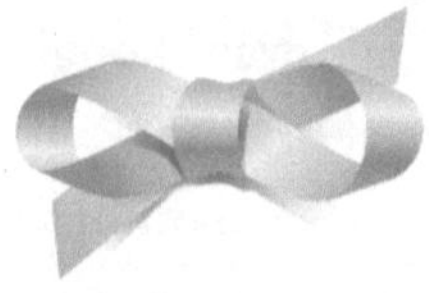

Dumb Dancer

I write to evade direct contact with reality or the floor of everything by describing it or imagining it as something much better than it is. I suppose you might call me a dumb idealist or a dumb dancer. There is no such thing as writer's block for me because I am compelled to do something symbolic, even if it is merely Art For Art's Sake.

I took a break from my usual evasions this morning to consider moving out of my writer's hovel because I noticed it is getting rather squalid after 15 years of habitation. You see, the older I get and the more wrapped up in imagining things and telling stories, the less inclined I am to clean the floor. It is not that I make a mess, it is just that even after I wash the floor and take care not to drop anything on it, it gets dirty on its own within three days, giving me call to wonder where all the little particles of debris, some of which look like sawdust left by the gnawing termites, are coming from.

The original paint job on the walls was poorly done, leaving uneven swaths of white and gray, and the grouting at the baseboards was just slapped on. Indeed, the grouting in the bathroom is one of the worst grouting jobs known to mankind. And despite a new roof, rainwater continues to leak into the bathroom cause the paint on the ceiling to flake and crumble.

The landlord used undocumented immigrants to barely maintain his buildings. He liked to chisel them down or not pay them at all, and he was proud of his frugality. He died, and his wife took over, and absolutely no maintenance is done now unless the tenant pays for it. The tenant must also his own supply air conditioners, refrigerators, stoves, electrical work and plumbing repairs. The city's code compliance cited the appearance of the building, so she made the tenants paint it. Everyone is on a month-to-month lease and at her mercy, to be evicted if a complaint is made. The upside is that the rent for the shoddy studios is about $300 to $400 a month below market. Another is the proximity to stores and the beach and parks.

Of course the weather in Miami Beach is great except for the hurricanes. Furthermore, a car is unnecessary if you want to risk being run over by one in a crosswalk. The society overall is somewhat lacking because many people come here to avoid society, and particularly its laws. There is an enormous economic gap between wealthy residents, many of whom are money launderers and tax evaders or persons whose fraud and greed has been legalized, and the virtual slaves who serve them and the tourist industry.

So what is not to like? The older I get, the harder it is for me to get up the nerve to actually move away, so this morning I looked around to see what I would have to do to stay in my unit in a complex that has finally been civilized after catering to drunken illegal immigrant workers and dope peddlers and other riffraff. I figured I could make my studio appear nice enough to have a guest over if I would dress five windows nicely, and re-grout or use grout paint on the floors, strip the molding and replace molding under the baseboards, paint the walls and not the ceilings, install one new light fixture, install a curtain to cover the closet area, and fix the rust in bathtub. That would cost about $4,800 if properly done, which I could count as a rent increase of $400 over 12 months.

But I have no lease. If the property is sold, which it might very well be, I would be out my expenditures for improvement costs. Another issue: if the landlady moved in another hell-raiser as in the past, I would want to move because I could not bear going through the hell that I did for three years in the past when the so-called chic

South Beach neighborhood was a virtual Central American ghetto thanks to the slumlords.

After engaging in that rather lengthy thought process and arriving at no decision, I determined to clean the floor. I'm glad I did, but that awful, blackened grout between the white tiles, some stained yellow hear the kitchen sink, is staring me in the face and giving me the horrors. Maybe I could fix that myself, but my body is not holding up so well lately. Why, I was exhausted, short of breath, just washing the floor. That gave me cause to think of the time I was in great shape and was in New York dancing eight hours a day. Even then I deplored doing what we called floor work.

You see, I used to be a so-called dumb dancer back in the day. Last evening I grew weary of television, so I turned to my cell phone to watch, with strained eyes plagued by cataracts, a dance choreographed by Pina Bausch. Much of the dance was performed very close to or on the floor, and it reminded me of how I was kicked out of a Graham class for remarking that there was too much floor work and that the dancers should get mops instead of using themselves as mops and getting themselves dirty.

Of course the earth is dirty. The ancients associated it with our genesis and referred to it as Mother Earth. Women are by nature more flexible than men, not only because their hips are broader to carry the race, hence they have a greater extension and their legs that enables them to proudly do the splits, but because it was strategic for them to be submissive from the beginning given the dominance of men by virtue of their greater size and strength. Of course there were Amazonian women back in the day, and some liberated woman today are proficient enough in the martial arts to dominate most men, in addition to employing the usual wiles to outsmart them and twist them around her fingers

Yes, there are male dancers whose long hamstrings can outstretch those of any female, and they are quite good at floor work. Stretching my hamstrings was of little avail to me. I recall a male dancer who found his hamstrings lacking after years of stretching, so he had them cut in several places to give him more stretch, but wound up crippled. Likewise, a dancer on tour tied his legs into a split on the bedposts in his hotel room. He tore his hamstrings badly while sleeping and was unable to finish the tour

No, floor work is not for me, not at all. I do my best to avoid it. Maybe I will sweep up the hairballs, lint, and termite sawdust, and then mop my floor with a Cuban mop after I write an essay about what happened to a guy with gout who tried to paint his grout.

Dancing With Women in War and Peace

In Fond Memory of Luigi Facciuto

That we dream a certain dream, fashioning it from bits and pieces of memories, has fascinated many an interpreter. As everyone knows, the brain keeps running while we sleep, and when we lightly do so, it is wont to tell a story to that unity of apperception we call the self, as if the storyteller were another person split off, or half the individual divided, and a mysterious half at that because we may not intuit or directly know the introjected subject we associate with the I as it organizes our self-reflections. Yet it has a motive, a theme, or fixed idea to be divined upon awakening.

I had not seen Jill Strauss for twenty years yet she represented that motive in my dream. She taught jazz dance for Luigi Facciuto, may he never stop moving, and I took her class from time to time when she substituted for him. I still take his class in my dreams although he went to the presumably Better Place this year, and she, a pretty little woman with a big heart, is almost always around, as she regularly was back in those days. I do not believe I had a crush on her, at least not consciously, though I did think she was quite cute. We both moved away from New York, she to California, me to Hawaii then Florida.

Jill starred in my dream last night. She was driving, and I was her passenger. I used to drive in my dreams, smoking cigarettes as well, until I realized with considerable alarm in one dream that I had quit smoking, and had no driver's license. She pulled into a charming shopping center. Judging from the Spanish architecture, we were in California.

I visited California in my youth, even stayed in San Francisco a few months, and thought Californians were weird. I liked the smaller cities, got to drive a big pink Cadillac convertible, and thought the traffic was atrocious.

I just heard from Drew a few days ago. He moved to California from South Beach a couple years ago. He said people were a lot nicer in California. I thought of moving out there. The San Bernardino shootings took place the next day, an hour's drive from his home.

The war drums beat incessantly, bombs are away and maybe a National Socialist American Workers Party will be founded, its militant members goose-stepping in brown shirts.

I felt comfortable with Jill at the wheel as she wheeled into the mall. We approached a two-story building with a wooden façade and big windows. A dance class was ongoing inside. The studio was huge, with a very high, vaulted ceiling. There were two huge murals of modern dancers painted on two of the walls. It reminded me of Ana Lessa's new Atma Beauty salon in South Beach.

Yesterday I encountered Ray Sullivan, a choreographer, sitting at a café in South Beach. We chatted animatedly at length about the great dancers and teachers we knew and had studied under back in the day, and bemoaned the fact that the current generation has missed the revolutionary philosophy of modern dance and along with it the passion that moves audiences to tears of joy.

Too many today are just doing technique, not dancing. The kids know little yet think they know everything, and believe they are entitled to dance choreography in their own, conceited way, instead of getting into and being engaged in The Work. I recounted, with some satisfaction, how a dancer told a top choreographer that a certain movement did not work for him, and the choreographer replied with, "Then you're fired because you don't work for me."

The arts bring out the best in people when art is loved for its own sake. Woe unto me, for I no longer sing, dance, and act, and have taken up writing about politics, which brings out the meanness in me, not to mention others. And what I write about is here today and gone tomorrow. I love history, but when I try to relate current events to their historical contexts, most people are just not interested because they are inclined to repeat well-worn mistakes.

So I am drawn back to art, to at least write something immortal to pass along the gifts that are not mine but of my kind. I have been preoccupied with death lately, in the form, unfortunately, of bad finales. Death is part of life, but art is about it all.

So Jill and I got out of the car in front of the California dance studio. She took my hand as I took hers, but not quite in the right way, therefore we made an adjustment until the form was perfect, and she led me into the studio. Finally I felt safe, and I awoke.

Just before falling asleep, I considered how women may now participate in combat alongside men, to actively engage in the massive murders legalized by nations. I felt uncomfortable about that.

Much of the difference between the sexes is cultivated. Still there are differences in strength and size, and in hormones: females are theoretically more nurturing than males. Female warriors are nothing new, really, and there are desperate times when women are needed to not only fight but to lead in battle instead of just throwing themselves off the walls when defeat is imminent lest they be forced to bear the children of the enemy.

If a woman wants to be a warrior and can qualify, that is fine with me. She should not be subject, however, to the draft. I believe women should be cultivated to make and keep peace among men through nonviolent means, just as she has done with the advance of civilization. She should be protected along with her children from the ravages of war.

Ray had complained about the notion that choreographers should be business managers and producers and fundraisers wrapped up in one person, which works the ruin of the choreographer's expertise and creativity, and distracts the others from their duties as well. And too many people in Miami Beach tend to think that the mere possession of funds makes them experts. Labor must be divided into functions, so each can excel. The lack of these divisions and their purposeful coordination is why organizations fail, especially small companies.

I once read an evolutionary theory that men were relatively peaceful when they lived in the forests somewhat like bonobos, and then became violent when they left the forest and had to forage more widely and fight other groups for their sustenance. As they did so, they grew larger and stronger. Females, on the other hand, remained small by comparison so they could be carried to safe places, for they cradle the race.

Maybe that anthropological theory is not scientifically justifiable. Cultural justification is another matter. I think the memory of it brought me to Jill in my dream. She is the pretty little muse who took me by the hand and led me back to art.

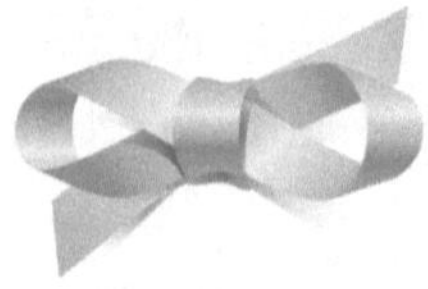

Keiko's Monophobia

How can I begin to tell you about Monophobia? I could consult the myriads of books on creativity, but then I might lose the impetus to speak. So I shall proceed to say whatever comes to mind. An improvisation if you please, since I have no plan.

I must admit that I am afraid to approach Monophobia, to waltz right up to it, take it by the hand and report back to you what steps were taken in 3/4. For it concerns the existence that has us all pinned down. We struggle to unpin ourselves, yet if unpinned we lose the point and cease to exist. That struggle is my starting point. I cannot stand here perfectly still. I have no choice but to be continuously active or gravitate to nothingness as the ground rushes to meet me. I must keep moving in the interim, one way or another. So, in this case, I must speak to you.

Keiko Fujii and her dancers came to Manhattan and reminded me of my own singular fear of existing, a phobia I attribute to the personal sense of the imminent loss of existence that my own existence implies. Her production of Monophobia, which premiered in the United States at the Sylvia and Danny Kaye Playhouse, was shaken out of her by the Kobe earthquake. There is nothing like having the earth ripped out from under you. Creative Destruction is awfully sublime. The thing in itself that is really no thing is a terrifying mystery beyond description. Nevertheless, we can describe some of the forms it takes. The question is: where to start.

Anywhere might do. Keiko started with the pas de chat, using it to describe the mythological underpinnings of the Japanese economy. It is amazing how she milked the pas de chat for all it is worth. No, the pas de chat is not the udder of a cow. It is a cat-like step that has become a formal element of the traditional ballet vocabulary. The dancer jumps quickly off one foot then the other, legs turned out at the hips, bringing his knees up in the air in rapid succession, with feet pointed and for a moment almost touching below, so that at the height of the movement his legs form a diamond shape. Of course, there is a lot more to it than that: it is a simple movement in the rough, but it takes the dancer years to polish the diamond.

To continue: Keiko's dancers, decked out in business suits, formed teams and executed several series of pas de chats across the stage. The simulated enthusiasm as well as the unison of the team members and the precise coordination of the teams vigorously shuttling about their business illustrated the virtues of the well-oiled Japanese business machine. To serve its purpose, the parts of a machine must move in opposition, as did the phalanxes of dancers as they moved in opposite directions to weave their illusion of happy workers laboring in their divisions for a common cause. However, as the workers continued with their rituals apace, the entire affair became rather monotonous. I began to notice that the whole industry was based on perfunctory pas de chats, alien components expensive to maintain. Technique is better left unnoticed. The workers were not dancing; they were doing technique. Even the smiles of the happy workers seemed contrived. The dream machine was running down. A couple of the machined parts began to squeak and broke off, annoyed by paperwork and laptop duties; information anxiety began to set in. Alas, the worker was overloaded. But, finally, the relief of the evening commute! The ranks were broken into their constituents. The dancers, however, did not bother to communicate with each other at the station or on the train; rather, each one got out his cell phone and proceeded to call home, finally displaying his most genuine smile, not for his traveling companions but for the invisible family on the other end of virtuality. But what if you don't have a family, what if you are single; for whom do you smile, your personal God?

Except for the sole male dancer Keiko traditionally utilizes, all of the male's roles were played by lovely women decked out in the business suits that frightened me because, though I look terrific in one, when I see someone in a power suit, I feel that someone is going to be crushed.

Never mind. Thou shalt not shout or lose thy cool. A well-oiled machine must not squeak. A happy worker does not need a future because she has nothing to cry about. Employees must not display genuine feelings, especially negative ones; although positive emotions are highly recommended for everyone, they are resented because they cause hard feelings in those who don't have them. Business is not the place for emotions. The romantic claim that all values are based on emotion is scoffed at by the rational businessman.

Thou shalt not get naked! Thou shalt not take off thy suit! Thou shalt not streak! Above all, thou shalt not whistle or sing on the job!

In a moment of disobedience, however, Keiko's dancers did shed their suits. It is not easy to shed the conventional mythologies, especially the mythology of the Japanese economy or any other economy where if it cannot be counted it doesn't really count. We want to strip, but our clothes are a security blanket.

Shed obligations. File bankruptcy. File for divorce. Quit your job. Disown your family and friends. Forsake your nation. Move offshore. Be cynical and be saved, you selfish traitor to your own social security! Ironic, isn't it, that almost any virtue defrocked makes all virtue look like vice?

Good grief! Just what is the healing answer to all this highly touted Creative Destruction?

Well, Keiko went back in time and donned the traditional kimono, a green kimono under which she executed ever so small movements with enormous implications. A mere lift of her foot gave one the impression that she had just traversed the entire universe. Moving upstage on the diagonal, the kimono unfurled behind her in a train that extended from one corner of the stage to the other, all to the rushing, rumbling and gurgling sounds of a waterfall. Then she ever so slowly turned and turned, reeling in the train, winding it about her feet into a pedestal. Disappearing under the green shroud of the remaining material, she finally emerged, an exquisitely painted "nude" in colorful tights, as if clothed by Nature, leaving her traditional chrysalis behind. She did a series of Grand Changement Italiens, jumping straight up from both feet, bringing her legs up rapidly into a diamond shape, hovering in the air for a moment. Yet again, as it should be, the classical ballet technique was invisible to the untrained eye. Keiko simply looked like a wild hummingbird cavorting about in accordance with her natural proclivities. The other dancers then appeared in the same native costumes so wonderfully designed by Keiko herself, and they likewise displayed instinctive tendencies.

Is this the healing answer: Back to Nature? Maybe so, but not as long as we have to think about it, so I'll leave it alone in the trance I briefly enjoyed. It was a retreat into solitude, an epoch, a momentous pause, an interlude eventually rudely shattered by Monophobia.

Enter doom and gloom with a room therein all pervaded by that familiar fetid fog mentioned heretofore in a clause cluttered with malicious malcontent. I see my life passing by on the stage. That must be my dismal uptown studio with one window facing the rank exhaust of the Chinese noodle shop. Ah, and nearly the same discordant, unsynchronized, rhythmic racket of the air conditioners and exhaust fans outside that window, music here for the modern ears, as accompaniment for the monstrous ogres now entering. There is an ocherous devil dragging an enormous white bundle on a rope behind him with all his might. It must be Saturday morning laundry!

I am shocked: this is about me! Several dancers are huddled together in a corner each shrouded in white. They must be the sycophants of yet another diabolical character, played so well by the sole male, creeping about with that two-pronged pitchfork. He must be the infamous binary system. Damn! I think he uses that fork to devour his sycophants! What great technology! The food cooperates with the fork. When Keiko comes out of her room she eventually embraces the ghastly instrument.

Keiko's tiny room in hell reminds me of the facades on those Holiday Inns that mushroomed all over the country years ago, facades made of glass and aluminum extrusions. Although her cubicle is transparent and my uptown hovel is opaque with merely a window, I think the song is still about me. The room is the mind; I am aware of a vast universe by virtue of cells in my brain living a warm and watery life in total darkness. And because my consciousness off it all seems to expand, the possibilities of what I might know seem unlimited—it is really my stupidity that gives me the sense of infinite expanse. My room is so tiny, my perspective so small. I live in a skull supported by flesh and bones. I am so small in comparison with infinity that I might as well be a point without dimensions. I am pinned down here! Someone please tear me loose, please get me out of here!

Keiko struggled with an enormous variety of movements in her cell. Perhaps that is how the human animal differs from her caged relatives; she dances his miserable danse macabre intentionally, hoping to somehow overcome the isolation of her limitations, to get out of here and become one with the all, to synchronize with the cosmos. Is this love of unity a fear of identity? Is our dance a game of camouflage, a nihilistic playing of hide and seek with the universe?

As modern dancer in original, iconoclastic sense, Keiko attempts to display the fullest range of movement; history is the progress of freedom, but what paltry limitations has this pinhead existence!

Eventually one succumbs on bed or couch. Not for long, however. "Never Stop Moving," is life's imperative. Depressed by ponderous gravity, feeling monotheism is monophobia and that the one sure thing, the monotonous reality, is death, that God is not dead because God is death, the devotee prostrates herself prone before her master; but then she twists and turns and now she is supine; now she tries to rest and shuts her eyes and voids her mind all to no avail. She shudders with hunger and ennui. She must have bread and the circus. She leaves the security of her room. She goes out to embrace her fear. Entranced by the not- voidable, she will willingly dance her dance with death.

Embrace fear. Is that the healing answer? Misery is inevitable, the argument goes, so console oneself with the knowledge that chance does not really matter because your misery would just take another form if not the present one.

So, you say you enjoy being alone, and while alone you do not give much thought to death. I too love being alone, but after a while I must admit my thoughts turn morbid. Acute awareness of my own existence prompts me to think of its opposite and I, in my solitude, cling precariously to the roots of depression lest I plunge into the abyss. For what I love I fear as well. The formation of my personality is the response to the fear that my life will be wiped out. I am a product of death. I think death makes the man and then takes him away. I love and fear my maker and although I love being alone I am driven by my fear of the same to desperately cling to others of my ilk on the chance that I may forget myself. Fat chance, for the relation further defines me and sets me apart from my relations.

I think of all this when I consider Keiko's Monophobia. It seems, however, that I seldom have much company. It was not a full house. The audience enjoyed the performance, but grew very weary during Keiko's prolonged, anxious movements within the confines of her own limitations. That is just how an anxious life can feel after a long while: extremely boring and sleep-inducing. Although the audience was enchanted by the early stages of the performance and was appropriately enthralled by the hellish scene, many people thought its life had come to an end and left, forgetting there was a third act to come as indicated by the programme.

I was so exhausted by Keiko's extenuated monophobic symbolics that I paid bare attention to her third act. I do recall a pleasant dance by the chorus all decked out in white space suits. Is that the final solution? To go where no man had gone before? To catch a ride on the tail of a comet?

I met with Keiko the next day. She seemed amused by some of my interpretations of her work, but was mostly silent. At one point, while struggling desperately for the meaning of life, I said: "I see people smoking, drinking, using drugs, chasing men and women and money, seeking information, so on and so forth. They look like they are trying to escape. I keep saying maybe there is no way out. Maybe there is no escape. Maybe there is nothing but misery ending in nothing."

Keiko seemed surprised, and responded: "That is Buddhism."

"If that is an answer, why don't you show it to us in your next concert?"

"Maybe I will.

"Call it Zero, or just 0."

"We'll see."

Keiko's Shinwa

Textual Narrative of a Dance Myth Created and Choreographed by Keiko Fujii

In the year 3,000 AD, a 200-year-old man is telling children a story about something that happened in Japan after World War II more than a thousand years ago.

"On the first day of spring, in the countryside near Ashiya, an innocent young girl named Keiko was dancing with the cherry trees at the edge of a lovely meadow. She was happy because springtime had finally begun.

"When Keiko was a baby, she got very sick one winter and lost her voice forever, so now she sang to the trees, birds, and cherry blossoms in sign language as she danced and danced with the cherry trees. Losing her voice had also made her very shy. When other people came near the meadow where she danced, she would run and hide until they had gone. There were so many people interrupting her on this first day of spring that she decided to go home and return the next day.

"While Keiko was dancing in the meadow on the next day, three young bullies snuck up behind her and surprised her. At first they surrounded and teased her, but then the ruffians got rough. One of the boys started to break off a branch of her favorite cherry tree. She tried to stop him from hurting the tree she loved the most, but he finally broke off the branch. Then he began beating the tree with the branch just to upset her.

"Keiko put herself between the bully and the tree to protect the tree from being hurt, but then he hit her several times with the branch and knocked her down onto the ground. The boys saw she was badly hurt. They thought they might get in trouble, so they ran away. Keiko seemed to be dead. She was lying on the ground at the foot of the tree. The spring breeze swirled cherry petals from her beloved trees all around her body. Her stiff arms were hugging the branch the boy had beaten her with.

"One hundred years later, in autumn, three men had a very strange experience near the meadow where Keiko used to dance. They were tourists who had walked to the Buddhist celebration of *Shakya Muni* in Saga, Kyoto. On their way home from the celebration, the three men stopped for a while to look at the beautiful maple leaves which were changing color with the approach of winter. Suddenly, before they realized how late it was, it was very dark. A cold blanket of fog covered them. They could not see their hands in front of their faces. Then it began to rain. The men were confused. They were all shivering from the cold. You could hear one man's teeth chattering in the dark.

"But the lost tourists were lucky this time. An old woman appeared out of nowhere and told them they could stay at her house that night.

"The tourists felt warm and welcome in the nice old woman's house after they had feasted and had drank plenty of her hot *sake*. Later that evening, the woman told them she was going to go into the woods to get some special firewood to make sure they would be warm all night. They offered to help her, but she refused their offer. Before she went outside to get the wood, she made them all promise not to go into the woodshed behind the house or even to look into it while she was gone.

"One of her guests became curious after the old lady had left, wondering why she wanted them to stay out of the woodshed. He asked his friends to go outside with him and take a look into the shed. They refused. They warned him not to break his promise. But when his friends had fallen asleep, the man decided to sneak out and peek into the woodshed anyway.

"The curious man went to the shed and slid open its door. He heard weak moans and groans coming from inside. He hesitated, then stepped slowly into the shed. He saw a vision of Hell inside. The shed was filled with gruesome zombies who were only barely alive, too dead to move except to fall and stagger and wriggle around the best they could with their rotten bodies all twisted out of shape. Many of them were missing an arm or leg. Some were missing feet and hands. The chopped-off body parts were on the floor of the shed, oozing blood. One zombie was trying to play football with another zombie's head, but he was so dead he could barely kick it. Others were sticking their hands into horrible gaping wounds in their bodies. Many faces had been smashed with a club. Noses and teeth were badly broken. Cheeks were swollen out of shape. There were bloody and broken eye sockets with eyes missing. Mouths and jaws were caved in.

"The zombies slowly surrounded the curious man. They wanted to suck the life right out of him.

"Well, the man who had broken his promise not to go into the woodshed was now paralyzed with fear. His knees weakened and he had to lie down on the floor where he wet his pants and vomited. Then he raised his head up and saw a strange light coming from the corner of the shed. He felt the light calling to him so he crawled towards it. He struggled to his feet and saw that the light was coming from a glass coffin. A girl in a pink dress was laid out inside the coffin. A strange power was pulling the man towards her. He looked up and down her body, trying to find some sign of life, but there was no sign because she was dead. He saw she had a broken branch from a cherry tree in her stiffened arms, as if she had been hugging it close to her bosom when she died.

"The nosy tourist stared at the dead girl for a while, then ran out of the woodshed and back into the house. He woke up his friends, shouting, 'There's a witch's den in the shed with zombies and a dead girl in a glass coffin!' Of course, they did not believe him. They did not want to get up yet because their heads hurt from drinking so much of the old woman's *sake*, but their friend kept yelling, so they went outside to see what he was so upset about. Sure enough, there were zombies in the shed, walking-dead people in a living Hell, and a dead girl in a glass coffin, just as they had been told.

"At that very moment, the nice old lady came back carrying a bundle of firewood in her arms. But when she saw the tourists inside the woodshed, she became very angry. Her body changed shape, taking the form of a huge spider with a witch's head. The spider-witch blamed the three men for breaking their promise not to look into the woodshed. She screamed she was going to kill them then and there.

"The frightened men struggled to get away. The witch's hair turned into threads which spiders use to trap their food alive. As she wrapped her spider hair around the curious tourist, the other men scrambled over each other and escaped. When the spider-woman started to run after them, the curious tourist untied himself and ran away too. All three men got away, disappearing into the woods. The spider witch screamed, "I will catch and eat you all someday!" Then she changed back into an ordinary old woman.

"After the tourists got away, it started to snow. The old woman began dancing slowly with the snow. She wanted to tell a story with her dance, a very sad story. But as she danced and the snow became deeper, her thinking became deeper too. She was not really an evil witch, but a good witch who warned and frightened people so they would not get into deep trouble. As she danced in the snow, she became young again. The snow melted and it was spring again. She was a dancing girl again, singing and signing again, whirling again with the petals of cherry blossoms in the breeze."

The End of the Long Winding Road

I am coming to the end of a long and winding road that I have always traveled at random without a goal in mind. I ran away from "home" right after my thirteenth birthday, and I have been running ever since.

When by chance I worked in hospitals as a teen and was called upon from time to time to take the dead to the morgue, I did not imagine at the time that their destiny would be mine. As I grew older, I kept running, from what I knew not then, and I took up dancing for the art of it because I really did not like exercise per se.

I also took up acting, and singing the Blues. I liked to sing about that Old Black Train as it approached the subway platform to take me to classes, how its light approached ever so slowly in the distance, but then suddenly arrived in a rush.

Now the rush is upon me, accompanied by I could of, would of, should of been this or that instead of being temporarily a gypsy, dancer, singer, and a part-time numbers man, and now a full-time writer to avoid the fate that is mine.

Having flown from love to love for Love's sake, I am unloved now, with, perhaps the exception of Jesus. Upon reflection of what I could have been, I am moved to say what I learned in all those classes.

My words of wisdom from experience are nothing new. Stay put, stick with it, and be somebody, It is with that in mind that I wrote, *Reflections in the Well*, demonstrating that even escapees on foot who follow that advice can succeed. It features postmodern dance pioneer Deborah Hay.

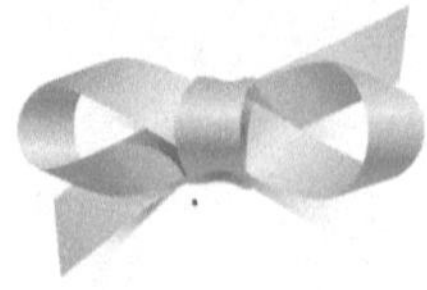

I'm With the Dancers

Sometimes I wonder how my prospective friend Fidel Castro, the scapegoat for all of Cuba's ills, including the neo-fascists' forty-year terrorist campaign against Cubans who stick around the island, can be so foolish. By gum, it seems that President Bush is losing the contest for World's Greatest Moron ("fool") after all.

Well, maybe the pattern of blunders are not always Castro's fault. Perhaps his leading bureaucrats should be terminated forthwith before the pre-emptive Bush Agenda is launched - at least Castro would be rid of the officials within his government who are presently privately drooling over the right-wing prospects.

Indeed, when a great man approaches his demise, one would think he would repent of evil and provide for a succession competent to realize the goods he had in mind; maybe he would step down as chief executive, to serve as chairman of the board on a part-time basis and to enjoy the golden years - smoke cigars, talk about the good old days, go yachting and snorkeling, those sort of favorite pastimes. But great men who are beyond good and evil seldom do that, for they are jealous of their personal power.

Just for example, we might start with the legendary Alexander the Great, who might have been poisoned by his own mother if not by his prodigious boozing, and who left behind a weak administration. Or take Tamurlane, who might have been poisoned too, and who might have fulfilled his destiny and saved the world from the future U.S.S.R. instead of setting up a vicious advertising circle - the towers of skulls. Or take Yassar Arafat, who could have made amends and left something worthy of a Nobel Peace Prize behind besides a reputation for explosives. Maybe Ariel Sharon, the former war criminal, will atone with the loving side of YHWH, and leave a legacy of enduring peace behind instead of something that reminds us of the worst enemy the Jews ever had - ironically, the anglo-american-saxon Roman-Nazis are frustrated Jews, and now have in Iraq their own large-scale Palestine.

Yes, it's time for a purge down south. Fidel Castro might first of all open up the world for his people by providing them with free Internet access along with sturdy Cuban designed and manufactured Internet access devices. Then Cubans would be understand who is really to blame for Yankee Imperialism up north, where the Northern European, WASPish culture predominates today regardless of race, color or creed. Cubans would soon discover whom the real friends and enemies of humanity are.

Castro should retain some competent Cuban Americans and sympathetic gringos to come down and help revitalize Cuba's social revolution along the lines of welfare capitalism. Fidel might realize that there are new ways to skin cats, then let go of the obsolete methods, provide for the future, and give his people voluntary cause to weep over his grave and monuments. If he handles things rightly, he might have due cause to envision himself as the Latin American messiah on his deathbed. As it is, we see one blunder after another. What is the Spanish word for "blunder"?

I'll mention one that came to my attention today (November 15, 2004). I noticed it because it was on the front page of the Miami Herald, whose publisher, editors, and reporters are committed to serving the "market need" of their readers, according to "race and ethnic background." That is, the market need of Cuban exiles who control Miami along with its "free" press.

The article about Cuba's most recent blunder appears to the right of another article on Cuban affairs: the plans of U.S. Senator-elect Mel Martinez, President Bush's former Housing Secretary, to use his

Senate position to further a "tough attitude on Cuba," meaning, of course, regime change - "a total change in the government." Martinez was on a special Bush committee to plan the U.S. led transition and reconstruction of Cuba. He was hand-picked by the Bush administration to run for the U.S. Senate, and his vicious and slanderous campaign against his opponent Betty Castor, implying that she fostered terrorism, was denounced by respectable journalists all over the world. "I'd do anything in the world," said Martinez, to see Cuba have the opportunity to do better.

But let's get to the Las Vegas blunder: '44 Cuban artists plan asylum bids' is the headline. Forty-four performing artists, in Vegas for a three-month 'Havana Night Club' review, decided to defect because Cuban officials threatened to jail them or take away their livelihood in Cuba if they stayed in Vegas for the review. I understand their concern, for I can testify from my personal experience in the United States that taking away an artist's livelihood is similar to killing him. The leader of the Cuban group, Ariel Machado, said the group had no intention of defecting until Cuban officials threatened them. After all, he said, they all have families in Cuba.

Well, many U.S. families have lost members to the bright lights of Vegas, and politics had little to do with the loss - patriots go home and fight the good fight. Those of us who were born and raised for a few decades in the United States have learned that all that glitters is not gold for us but is mostly for them.

But that is not the point here. The point is this: Castro, who was known for his chess-playing public relations skills must be losing his grip. Threatening the performers into defecting has provided the neo-fascists with yet another public relations coup. Whereas, if Cuba had let the performers remain, and had had an agent visit them daily to encourage them to represent the good things for Cuba, then people who saw the show and read about it might say, "Why, that is beautiful. Maybe Castro is not such a bad person after all if he lets that sort of thing go on in his country.

By the way, I am with the dancers, whatever they do. I hope to return to dancing soon, and would love to take classes with the dance masters in Cuba.

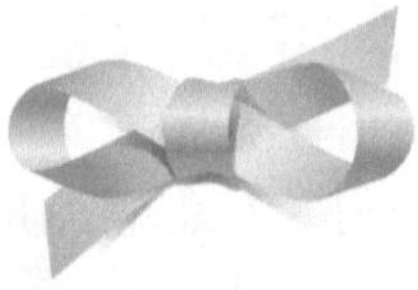

My Masterpiece Refused in Miami!

I submitted a masterful letter of approximately 500 words to the editor of the Miami New Times a few months ago, criticizing an example of the publication's liking for derogatory personal aspersions instead of facts. The free street rag's increasing fondness for vulgar allegations and virtually interminable pieces on irrelevant subjects has ruined its former reputation as an alternative paper willing to take controversial subjects much too relevant to what is really going on in Miami for publication by Knight Ridder's bilingual *The Miami Herald/el Nuevo Herald.*

"I had mixed feelings when I read April 7, 2005 The New Times article, 'Colorful Personalities', about the personality clashes at Art Center/South Florida, an art colony located on South Beach's famed Lincoln Road Mall. On the one hand, I was chagrined by the focus on the bickering instead of the art exhibited. Little was said of the art itself, other than the inference drawn from the mouths of disgruntled dissidents: that the art must be of poor quality because of the authoritarian regime of the institution's current chairman. The reporter, Forrest Norman, did make a general positive statement about the center in the first sentence of his leading statement, but then used his "blessing" as a license for a protracted revelation of the carping 'turmoil', to which I received a swift response Then editor said my masterpiece was "very long," and asked me to send over a shorter version. Without my cooperation, he said, and given his editorial restrictions, he would be unable to run it.

I replied that my submission comprised such a fine work of organic art that I could not bear to mutilate it. However, since I am a cooperative sort of person, I gave him permission to run it, just as it was written, as an article. Surely my piece would not be "very long", as an article, not given the average length of New Times articles. To further cooperate, I waived my fee.

No thanks, replied he, and I replied, no problem, I shall put out the word worldwide, to whomever it might concern, that he had rejected my little masterpiece. To which he suggested that I simply copy our email exchange - this is the virtually verbatim summary of the momentous transactions between us.

I was not offended by Mr. Mullin's refusal - not at all. My reputation as the leading Refusé in my field would have been ruined by his acceptance. I took quite a risk with my counteroffer, for he could have had the work gratis and on an all-or-nothing basis. I certainly would not butcher my baby to appease the editorial restrains presumably imposed by his publisher. Would we ask Dali to cut Jesus out of his painting or amputate his arms outstretched on the crucifix simply to suit a gallery director's narrow sense of proportion? No.

Ah, but forgive me, father, for I believe I have misjudged Mr. Mullin's rejection of my counteroffer. My letter may have been too long for a mere letter; but it was also too short for a regular article, given Mr. Mullin's editorial criteria! My letter was 1,200 words in length, in contrast to the 450-word published report it appertained to. The New Times editor ran a 3,300-article, about a hip-hop studio king's diet, in the same issue as the 'Colorful Personalities' report. The 3,300-word piece was entitled 'Organic Produce'. Its composition did not comprise the "organic art" or artful excretions of my own that I had with good reason bragged about to the editor. Organic art evolves from life as life is felt. 'Organic Produce' was a well-crafted report issued in accord with the generally accepted accounting principles of journalism. It was an impersonal account or narration of facts, posing as the truth about the superficial aspects of its subject.

I am glad it finally dawned on me that my letter was obviously too short to be an article. To maintain my reputation as the foremost Refusé in my field, it would behoove me to flesh out my letter a little and beef up my composition on the whole, that it may correspond to The New Time's ideal model, at least in respect to its length. My little masterpiece will then be a great organic masterpiece. Of course I shall do my duty quite naturally and before your eyes, in accordance with the philosophy I learned from my jazz dance master, Luigi Faciutto, who, when choreographing, used to say to us dance grunts, "This just came out. Now it is our job as dancers to make it smell good.

"Not that the editor of The New Times will accept my organic elaboration. His rag is a free, weekly periodical. Notwithstanding their parochial and pop-culture content, free weeklies are, in respect to journalistic style, frustrated major daily newspapers. We find hardly anything really new in the news or in the times it reflects today. The journalistic style of most papers and magazines is scarcely artistic: it resembles an inorganic machine, and poses as impersonal and as objective as the printing presses. It is designed to inculcate obedience to the "market needs" of the power elite who own the machine and control the major means of production. No, the romance or spirit of artistic reporting and commentary is seldom found in any journal or periodical today - everything is broken down into bits and pieces, into incoherent fragments - any artful organic elaboration is resented and feared as an insult and threat to the technical process.

Much of the "news" today, seemingly devoid of arbitrary emotions, political and social prejudices, is not what it seems to be: it is a sales pitch; it is dogmatic propaganda. The creative talent fled from the “art of journalism” to novel writing some time ago; the artistic journalists do write entertaining nonfiction books as well. The subjective, first person is virtually anathematic. The 'I' appears here and there, in feature stories and the like, but that 'I' is usually an empty perspective, a dead fact instead of the "fact" of a continuous event. And that is why the people in the boxes above know very little about what is really going on in the street, for they do not care much for the man in the street any more. Such is the art of journalism today, a product of our disintegrating culture.

Of course art is contemporary or produced in its time. Our most popular art, dubbed Contemporary Art, enjoys unprecedented commercialization and popularity at present, but its time shall soon pass away. Each producer would corner the market if he could. He would differentiate his product from others, isolate it and place it rightly in hopes that it will stand out of its context and appeal to the consumer. He would have his art mass marketed in big-box stores if not in the White Box of Contemporary Art galleries (the walls are painted white, the wood floors are polished) despite the declaration of a "theme"; but there is no underlying theme besides the cult of the original artist and gilded individual. Of course the consumer is easily deceived by what he sees and believes and what he sees and hears because his conscience has been fragmented and repressed in the competitive process of democratic consumption. The consumer is free to buy or to buy; shopping and consumption constitutes his freedom; he does not want so much the things in themselves as the demon of the fetish, the feeling of power endless conspicuous consumption provides.

Very few craftsmen have the talent for representing the organic reality of the living person, a continuity that is necessarily romantic: What is love? Love is your life. What we get today from the craftsmen is a face, an image, a flat, superficial view of things, without depth or breadth. The death of spiritual culture is a shame, especially where the free weeklies are concerned, for many of them proceeded with high hopes of providing a viable alternative to the materialist atomization of humankind via the cult of gilded individualism.

Let the gold glitter, but with the talent of gold give us a good tale to boot! Not that a 3,300-word account in the Miami New Times about a hip-hop studio king's diet plan is of minute interest. Without a survey of a representative sample of readers for their opinions and a statistical tally and analysis of those opinions, we have no way of knowing how many people were actually interested in the article or in the free weekly for that matter. We know not how many people would actually subscribe to the paper if they had to pay for it. And in the absence of reliable independent surveys, most advertisers do not know for sure how much additional business their advertisements bring in.

Contemporary Narcissism

No doubt the 3,300 words of 'Organic Produce' had a substantial audience given the cultural mentality I have enjoyed while riding the buses every day. The article revealed how Timbaland became one of the most influential and innovative record producers of the last decade; bought an $8 million house; hired an expensive trainer; went on a creatine - supplemented diet, reduced from 331 to 222 pounds thus far; and wants to become a bodybuilder because communicating an image of perfection is seen as the key to maintaining celebrity today.

Nowadays the ideal of perfection is a rock-hard body. Timbaland is sure that his new body and outlook will make his new album "way hotter" than the others. "There's going to be some jump. Plus, how I look, that's what's going to kill it. Appearance is anything," he said. He wants to teach the youth the lesson he is learning so well: "Your outer being is who you are as a person. People say no, but your outside effects who you are inside." Our young buck keeps natural models in mind: "I don't want to be lean and cut, I want to be buck. I just like that look. When you see horses, or animals, like you see a monkey or gorilla, like, the cut. It's a freaky look. When you keep working out, you get to be almost like an animal. I like the veins popping out. I love all that."

There are two sides to every coin in our dimension. I have no problem with tails if heads are honored. After all, I was a dancer - I am still a dancer of sorts. A healthy body and good appearance are certainly important. But we must deliberately cultivate the mind as well; mind and body may be one, but we are able to elevate the mind in our favor; the mind must be superior to the body, at least for those of us who walk upright, with our heads in the heavens, and our feet on the ground.

Personal image is overemphasized by the cult of gilded individualism. The rage for superficial self-surveillance and relentless self-promotion in the war of all against all for sake of the Idol Competition renders the self dependent on consumption of ephemeral images, leaving it without any metaphysical ground to stand on. Christopher Lasch (*Culture of Narcissism*) once pointed out that narcissism, contrary to what one might think, is not based on self-love but rather on self-contempt if not self-hatred, for it is a defense arising from the fear of retaliation for one's own aggressive impulses.

His generation's culture of narcissism arose from the evolution of the culture of hypocrisy derived from the rise of the city slicker and carpet-bagging confidence man around the turn of the century when the scientific-industrial revolution and world war opened up the pursuit of happiness (property) to more ordinary people. What counted were deceptive images and styles, smiles and other veils of generosity masking selfish, competitive motives. "Getting ahead" was the order of the day, hence self-realization was based on the devaluation or lowering of others at home, at school, and in the workplace.

Not much has changed; for instance, I have confidentially interviewed several employees of Miami businesses that advertise their "integrity" and "honesty" - meaning other businesses are corrupt and dishonest. Most employees condemn outright theft, yet admit that many "deals" are deceptive and are intended to take in the unwitting and credulous customer. Managers spoke in terms of "manipulating" both customers and employees. All confessed they were loyal to themselves and not to their employers, whose hiring and firing practices they believed were arbitrary. All this is common knowledge. Politics is even worse, except that deception and lying are more obvious and even espoused by political philosophers as necessary to get anything done in a democracy. Hypocrites control the government: our democracy is a hypocracy.

• • ❧ • •

HAS ANYTHING AT ALL changed since Lasch's summary critique of typical American image? We still have the usual fear of dependence, inner emptiness, repressed rage, oral cravings, fear of old age and death, decline of play spirit, fascination with celebrity, deteriorating sexual relations, and devaluation of others. But we want healthier, better looking personal images today. The fat man and the skinny woman are out of fashion – “fat” and “skinny” are politically incorrect terms. Lean and mean is all right. Buff and tough might do. "Buck" and "cut" is better, for that will "kill" the competition.

In fine: What you see is what you get, and how you look is who you are. We must give credit where credit is due, and say the posing today is less hypocritical, for the ideals that man falls short of have diminished with the dementation of culture. The mental/moral side of the coin is forgotten - the mental aspect used to be called "moral" because mind chooses conduct. The idols and those who idolize them have their heads in the sand, the barren soil produced by the atomization of social persons into individual competitive units mechanically manipulated by the mass culture they really have no power over.

Wherefore more attention must now be paid to the old platitudes; such as, appearances are not everything; appearances are deceiving; clothes do not make the man; and the positive affirmation of substance and principal over fleeting, arbitrary forms. "Dumb" dancers, body builders, musicians, and everyone else who really wants to be liberated are well advised to get a liberal education, either on their own or in schools. They would do well to write as many brilliant essays as they can; and the wordier the better if the words flow naturally along the Way. Writing about works of art, for instance, teaches us to question the images we behold, to be at once critical and self-critical in the examination our preconceptions and prejudices; a practice that is useful and applicable to any endeavor the person might choose to pursue.

Now I have articulated almost 4,000 words to this point. There exists a very slim chance that my articulation will suitable for an article in The New Times. The editor or his master might think my subject matter is inappropriate for his periodical. Perhaps it is too snooty or intellectual or academic, and not the cool talk about the cool stuff his readers like. Yet he has published an article about the controversial bickering at Art Center/South Florida, and he has refused several of my brilliant and edifying articles about the art actually displayed there. His editorial constraints are obviously discriminatory. I have trashed his pop-art, and he has trashed my masterpiece, but we are not even.

I have often gone to bat for the proponents of the vulgar arts; for instance, in my celebrated 'In Defense of Assholes'. But I have done so with the understanding that I should have a right to get my say-so in on an equal-time basis every once in a while. As far as I am concerned, artists should have their da-das providing I can have my blah-blahs! If they must refuse my work as if it were garbage in comparison to their own excretions, then I shall have three words for them as I turn my back on them and get on with the elimination of my mounting backlog.

Modern Dance – Serious Business

Anna Sokolow's Player's Project, presented at the Riverside Dance Festival in 1984, may be summed up in two words: Serious Business.

I expected to see some historical modern dance, and that's what I got. Ms. Sokolow began her career with Martha Graham and Louis Horst, and went on to form her own group in 1937. Graham's probable influence was evident in Ms. Sokolow's 'Lyric Suite' (1953), in the form of contractions, spasmodic releases and ponderous attitudes. Furthermore, during the 'Adagio Appassionato', a softer sort of round dance by four lovely ladies in red gowns, I expected Graham to come onstage any moment. She did not, but Dian Dong, Kathleen Quinlan, Risa Steinberg and Susan Thomasson did an excellent job with the choreography.

During the intermission, I conversed with a matronly gentlewoman on my left. We noted how the audience consisted of mature men and women and young artists (many of the latter were dancers). The middle generation was markedly under-represented. She remarked that Anna Sokolow had been around for many, many years, and asked why I'd come to see her work. "To see the real thing," I replied.

Following the intermission, we watched 'Ballade' (1965). I do not remember much of it, except that it was a ballet, and that my attention was diverted by the wonderful music of Alexander Scriabin, played live and marvelously so by Richard Justin Fields.

During the pause, my new acquaintance waxed enthusiastic about the music, then asked me if I liked the dances. I said, passing over the ballet just presented, that only the very best of ballet turns me on. However, I said I did enjoy 'Lyric Suite', which seemed to be a modern dance representing various emigrants landing in America (I did not have the slightest knowledge of Sokolow's intentions).

I further remarked that I enjoy the modern form of dance not because it arouses me emotionally, but because it makes me think. My seating companion rejoined that she had been attending modern dances for a very long time, and found them boring. I had noticed that she had fallen asleep during 'Ballade', and was about to ask her whether her boredom was due any distinction between ballet and modern dance, or if the music simply lulled her into a pleasant nap; but the show continued before I could ask.

'Steps of Silence' (1984 Premiere), with an introductory narration from THE FIRST CIRCLE by Solzhenitsyn, concluded the program. The impressions given here of prisoners did not inflame the passions. However, the choreography effectively and efficiently achieved its purpose: to recreate that dull affect of shuffling prisoners limping zombie-like to occasionally huddle together here and there. They looked like brainwashed, empty shells devoid of any capacity for passion. And in the end, they were blown across the stage of life along with the newspapers that reveal, all to no avail, their most miserable plight. No, nothing spectacular here. But long live Anna Sokolow, still true to the modern tradition.

As the cast took its bows, not one smile was to be seen on a face. Yes, I thought, this is very Serious Business!

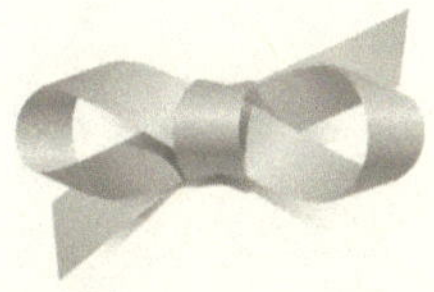

My First Dance Teacher Recommended

19 August 1993

Dean Wayne Miller

CASUAA

3211 Providence Drive

Anchorage, Alaska 99508

Dear Sir:

I am taking this opportunity to commend my first dance teacher, Ms. Jill Crosby, for inspiring me to move towards unity in mind and body.

Because of my experience over the several years since that first class with Jill, I know now that if it were not for her initial encouragement, I would have surely abandoned the course that has brought me to a much better state of being than the desperation I was feeling before I started moving.

It is my great pleasure to know Jill. I am very proud of her. She is a fine example of an ideal teacher. She has persevered where most would have given up long ago, especially in the area of her own education. I seldom meet a professional academic who can suspend judgment long to learn anything, And in practice, I have a profound respect for a tech who also learns how to teach from her students.

As evidence of Jill's influence on my lfe, I am enclosing something I wrote shortly after taking her class, some photographs of me demonstrating a Luigi style combination at Carnegie Hall, and copies of photos from my latest Lincoln Center performance.

Sincerely,

David Arthur Walters

Pooh Kaye's Punkmodern Object Relations

Now that postmodern dance adherents are becoming more and more concerned with communication and theatricality, the assaults on intelligence devised by dancer/choreographer Pooh Kaye for her Eccentric Motions company deserve a special term within the nomenclature. Perhaps punkmodern dance would be most appropriate. Some people just prefer to call it absurd or ridiculous. Nevertheless, at least in my untrained opinion, Ms. Kaye conducts legitimate experiments that have their redeeming qualities.

Accompanied by the composer John Zorn and Musicians, the Eccentric Motions put on quite a free show at Cooper Union in December 1984, proceeding with two videos: "Sticks on the Move", in collaboration with Elizabeth Ross, and "In the House of Floating Paper." The videos provided us with an unusual variety of bizarre object relations, a fascinating if not aesthetic experience for the layman as well as for the experienced psychoanalyst.

In the video "Sticks on the Move", the objects were "movie stars". However, they were not your usual sex objects. Rather, they were peculiar, uniformly oblong motion picture personalities; to wit: several four-foot long four-by-four boards! Instead of being moved by carpenters, people were weirdly moved by the boards, as those wooden performers slid and tumbled, skidded and hopped madly down the avenues of the city.

And in the video "In the House of the Floating Paper," a dancer rode around on a typewriter, another dancer was wheeling around on a swivel chair, somewhere in a deserted office building abundantly decorated with graffiti. The typewriter spewed forth colored papers, which then moved about the floor with a cast of dancers who appeared to be blown about with the colorful trash according to some law at once both natural and unnatural. After all that traipsing around with what appeared to be colored newspapers, I was unable to recall what the dancers looked like, but the objects were unforgettable because of the manner in which they were presented.

In both videos, the human beings defied the laws of gravity as well as the law of good taste.

Yes, youth is rebellious! Pooh Kaye came on stage then with her company of young dancers and blew us away with "Wild Fields", a work commissioned (1984) by the American Dance Festival. The movements were unpredictable, absurd, outrageous, and beautiful. Sometimes the poses taken were so extremely amusing that a toddler in the audience laughed uproariously. Serious critics kept their giggles and their consternation to themselves, for dancing is a serious business: there is no humor in the heaven of fine art, at least not for them.

Be that as it may, "Wild Fields" is a carefully choreographed sort of anarchy not entirely devoid of meaning. Its dynamic images evoke definite emotional responses. On the whole, I was mindful of a disorderly finding of order, of wild insects, weeds, and people exploring their fields of action and finding therein the limits of freedom. During the subsequent intermission, I found myself sketching out some directions and drawing stick-figures representative of the positions and movements I had seen the dancers perform. The whole thing seemed to be a sort of goofy ballet.

Following the intermission, we were treated to an awfully nerve-wracking, mind-splitting, unmusical concert by John Zorn and company, the same being interpreted by the dancers in "The Return of Doctor Chaos: An Improvisation System for Dancers." The dancers, each in turn and all out once, found some kinetic clamor coincidental to an ear-shattering racket, which would undoubtedly be banned from Times Square as hazardous to the health of New Yorkers!

Despite the din and commotion, my mind began to wander aimlessly. I was burned out. Then I considered how that feeling of indifference and boredom was identical to the feeling I had experienced while watching carefully contrived ballets; that is, before I learned the ballet vocabulary by performing it myself, and hence became intrigued by it; of course, some ballets are wonderful exceptions, where technique is not even noticed. Yes, both extremes, organization and disorganization, can exhaust the innocent observer. Without contrasts, since our perceptions are based on differences, our attention span is too short to span the redundancies.

Yes, I thought, we can pretend to enjoy something when we are bored with it. We can clap loudly to break the monotony, to acknowledge that we recognize something familiar, to agree that we know a work of art when we see it! Or, alternatively, we can stop pretending, start analyzing the challenges, even the monotonous meaningless ones. As my attention drifted back to "Dr. Chaos", I realized that his antics were also therapeutic, that, in the sheer demonstrative madness of his patients there is a wealth of ideas.

At that point, the musicians announced they would perform one more number for us. Most everyone got up and left in a hurry. A few of us lingered for a while. For what, we were not certain.

Pooh Kaye, I longed to see you ripen. Where are you now?

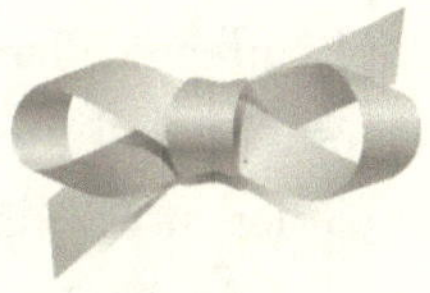

Linda Diamond's Charade

Dear Linda Diamond, Although a few years have passed since we performed *Charade* at Lincoln Center, I still think of our association often and with the warmest regard. The whole experience was a success for me during a time of great difficulty in my personal life.

It is often said that, in order to realize the best possible future, we should focus on past successes rather than failures. I think many dancers, admonished daily for their mistakes, forget what they have done rightly. Therefore, it may be useful for you to have in hand this contribution of my regards concerning our successful collaboration.

Foremost in my mind is the freedom of expression we shared as a team under your leadership. You brought together dancers differing up to forty years in age, from novice to professional levels of accomplishment, and under your firm guidance you molded us into a well-prepared performance unit; yet, at the same time, I believe each participant felt he or she was in touch with their own unique identity. I remember very well your response when I ask you for a detailed directions for a few sections: "Do I have to tell you everything? Make something up. Just be there in time." Once thrown into the water, I began to swim. You may recall how adamantly I refused to change some of the movements I had created, saying, "This is mine!" Thank you for encouraging me to give something personal to the audience.

Furthermore, I admired your intuitive ability to identify key social issues and to draw your audience into the choreographic abstractions in such a way that many of its members, regardless of their diversities, we're deeply affected. I recall the outburst of the man in the audience who stood up and cursed the judges and ranted about the telephone companies after 'Telephone Tango', and the intent looks on the children's faces in the audience during 'Plea for Custody'. And, as you know, there were some uncanny coincidences between the dancers' lives and the choreographed subject matter. I do hope you will pursue your work with social themes; it is a modern tradition that is often neglected; given the current, postmodern aesthetic, your work is a counter-revolution, one that enables us to get in touch with our real feelings regardless of the age we live in.

Your own performance as a dancer was superb. I marveled at your perseverance despite your injuries and the fact that you had to personally handle every aspect of the business: the costumes, promotion, ticket sales, photographer, staging, etc. And I was grateful, especially considering the stint of your financial resources, that immediately prior to the performance you paid each dancer in cash.

Speaking of business, of course you are in a most arduous one. You know only too well that the final reward of a dance career is often no more than fleeting memories and a few mementos in a scrapbook. We are fortunate that you love Dance, that you devote your life to it. I fervently hope you are more amply compensated in a tangible form someday soon; that, at the very least, the business tasks become easier for you so that you can dedicate yourself even more to the essence of your calling.

I hope you will consider from time to time the above references to our collaboration. You are well aware of my credentials. I have made these true remarks because I respect you and wish you well in your career.

Thank you very much,
David Arthur Walters

NOTE: Linda Diamond is a well-known New York choreographer with roots in South Florida. She was closely associated with modern dance pioneer Anna Sokolow, and is especially acclaimed for her choreography honoring Sephardic Jews.

I wrote the above letter to her on my 51st birthday, January 9, 1997, after performing with Linda Diamond and Company in the Premier of *'Charade'* at Lincoln Center in New York. Our satirical performance portrayed a divorce custody case where I played the father and Linda the mother. The girl with curly hair is Toni Kline, who is now a top cancer researcher in California. Chrissy Mulvaney is the other judge. Alexandra Robertshaw, now in her 30s, is the little girl. Her brother Ben was originally going to do the part at age 6, but his friends made fun of him at school so she inherited the part because she was with him when her mother went to drop off Ben for rehearsal and he desisted. Alexandra was amazing. She had many of her schoolmates in the audience and was not about to let anything go wrong, so she served as our virtual stage manager, running about between scenes setting up the props that we had forgotten to place. Chrissy Muvaney played the main judge, not seen in the photo above.

Linda and I danced a duet to Leonard Bernstein's West Side Story tune, 'Got a rocket in your pocket,' in a fight scene. The three judges appeared and took over the child after the fight scene. The promotional photo is of the final scene, 'Blinded Justice'. The little girl is being carried off on the shoulders of the judges as she expresses herself in pantomime to the effect that justice stinks and one had better see nor speak evil. The American flag fabric was donated by fashion designer Valerie Porr, an expert on borderline personality disorder. She had just had a party for the Democratic presidential candidate. She had no idea it would be used in this particular dance.

When we rehearsed outdoors on 6th Avenue, a lady in a car drove up and said, "This is very interesting, but would you please stop dragging the American flag around on the ground!"

The man who had ranted during the performance was lurking outside the backstage door when we exited. He congratulated us for our performance and proceeded to agonize about his divorce. We thanked him and hurriedly hailed a cab.

'Charade' was also performed as guerrilla theater at the New York Hilton Hotel on 53rd and 6th Avenue, on August 8th of 1993, for the American Bar Association Convention. The dancers donned their costumes and proceeded with a surprise performance much enjoyed by the lawyers present, I later heard. I was unable to perform with the cast because of other commitments. I was, however, nearby, I believe on the Avenue of the Americas, where a woman who had become distraught over her divorce had hurled herself naked out of a window onto the street below, fortunately missing the pedestrians on the sidewalk, just as I walked by.

The playbill for the American Bar Association performance was entitled 'Demonstration, A Notice to All Legal Reform Activists.'

"To voice our anger and to put the American Bar Association on notice that we, as consumers of legal services, demand legal reform. Nothing short of sweeping change will be tolerated. The final scene of charade, entitled 'Blinded Justice,' will be performed in view of the recent horrors which many people have experienced at the hands of judges who have defied and violated our basic constitutional rights and who have been directly responsible for ruining many lives of women, men and children. This choreography by Linda Diamond was created to make a statement concerning what is happening right now."

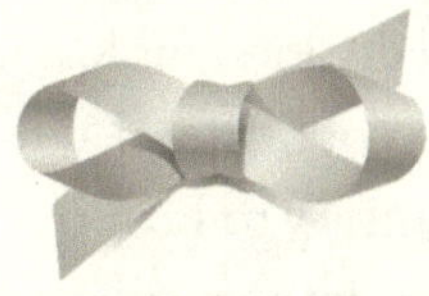

Life on the Run – The Trinitarian Tango

Life proceeds with a bang and flees madly against itself for dear life. Its existence depends on flight for its essence is flight. By inner necessity a life would persist forever if it could, hence it would fly from its origin instead of returning home.

Nevertheless a human animal composed of enlivened mud often wants to go home and collapse into mud, leaving alienated life in discrete bodies behind. Perhaps he would pause at the soft mountain to have a last sip of the ocean of milk and take a last glimpse of the white light at the end of the warm tunnel.

This last taste and sight of a primitive beginning subsequently obscured by its accretions is a contradiction always more or less wanted, as if the precious life launched into existence were under sway of an overpowering gravity all along, and must sooner or later fall back on itself with fuel expended, the madness of its partial identity finally exhausted with a sigh.

Why, then, did life run away from home in the first place, against its will as it were? It had no choice in the first place. It ran away from itself, and Strife was its name. Returning to itself, Love is its name. And "From paradise to paradise" might be said over the grave if the truth were told, and some do mention the Better Place.

The life-line no matter how straight curves in maximum extent, and end meets end. The arc along the way cradles all. What is this attraction that pulls at a distance no matter how remote? What would bring an end to all vicious cycles, striving trajectories and relentless orbits? What would have minds fall in Love and bodies into Cosmic Fire to be consumed? Empedocles called it Eros or

Love, and he imagined all distinctions lost in a single Sphere without limbs, hair, or genitals. Eris or Strife, glad to make the distinctions of identity, was of course contrary to Eros.

Sigmund Freud, whose monistic pleasure principle failed to fully account for every sort of self-destruction, admired the dualism of Empedocles' Love vs. Strife. Incidentally, Pierre Bayle saw that the Dualism of Zoroastriansm was far more logical than monism. Christianity poses as a monism but its one god secretly needs a devil, the worldly one, the only real monotheist despite his hate for God, for he loved God so much he refused to love man. Apparently the Zoroastrians forgot why they had persecuted the Manicheans - for confusing demons and angels: under Christianity's influence, the Zoroastrians took up Zurvanism, confusing good and evil again.

Freud soon fell silent about his stated contrary to Eros, the so-called death instinct that he named Thanatos, after the relatively harmless Greek transporter of the dead. Now Eros has a product in the self-sacrifice of lovers: the annihilation of two lovers struggling in each other's arms results in another life from union, hence that union is said to be one by virtue of a higher power. In the erotic case we prefer to speak of Eros, although Thanatos plays a part, and biologists say he improves the race by the periodic mixing of seeds. But of course, for it takes two to tango whatever their names might be; say, anabolism and catabolism, and so on.

But let us not exaggerate one pole over the other along the continuum lest we upend it. Better strive for the Golden Mean. In death religions we find Thanatos curbing pleasure - the cultivation of virtual suicide in the name of love, the object of which seems to be, despite the promises, Death. And in war Thanatos works overtime for the massive self-murder is no longer virtual - Freud carefully noted the similarity between religious and military organizations and the danger that erotic love between individuals poses to their sacrificial cults.

Returning to Empedocles, who reputedly ended his life by jumping into a volcano and was until then an early psychotherapist or metaphysical doctor among other things, his cosmology presented a sort of doubling movement that brings to mind Einstein's cosmological constant. Maybe the universe was born with a big bang and expands so far until it starts to fall back into itself under the force of gravity and implodes, or whatever. But maybe there exists a force of repulsion besides a force of attraction. Einstein thought so for a while, and came up with his cosmological constant. He used it to balance the expansion/contraction of the universe, making it "flat" - actually, it was a way of cheating by forcing the cosmic books to balance with a variable number: x. The constant was anti-gravity, an independent force. However, unlike Freud, who simply fell silent about the death instinct which he needed to balance the life instinct, Einstein threw his cosmological constant away and re-embraced the monistic view. Now evidence had come to light in favor of the antithetical constant.

Well, now, if we are dualists and individualists we might conclude that the loving centripetal force that unites disunity in unity - that unites all in a hairless, limbless, undifferentiated, perfect sphere without genitals - is really the Grim Reaper who loves death or nothing in particular. While, on the other hand, we might think the centrifugal force that disunites the sphere without members into striving members, loves the variety of life hence life itself, for life is a struggle, a variance.

A vulgar speculator might propose a hairy hermaphroditic deity with limbs who could not love his/herself unless s/he created a universe to hate itself so s/he could save it by loving it to death. The more sophisticated logic-jugglers among us will certainly come up with a much better and more extensive explanation. As for dualism, either/or has its attractions, but I prefer to dance the irrational Trinitarian Tango.

Why Go There When God Is Here?

Ortega y Gasset made an obscure allusion to the Doctrinaires, saying they were misunderstood and were well worth studying. He mentioned none of them by name, so I looked them up and read their works. He was right.

I encountered Gustav Flaubert and many others including Albert Camus as a consequence of my studies of the Doctrinaires. Camus was trained in philosophy but he took up writing novels. He remarked in his diary that a good novelist must be a philosopher. I believed by "good" he meant immortal or something of the sort. Camus became one of my favorite authors. I read almost everything he wrote, and, given my distaste for fiction, that proves my fascination with his work - Melville is the only other novelist whose complete works I have read.

That is not to say that I enjoyed Camus' novels - I did not. His writing seemed as dry and parched as the Sahara desert. He is one of several existentialists who denied being an existentialist, and caused me to declare, "Existentialism is a dead end." But I eventually emerged from the other side of the dead end into nothing, and realized that Nothing is perfect.

I perused several marvelous critical assessments of Camus' work. I wondered why the critics were not writing novels themselves, because they certainly made Camus' novels interesting! I came to the conclusion that he was a great master because he laid down true lines for critics to wax eloquent on. Without such creative masters around, critics would not have much to say.

A dance teacher who had a reputation for giving the greatest dance class in New York happened to be the disciple of Luigi, a great master of jazz dance. But once he stopped taking classes with the maestro himself, once he gave up the lines he had learned to follow in his own way, his classes were not worth taking. I should have listened to the maestro in the first place, when he said, "Why go there when God is here?"

I shall reread Camus. Maybe I missed something.

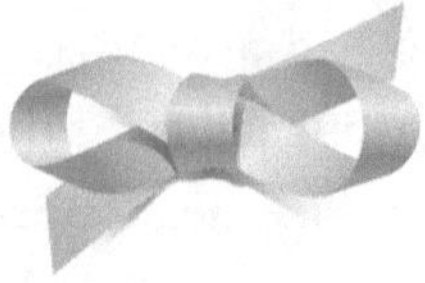

The Great Dance Master

It has been my good fortune to study jazz dance with one of the greatest jazz-dance masters the world has ever known. Not one of the hundreds of factual articles written about him fully expresses the secret of his success, why he has inspired thousands of students from all walks of life. We call him Luigi, and we know his secret. Luigi is a lover.

Luigi loves everybody, dancers most of all, because he has found himself in his occupation and is not ashamed of his discovery. He possesses the innocent vanity necessary for all great masters, the courage to persevere in the faith that he has valuable gifts to offer. Although he sees himself in the mirror of the world, he is not arrogant or selfish. Rather, he is the picture of generosity, for he constantly strives to improve his image by bringing it into harmony with the feeling of love that makes all differences superficial.

Luigi has a keen eye for dance lovers. He prefers the beauty of a 600-lb. gorilla who dances lovingly to the meticulous drill of a 95-lb. beauty just doing technique; yet he loves her too, for no matter how dull life seems, he says we must "never stop moving."

Dancing is Luigi's greatest passion. However, dancing is only a fleeting reflection of his love for learning something new. He learns how to teach from his students by studying them and asking himself how he can teach more wisely. He comes to class with his curiosity, genius, and extraordinary experience, finds music that fits the mood, and choreographs something on the spot, always searching for the best way to express feelings. His search encourages students to seek. If he sees in their efforts something he likes, he will clean it up and use it. If the final dance does not, like his mother's spaghetti, "feel right", he'll say "This stinks, but our job as dancers is to make it smell good until we get rid of it."

Luigi's secret is not the visible motions we imitate until we find our own way, but rather the invisible spirit that creates and supports all the forms and fashions. When Luigi advises us to "use space as your ballet barre," he refers us to the universal standard within that supports every object: the feeling of love. I once asked him what I should do with my hands, because they just did not look good. "Connect them to your heart," he replied without hesitation.

A great teacher brings us to the spirit within almost unconsciously, sometimes even against our will. When we are no longer with him, by reflection on his example we connect with the source of all activity and find, to our surprise, that we have been unknowingly enriched. We realize then that the most valuable lesson is given not by command but by affection. This is the classical romantic tradition, the legacy of our freedom, and the secret of Luigi's success.

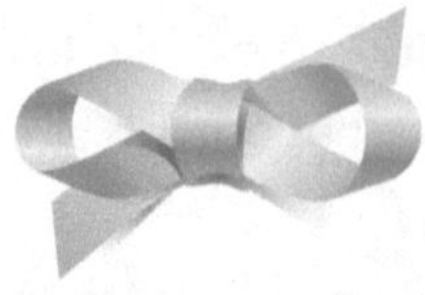

The Kaiser's Ballerina Dropped Dead

Kaiser William II took the throne when powerful new technology was being developed, and he was not about to give it up during his right-handed move to personal sovereignty. That move was engineered behind the throne by his best friend, Phillip Eulenberg.

Eulenberg was responsible for Prince von Bulow's rapid rise to the chancellorship in 1900. He was also a cause célèbre of the homosexual scandal that was shocking the Fatherland and embarrassing the Emperor in 1907 at about the time his embarrassing interview with a reporter was published in England.

In 1906, a homophobic muckraker and militant nationalist by the name of Maximilian Harden, convinced that a "weak" homosexual ring, even more internationalist in character than the Socialist International, was conspiring to seize control of the Empire. Harden used his rag, The Future, to charge Eulenberg and others near the Emperor with homosexuality. He claimed to have liberal ideas about homosexuality, yet he felt it had no place in manly politics, which should be more concerned with the art of war than that of friendship. He went on to advocate unrestrained submarine warfare during the Great War, after which he converted to socialism.

Phillip Eulenberg was a relative moderate gentleman, a diplomat with an interest in the arts as well as politics who rapidly rose to become the power behind the throne. He preferred diplomacy to war, believing war was too risky of a course for Germany to follow.

His personal affection for William led him to oppose the 'New Course' of liberalism and to support the personal regime of the sovereign who would run his government in the Prussian way, from the top down through his ministers. Eulenberg sponsored Prince von Bulow for the chancellorship because he believed the Prince would augment the Imperial cult of personality and wholeheartedly do the Emperor's bidding, but Prince von Bulow turned out to be a slippery eel and one who added to the Emperor's extreme discomfort in 1907 by delivering a speech to the Reichstag, assuring Germany that he was disgusted by the suggestion that Germany and its Army had been corrupted by a homosexual ring reminiscent of decadent Imperial Rome.

The moral rectitude of the Imperial couple was beyond question, he said, implying that gays in the military defamed the Empire. The Imperial family was a perfect model for Germany. It was outrageous to suggest that Germany was some sort of Sodom. It was time to put an end to the gossip.

A gaffe erupted over an interview William gave to the *Daily Telegraph* erupted in the midst of this gossip about gays in the military. He happened to be the grandson of Queen Victoria and an honorary admiral of the British navy. He had expressed his affection for England therein, contrary to the sentiments of his countrymen, and said the English were "mad as hares" for suspecting him of bad intentions for his diplomacy in Morocco.

A sort of People's Court of Justice was duly convened in the Reichstag. The Chancellor's defense of His Majesty was tepid. Yes, the Kaiser had observed the constitution; he had the Chancellor sign off on the interview before it was released. Yes, the Chancellor and the Foreign Office had been inattentive and had unwittingly allowed the indiscreet interview to be released; for that the Chancellor took full responsibility and offered his resignation, which the Emperor had refused. Yes, there were plans to reform the Foreign Office bureaucracy; the legislators laughed at that statement. However, or so the Chancellor implied, the buck stops with the Emperor for making his characteristic statements in the first place. To wit: the Kaiser is personally responsible, and His Majesty must refrain from such "incredible mistakes" during the future course of his public and private life:

"Gentlemen," the Chancellor said, "it is certain that the appearance of this interview in England has not produced the effect His Majesty desired; that here in Germany it has caused the profoundest emotion, the gravest heart-searching and regret. His knowledge of this—these last few days have convinced me of fit—will cause His Majesty, even in future private conversations, to maintain that reserve indispensable to the interests of any consistent Foreign Policy, and to those of the authority of the Crown (Bulow notes a burst of applause, particularly from the benches on the Right.) "But if this were not so," (Bulow says he added, to the "prolonged acclamation of both National Liberals and Conservatives"), "neither I myself, nor any successor of mine could accept the responsibility of office." And that was not all.

Now William had always deeply resented criticism even in private, so we should know without asking how he initially felt when he heard that Chancellor von Bulow's defense amounted to a confession of the His Highness's ineptitude before the entire German nation and his willingness to be a good boy now!

He was livid, to say the least. He allegedly burst into tears and accused the Chancellor of judicial murder for the defense presented to the Reichstag by a Chancellor in whom, as the Chancellor later said with some amazement, William had placed his "child-like trust" in to handle the fiasco. Up to that extremely embarrassing point, the Kaiser had not totally collapsed.

According to *Prince von Bulow Memoirs*, William did suffer a bit of a shock short after the interview was published:

"A dark foreboding ran through many Germans that such clumsy, incautious, over-hasty—such stupid, even puerile speech and action on the part of the supreme Head of the State, could lead to only one thing—catastrophe. The Emperor himself, if only for a passing instant, felt the earth tremble beneath his feet."

Before the Reichstag interpolated the Daily Telegraph hearings into its proceedings, Prince von Bulow recounts that William had planned on visiting Kiel and Hamburg, but he was advised not to do so because hostile demonstrations were expected. On 31 October 1908, three days after the interview was published, he visited the Chancellor:

"He was," wrote Bulow, "as he always was at moments of crisis, very pale, very pitiable."

Bulow insisted that he told the Emperor what he would say before the Reichstag, that it would be a declamation against the sovereign's personal intervention in foreign policy. He claims William then grew calm, placed his child-like trust in him, and said, "However you do it, get us out of this, bring us through."

Despite the "unpleasant shock" Bulow said His Highness initially experienced, we hear from other sources that, on 4 November, William did not seem to have a clue about the grave damage to his image the interview had caused.

On 6 November, he sent the Chancellor a cheery note. He slapped another concerned official on the back, saying he ought not to worry, the gaffe would blow over; there was a silver lining in every cloud. He went off stag hunting in Austria, and then visited his best friend Prince Furstenberg at Castle Furstenberg for a week.

On 10 November, while the Reichstag was listening to Chancellor von Bulow's speech, the Kaiser was enjoying a Zeppelin launching at Castle Furstenberg; he loved the sea most of all, but he foresaw the virtue of air power and said that the air show had been "one of the greatest moments in the development of human culture."

So it was not until the next day, on 11 November, when he received the news of the Chancellor's so-called "defense" of His

Highness, that he was outraged. However, he was not completely mortified until several days later, on 14 November, during a tragic episode at the Castle.

"During this whole affair I underwent great mental anguish," wrote the Kaiser in his Memoirs, "which was heightened by the sudden death before my eyes of the intimate friend of my youth, Count Hulsen-Haesler, chief of the military cabinet."

The Kaiser was being entertained after the Zeppelin show by his best friend and personal advisor, His Serene Highness Prince Maxmilian Egon zu Furstenberg, German-Austrian grand seigneur, multi-millionaire, the power behind the Imperial throne that replaced the scandalized Phillip Eulenberg.

Prince Furstenberg was a very handsome man; his wife apparently kept an eye on him, so there is little suspicion that he was up to hanky panky within the inner Imperial circle. He was in fact the perfect friend to have around during bad times. Not only was he brutally honest with the Kaiser, he loved to tell vulgar jokes and stories and to stage entertainments to distract William from his royal troubles.

The entertainment included General Hulsen-Haseler, dressed up in a tutu. He was an excellent dancer and had on other occasions performed as a ballerina. This time he had a heart attack immediately after his exertion and dropped dead.

The guests hastily redressed the body and laid it on an improvised bier. This whole affair at Prince Furstenberg's castle only served to add to the "November Storm" over the Daily Telegraph interview raging in Berlin. Emil Ludwig represents the scandalous version well in Wilhelm Hohenzollern, The Last of the Kaisers (1927):

"It was Durer's Dance of Death come true. But the Emperor did not read the writing on the wall. He did not see that once again a mightier hand than his had pointed threateningly to follies and frivolities. Encircled by anger and resentment of sixty millions of active fellow-creatures, one man sat, inactive and provocative, drowning his mortifications in music-hall songs and jokes, in shooting parties and ballets, and allowing exasperating tales of Court-life to circulate among the people. Now, when finally one of his most prominent Generals had appeared as a ballerina before the highest society, disgracing the most illustrious class in the land, behold! The hand of Heaven was put forth; it struck the abject courtier to the earth. Upon the wall of the castle at Donaueschingen flamed the great Mene Tekel, that now at last the roistering King might look into his heart. But the King was looking into quite other places."

SEE: *The Memoirs of Prince von Bulow* (1932)

Whatever Happened to Mark Barenboim?

Mark Barenboim was born a Jew in the U.S.S.R. He wanted to be a composer. Rather, he was a born composer, and his destiny had put him in the hands of Russian composers at an early age, one of them being, I think, Aram Khachaturian. Despite the anti-Semitic discrimination he suffered, or because of it, Mark's early compositions were masterful. He was widely regarded as the genius destined to follow in the footsteps of the Russian masters. Then he decided to use all the money he could raise to buy his way out of the U.S.S.R. and immigrate to New York. He received a Charles Ives Prize in 1987. Although he considered an American education to be quite inferior to a Soviet Union education, he committed himself to obtaining a doctorate at Julliard because he believed success in America was more a matter of credentials than of genius and skill. While there, his advice was occasionally sought by the most famous composer in America, or so he said.

At first Mark supported himself playing for Bar Mitzvahs and accompanying ballet classes. But he was too creative to fall into the class routine. For one thing, he would get up from the piano and give students corrections. He was not a dancer himself but he had been an accompanist for two of the top ballet schools in the Soviet Union, therefore he knew what was going on, and he just could not just bear to stand by in America and watch students get a bad education.

That is how I met him. He came over to me at the *barre* one day, and said, "Why do you want to do it that way?" He demonstrated a *ronde de jambe en l' air*, circling his leg around in the air "This is the way it is done." To which the teacher responded, "Mark, I am the teacher here! Go sit down and mind your own business!"

He also greatly annoyed teachers with his musical improvisations during the routines. Musically inclined students were inspired, but it was all too distracting to others, especially when he went into one of his frightfully surprising variations on 'The Rites of Spring' during the petite allegro segment of the class.

I liked to chat with Mark before and after classes in Manhattan. He was a creative or "Crazy Russian." What was not to like? I was reading Gogol, Pushkin, Dostoyevsky, and Solzhenitsyn at the time, and my favorite composers were Russian. And he had a heart of gold. He knew that I was living in a crummy but still expensive hotel room, which was actually the bathroom of a formerly large apartment, while eating meagerly and spending a small fortune on dance classes.

"Why do you want to live there when you can live in Queens at my place until you can save up a deposit to rent a studio?" he asked, in his characteristic "why do you" way of making recommendations with a question, so I took the couch in his living room, and rode the Flushing train every day.

The living arrangement was not intolerable. The living room was spacious, with a few pieces of furniture. There was a painting of Jesus Christ suffering on the cross, placed on the wall near the piano so the pianist could see it. Mark was a frustrated painter, with Jesus as his only subject, which I thought was rather odd for a Jew. The one bedroom was also large, with a comfortable bed, chair, and an electronic piano—I had the bedroom when he was away.

He was a chain smoker while composing. That was a drag because I was trying to quit. He worked on his symphony in the wee hours of the morning the kitchen, and kindly kept the door closed to save my lungs, but then the kitchen reeked of tobacco for breakfast. I was not without sin: he had to advise me to rinse out my sweats before storing them for the weakly wash. "Why don't you want to rinse these smelly things before putting them in the laundry basket?"

Mark had what I called an immigrant inferiority complex that moved him to frequently brag about his native artistic superiority over Americans as well as the superiority of a Russian education. I thought he would be closer to the mark if he attributed his talent to the Jewish intellectual tradition. However that may be, he gave rather amazing piano lessons to virtuoso students in the living room.

He emphasized "Feeling." He wanted his students to know about the lives of the composers, and to imagine how they felt during the time of composition. He "saw" what he heard. He did not need sheet music to play a large segment of a composition his student had just played without feeling. He would stop the student, sit down at the piano, and say, "This is how Scriabin felt about this," and play a moving rendition, although he had not played it before.

Embarrassingly, he liked to play Bach on the electric organ while making love with his girlfriend, a Korean pianist. Indeed, he had a thing for Bach: he saw colors and had mystical experiences with Bach's music. He tried to explain the architecture and mechanics of Bach to me, how and why the structure of his compositions had a profound psychological effect. He would also explain why certain popular tunes had their appeal.

It seemed that Mark was bound for success. A Russian dance company had commissioned him to compose a symphony. And then, two weeks before he would have surely won his doctorate, Mark drove his car head on into a telephone pole. There was no explanation for the accident, except that he had "lost control," which aroused my suspicion that he may have had an accident on purpose to avoid success. Fortunately he was not killed, but he was disabled for many months. After a long rehabilitative period he took up cab driving; the last I heard it was his permanent career. No doubt Mark is serving the public well if still alive. Nonetheless, the loss of his genius is regretted by me at least.

It was as if he wanted to fail. He did not drink or use other drugs except tobacco. He was an attentive driver. I do not want to misjudge him—maybe the long hours put him to sleep at the wheel. Still, I speculated that he was fated to fail because the Soviet Union taught him that Jews cannot be great Russian composers. Yet Jews have risen to the top of every field despite being told they are inferior, or in spite of it. I have not been able to reach him. I did save enough money to make a deposit on a tiny, illegal sublet in Manhattan, so I had moved away before I heard about the accident. Now I Google his name ever so often.

I Lost My Ass

It is becoming increasingly difficult for me at my age to walk the two miles to see my friend Liz on the Bay. I insist on walking back although she tries to call me an Uber. You see, walking is my basic struggle to survive.

My father warned me when he was 90: "Never let Them give you a walker because then They will warehouse you in a poor old folks home, take your social security benefits, and beat you for spitting out the food."

He was a great walker, and I followed suit. I have had cars but I finally rid myself of the nuisance, and I stay away from public transportation so walking is my only means of transportation.

But now my legs feel like lead weights and my feet hurt. I blame it on my cheap shoes, yet that was never a problem in the old days when I was accustomed to standing or walking all day on sidewalks in shoes with stiff leather soles. As far as I am concerned, the fancy athletic shoes weaken feet. They just cannot sell enough of them. Nowadays a person is advised to have four different kinds of shoes to match his daily functions. I would rather go barefoot.

I sat down twice to rest on my way to visit Liz last Sunday; once on a low wall on the Bay, and again in the park in front of her building, where I was greatly amused to see how delighted a little boy was when his dad kept kicking a soccer ball away from him no matter how hard he tried to keep possession. Life for him was an end in itself.

Some kind of bug bit my ass while I was sitting. The resulting furious itch led to my discovery the next day that I have lost most of my ass.

I did not realize I had lost it before. I am not accustomed, as are many women, to looking sideways or over my shoulder in the mirrors to see how my ass is doing, and perhaps taking a picture of same. You know, someone ought to create an Assbook application for posting assies.

I located some anti-itch cream, took it into the bathroom and tried to get a glimpse, in the mirror over the sink, of the bite. There was no protruding ass there to see. I had lost my ass!

How could that be? When I was young man, so-called friends called me a fat ass. They said I walked like a duck and that my ass wagged. Yes, they made homophobic remarks, even intimating why I should stay out of prison.

A man at Crunch Fitness told me, when I mentioned my missing ass, that gay men are getting buttocks implants nowadays, but that is not for me, I really do not need much of an ass. A little handful on each side is just fine for the things I do. But still!

What had happened to my ass? Well, I became a dancer for a decade, and deliberately improved my walking gait. I also got rid of my car and driver's license. It now occurs to me now that I had unwittingly walked my ass off if that is at all possible.

Forgive me for being so asinine for raising this subject. Maybe I like to make ass, or maybe I have become a horse's ass. I hope not. Anyway, I sure wish I could get two or three better pairs of cheap shoes. My feet are killing me, and Walmart is ten miles away.

My Recurring Dreams

I used to have two really bad habits, driving and smoking, including smoking while driving, which I continued to do in a recurring dream although I had quit smoking and let my license expire.

I often dreamed that I was driving my beloved Mark IV Lincoln Continental down the mountain side to my stone castle beside the ocean in Kona. I am smoking a Russian cigarette and listening to a Moody Blues tape. The taste of the tobacco is repulsive, and it occurs to me with some dismay that I quit smoking. And then I notice in my rear view mirror that a police car is moving up behind me.

"Oh no! I don't have a license! I will be arrested!"

I awake with a jolt. I remember that the stone castle is the Kona Inn Hotel, where I checked in after Rene told me I should go live in my car since it was costing more than the mortgage on the house. I wonder if she quit smoking too. We were eventually divorced, to my everlasting regret. If only I had persevered, there was enough love there to save the marriage.

I no longer have that dream, nor do I dream anymore that I am on the run down streets, through the woods, and crawling under houses and onto rooftops because I am wanted for some sort of felony and have escaped from jail. I wake up in a sweat with sheets wrapped around me, wrack my brains, and realize with some relief that I felt guilty for nothing, or, perhaps, for not being the good man I should be.

And then there is the descent into hell where, of course, there is big furnace guarded by an underworld creature, a dragon with red scales. The dragon seems wise, and would advise me how to avoid being incinerated. He says something profound, but I cannot remember what he said when I wake up—perhaps dragons do not speak English.

I woke up and abandoned my career the last time the hellish dream recurred. I was on the verge of success at the time. My withdrawal from the habitual pursuit of happiness in the form of property frightened me so badly that I am still in shock. I lead an impoverished author's life, which is a cowardly life in comparison with that of a man of action. Ironically, active people sometimes retain me to discuss metaphysical subjects with them.

The underworld does have it attraction for dreamers. I often dreamed of grave digging after watching the war news. I called the grave digger "the Grim Reaper." The cemetery was an abandoned battlefield strewn with corpses. All the trees and shrubs were also dead. I stopped having that dream after I realized that I was too was a Grim Reaper. I had balked at material success, forsaking it for art for its own sake, and almost jumped off my nineteenth floor terrace to perfect the war against myself.

And lately another earth-moving dream, something to do with landscape architecture. I am standing on a large earthen berm or maybe a natural bank by a stream. The architect is warning me that pipes must be installed under the bank. Otherwise, water running underneath it will wash it away and I shall have nothing to stand on. I interpreted that as a health warning, to take care of a plumbing issue.

Yes, I believe dreams may be prophetic, albeit rarely. For instance, I dreamed of a dancer I had not seen for twenty years. She lives in California. She took me by the hand in my dream, and led me back to the arts. She actually showed up in Florida, two blocks from my place the day after my dream, as evident from her Facebook posts. I contacted her on Facebook, and she promised to call me, but she never did.

I have been daydreaming of living in a penthouse for a few months instead of in my present squalor in a South Beach ghetto. We humans can get used to almost anything, and it no longer seems good or bad. I lived in luxury, in paradise, in a grand condo beside the Pacific with whales blowing by, and it eventually meant nothing to me. Now many people, especially a million Syrian immigrants, would love to live in my present hovel, which I forgot was a hovel until shortly before Christmas, when I perused a real estate vanity magazine, and then I penned 'All I Want for Christmas is a Penthouse.' Mind you that I am not a penthouse panhandler, as I have contributed much of my spirit if not cash to humankind, and I have more to give.

Indeed, I yearn so fervently for penthouse life that I have considered looking for a job although I'm afraid it is too late for that unless some publisher sees profit in giving me a desk, an editor, and a stipend. My time is short, but I already have a huge inventory.

Yet that is not the dream I had. I dreamed a very old dream. I am standing in warehouse. The sign on the back door said "Atlantic Metal." Two muscular young men, partners, whom I am seeing about a job, are engaged in loading fabricated sheet metal on pallets. Their clothes are grimy with machine oil and dirt.

"I see this is real work, dirty work," I say.

"As you can see, we need someone right away to load the trucks," said one partner.

"Would I have to lift over forty pounds?"

"Yes, some of the steel extrusions weigh two hundred, so the men on each end must carry one hundred pounds."

"Well, I have a hurt back. I am an office man although I operated a lathe when I was a kid. I do words and numbers now."

"What kind of experience do you have?"

"I have a lot of experience. What I like to do is save up enough money to quit and do my art."

"That won't do at all."

"This time I will die on the job given my age," I offer.

They are not so sure, so we get in a truck and they show me around the industrial site, asking me for my opinions on things, and I wake up, realizing I had just had a variation on an old recurring dream. What it means I can divine. Whether it is prophetic I cannot say.

I Do Not Believe in Writer's Block

It is better not to believe in Writer's Block. Just write at least five to seven days a week. It becomes a habit that is hard to break.

It is harder for me NOT to write than to write. I will write about anything at any time, including Writer's Block.

Sometimes writing is not very much fun. The writer usually works best alone, and she might really want to be with friends, she might even be trying to impress people with her writing, to get some approval for herself because she is lonely; but, alas, they are not around when she is writing, and they might not care to read her work anyway. She must love to write for other reasons such as For the Hell of It or Just For Fun in order to continue writing.

The writer might think of writing as a job, therefore she might have trouble being her own boss. She might be having Worker's Block! Especially if she has a deadline to fill.

For her writing is a job, but so what? Sometimes she does not want to go to work, but she does anyway, and once she gets started, it is not so bad, and she gets so interested in the work she forgets that she did not want to come to work in the first place.

A writer might be having difficulty writing because, when she is not feeling 'inspired' to just write something down, guided by her 'genius,' she does not know what to do or how to do it. That is what technique is for: a master artist does not produce a masterpiece every day, but she produces something, and, because she has practice, the production is not bad. A great actor does not give an inspired, command performance every night, but her technique or 'Method' alone will get her through a passable performance, and sometimes the audience does not know the difference because of their own subjective judgment.

The main thing is, if you would be a writer: Never Stop Writing.

I was once told to never stop writing when I was a very young man. My submissions were often rejected, but many editors wrote me encouraging letters and asked me for more submissions. I stopped writing because I wanted to dance instead, then I got lonely for dollars and started chasing them. I will not say that was a mistake, but if I had followed the advice of the editors, I would be a top writer today, not just a writer, but an AUTHOR; there is a big difference, because an author is an authority in his field.

And you may never be a great writer or author, but then again you might be; there would be no great writers without those who are less than great. It is up to you to find out, and even if you find yourself in the middle or on the bottom, you will continue to write if you get into the habit of writing and love writing, and that will help you with your "Day Job."

As for me, I love to write. I never have Writer's Block. I hesitate sometimes; sometimes a single paragraph takes me an hour to write, but then things start to flow.

But all the above might be because I am nuts. So please do not consider the foregoing as sage advice, but as the personal opinions of a writing maniac who does not recommend writing as a career to anyone. If you do it mainly for the money, it ain't worth doing, in my opinion as a literary slut.

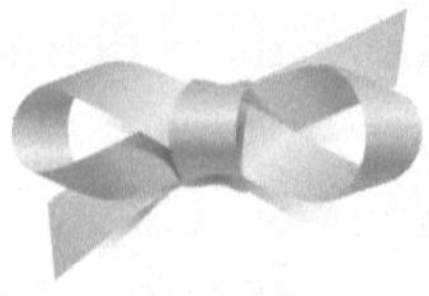

Women in War and Peace

That we dream certain dreams fashioned from bits and pieces of memories has fascinated many an interpreter. As everyone knows, the brain keeps running while we sleep, and when we lightly do so, it is wont to tell a story to that unity of apperception we call the self, as if the storyteller were another person split off, or half the individual divided, and a mysterious half at that because we may not intuit or directly know the introjected subject we associate with the I as it organizes our self-reflections. Yet it has a motive, a theme, or fixed idea to be divined upon awakening.

I have not seen Jill Strauss for twenty years yet she represented that motive in my dream. She taught jazz dance for Luigi Faccuito, may he never stop moving, and I took her class from time to time when she substituted for him. I still take his class in my dreams although he went to the presumably Better Place this year, and she, a pretty little woman with a big heart, is almost always around, as she regularly was back in those days. I do not believe I had a crush on her, at least not consciously, though I did think she was quite cute. We both moved away from New York, she to California, me to Hawaii then Florida.

Jill starred in my dream last night. She was driving; I was her passenger. I used to drive in my dreams, smoking cigarettes as well, until I realized with considerable alarm in one dream that I had quit smoking, and had no driver's license. She pulled into a charming shopping center. Judging from the Spanish architecture, we were in California.

I visited California in my youth, even stayed in San Francisco a few months, and thought Californians were weird. I liked the smaller cities, got to drive a big pink Cadillac convertible, and thought the traffic was atrocious.

I just heard from my friend Drew a few days ago. He moved to California from South Beach a couple of years ago. He said people were a lot nicer in California. I thought of moving out there. The San Bernardino shootings took place the next day, an hour's drive from his home.

The war drums beat incessantly, bombs are away and maybe a National Socialist American Workers Party will be founded, its militant members goose-stepping in brown shirts.

I felt comfortable with Jill at the wheel as she wheeled into the mall. We approached a two-story building with a wooden façade and big windows. A dance class was ongoing inside. The studio was huge, with a very high, vaulted ceiling. There were two huge murals of modern dancers painted on two of the walls. It reminded me of Ana Lessa's new Atma Beauty salon in South Beach.

Yesterday I encountered Ray Sullivan, a choreographer, sitting at a café in South Beach. We chatted animatedly at length about the great dancers and teachers we knew and had studied under back in the day, and bemoaned the fact that the current generation has missed the revolutionary philosophy of modern dance and along with it the passion that moves audiences to tears of joy.

Too many today are just doing technique, not dancing. The kids know little yet think they know everything, and believe they are entitled to dance choreography in their own, conceited way, instead of getting into and being engaged in The Work. I recounted, with some satisfaction, how a dancer told a top choreographer that a certain movement did not work for him, and the choreographer replied with, "Then you're fired because you don't work for me."

The arts bring out the best in people when art is loved for its own sake. Woe unto me, for I no longer sing, dance, and act, and have taken up writing about politics, which brings out the meanness in me, not to mention others. And what I write about is here today and gone tomorrow. I love history, but when I try to relate current events to their historical contexts, most people are just not interested because they are inclined to repeat well-worn mistakes.

So I am drawn back to art, to at least write something immortal to pass along the gifts that are not mine but of my kind. I have been preoccupied with death lately, in the form, unfortunately, of bad finales. Death is part of life, but art is about it all.

Well, I dreamed that Jill and I got out of the car in front of the California dance studio. She took my hand as I took hers, but not quite in the right way, therefore we made an adjustment until the form was perfect, and she led me into the studio. Finally I felt safe, and I awoke.

Just before falling asleep, I had considered how women may now participate in combat alongside men, to actively engage in the massive murders legalized by nations. I felt uncomfortable about that.

Much of the difference between the sexes is cultivated. Still there are differences in strength and size, and in hormones: females are theoretically more nurturing than males. Female warriors are nothing new, really, and there are desperate times when women are needed to not only fight but to lead in battle instead of just throwing themselves off the walls when defeat is imminent lest they be forced to bear the children of the enemy.

If a woman wants to be a warrior and can qualify, that is fine with me. She should not be subject, however, to the draft. I believe women should be cultivated to make and keep peace among men through nonviolent means, just as she has done with the advance of civilization. She should be protected along with her children from the ravages of war.

Ray had complained about the notion that choreographers should be business managers and producers and fundraisers wrapped up in one person, which works the ruin of the choreographer's expertise and creativity, and distracts the others from their duties as well. And too many people in Miami Beach tend to think that the mere possession of funds makes them experts. Labor must be divided into functions, so each can excel. The lack of these divisions and their purposeful coordination is why organizations fail, especially small companies.

I once read an evolutionary theory that men were relatively peaceful when they lived in the forests somewhat like bonobos, and then became violent when they left the forest and had to forage more widely and fight other groups for their sustenance. As they did so, they grew larger and stronger. Females, on the other hand, remained small by comparison so they could be carried to safe places, for they cradle the race.

Maybe that anthropological theory is not scientifically justifiable. Cultural justification is another matter. I think the memory of it brought me to Jill in my dream. She was the pretty muse who took me by the hand and led me back to art.

Sometimes dreams allude to the near future. Jill flew in one day from California and stayed at a Miami Beach hotel three blocks from me. We spoke briefly on the phone. She promised to arrange to see me, but she did not get back to me. I sent her this account of my dream. I never heard from her again.

Dancing Assets Protested In Nation's Capital

May *Raucous Laughter Prevail?*

Paul Schwartzman, a reporter for the Washington Post, admired what he called the "raucous" or shameless laughter of one Elizabeth Calamari's, 66, in his 19 December 2019 coverage of a small group of wealthy Kalorama neighbors protesting an old "gentlemen's" strip club, newly named "Assets" by Jeffrey Schaeffer, 55, the son of taxicab king and real estate investor Jerry Schaeffer, 74. Ms. Calomiris referred the article to me and I engaged in some raucous laughter myself at his stereotypical treatment.

The well-mannered demonstration of the neighborhood notables was staged in front of the elder Schaeffer's magnificent mansion in Kalorama instead of in front of the strip club itself, which is four blocks northwest of Dupont Circle at the intersection of Florida and Connecticut Avenues, a lower corner of the classy neighborhood named Kalorama, adjacent to the Sheridan Circle neighborhood. Mr. Schwartzman noted that it was unusual for Kalorama neighbors to take exception to one of their own.

Kalorama is a relatively elevated area that looks down on Washington and lies north of the original city boundaries. It fondly embraces elegant mansions, fine apartment buildings, embassies, chanceries, churches and private schools. It became a social and political center after Joel Barlow bought an estate there in 1807 and gave it the Greek name for all-around goodness or broad beauty. Residents proudly note that Thomas Jefferson frequently visited Kalorama back in the day, and Robert Fulton demonstrated his torpedoes and steamship designs to members of Congress on the estate's millpond. The current neighbors are mostly liberal hence showed their disaffection for Ivanka Trump and Jared Kushner when they moved into the hood. The Obamas were more than welcome.

Besides Ms. Calomiris, the protestors named by Mr. Schwartzman included one Marie Drissel, identified as a woman who lives in a "townhouse" at the "far end of a long block" away from Assets, Donald Friedman, 74, a prominent lawyer and president of the Sheridan-Kalorama Neighborhood Council, and Jim Groninger, 74, a recently arrived resident who runs a biotech company and recommended Amsterdam as an ideal location for Assets.

Mr. Schwartzman, who did not disclose his own age despite repeated requests, is a political columnist who was well known at the New York Daily News for his celebration of the rise of Rudy Giuliani, 75, as mayor of New York, 396. In fact, he carefully included in his piece the ages of all but one of the protesters, Marie Drissel, 73, whose age he took care to ascertain but for some reason failed to report. He mentioned that Mr. Friedman was accompanied by two Shih Tzu spaniels, but he did not provide their names and ages: "Two of the demonstrators arrived in a Cadillac. Friedman stopped by with his two dogs, a Shih Tzu and a Shih Tzu spaniel." (sic)

His angle on the story was that a few wealthy old white fuddy duddies, horrified by the new sign on the club, were making an ass of "Assets" in front of their neighbor's house in an attempt to shame him into closing it down. Ms. Drissel, the master organizer of the protest, provided her assessment of word Assets on the sign: She said it was "crass" and said she knew what it meant the minute she saw it.

Formerly the Royal Palace, the Assets strip club has been an insult to the neighborhood for decades. The neighborhood forged a Settlement Agreement with it back in 2001, signed by Vinh Quy Nguyen for Fabwill Inc. dba Royal Palace. He promised to keep the sidewalks in front of the place clean and unobstructed, not to display advertisements of any kind referring to dancing or anything related to sexual activity, not allow any noise from individuals to disturb residents, not to change the hours of operation with obtaining prior approval from the city, and not to lease or use any part of the entire building for sex-oriented business.

Ms. Drissel, as Washingtonians well know, is the famous DC finance watchdog and dog lover sometimes referred to in the District as "Ms. Rottweiler" and "Ms. Pittbull," compliments Marion Barry yelled down the hall at her one day when he was with reporters at City Hall—she reserves other, far more saucy details of her battles with Mr. Barry for inclusion in her memoirs.

She sports a masters in Finance with honors, studied up to her comprehensive exams for a Ph.D. in Public Administration, and took a year of law school at George Washington University before taking up a career in budgeting and finance. She served as a liquidator in the S&L debacle, and was the CFO/HR Director of World Links, an NGO spun out of the World Bank to establish computer education in underfunded schools. She has been a civil rights activist since she was a teen. Liberal minded as well as a proponent of law and order, she opposed, for example, legalizing online gambling in the District.

More recently, Ms. Drissel opposed legalization of prostitution, although she said arguments on both sides of the question were persuasive. The defeated 'Community Safety and Health Amendment Act of 2019' was advanced in the District of Columbia to increase public health and safety in the District by removing criminal penalties associated with sex exchange. The bill would have repealed statutes that criminalized adults consensually engaging in sexual exchange while upholding existing laws prohibiting sex trafficking.

Strippers are not necessarily prostitutes, yet prostitution is naturally prevalent around strip clubs if not within them, at least before prostitution went underground with the Internet. Closing strip clubs on Chicago's Rush Street in the 80s, for example, allegedly reduced prostitution arrests in their vicinity by 80%. On the other hand, legalizing prostitution may eliminate as many arrests.

It is even offered that prostitution should be legalized because it is healthy. The notion is hardly novel. Prostitution was sacred and ritually practiced in caves and temples, and primitive religions were rooted in sexual conjugation prior to the advent of Protestant protest of natural or diabolical urges; nevertheless, Catholic licensing of brothels financed many churches. Prostitution was once legal in most of the United States. Its proponents argued that it is a necessary evil that protects unmarried women from being ravaged and lessens violence and terror by providing a release for basic urges. Feminists claimed that its aggressive women led the rise of female power. Courtesans were once the mostly highly educated members of society, and they, in turn, civilized brutal men. Lenin declared marriage to be legalized prostitution while Marx thought labor was mass prostitution

Moriah McSharry McGrath, in her 2013 feminist thesis, 'Neighboring in Strip City: A Situational Analysis of Strip Clubs, Land Use Conflict, and Occupational Health in Portland, Oregon', said that strippers have a hard job and they need to be protected. They are, she pointed out, unorganized independent contractors with no benefits, entirely at the mercy of businessmen, and looked down upon by society. She interviewed strippers and officials and residents in her home town. The bottom line for her is alcohol causes misbehavior and not the sex business. She said there is no conclusive research associating strip clubs per se with crime, so regulation is driven by public perception not empirical data. Further, police enforcement helps curb all crime. Some well-kept clubs are accepted in some neighborhoods while others are not, so residents' opinions are divided wherever they happen to be

Katherine Frank, a Washington, D.C., anthropologist who claimed she is a feminist, stripped in clubs for six years to research the Ph.D. dissertation that became her book, *G-Strings and Sympathy: Strip Club Regulars and Male Desire* (2002) — She did not say she financed her education with the proceeds, a practice I discovered when I stayed in a San Francisco hotel with a lobby in between the strip club and dressing room. She concluded that men desire different kinds of bodies, not some standard ideal body, and that the clubs actually save many marriages because they can be at one with their fantasies, although she would not want her husband in one because of the expense.

Nevertheless, Ms. Drissel wants Assets shut down for good. "I do not believe there are long term careers for women nor men in the world of strip bars," she told me. "Further, there is a lot of information about labor law violations, no health benefits, only cash received for services, inability to establish financial histories, and also for the trafficking of young children in the world of strip bars." Furthermore, she said she does not believe a strip club let alone a bar or nightclub is economically viable along that commercial strip at the foot of the Sheridan-Kalorama neighborhood — Sheridan Circle with General Sheridan's statue is at one corner of the area.

Jerry Schaeffer bought the corner of Florida and Connecticut Avenues in early 2019 for considerably more than the assessed value. Ms. Drissel believes a tax free exchange may have been at play to make the transaction more attractive. Apparently the adult entertainment license came with the building, which was then inhabited by the old strip club, the Royal Palace, which was not known to do much business, and the Fab Lounge upstairs, closed since 2016, which has an interesting history including being a meeting place for a sex-workers trade organization.

"So many people do not know the history of the Royal Palace and Fab Lounge," she told me. "They have not been good neighbors. The Royal Palace hardly had any clients after Fab Lounge closed in 2016. Many of us have lived in the neighborhood long before it was a strip club. We met with the owners and they ended up hiring off duty police officers to sit at the bottom of our streets to keep the drunks from tearing up our cars and properties and awakening us at night with their noisy fights." There have been few liquor license applications in the immediate area.

The strip club and the "sports bar" now being built above it do not seem to be the highest and best use of the property. Jerry Schaeffer said back in March 2019 that he had considered leasing it to Wawa, the expanding convenience store chain, but there was no demand for anything but a strip club. That may be because his son Jeffrey, listed as an officer of the company operating the strip club, wanted the place for his wife along with its cash income.

Mr. Schwartzman's prejudicial narrative jibed with the race card played by that wife, the nightclub's purported owner, Saxton Gabrielle Miller, 26, a beautiful black woman whom the reporter engaged in conversation while she threw stacks of dollar bills around as scantily clad dancers wiggled around. The club has been advertised as woman owned, yet her name had yet to appear on the official documents.

Unfortunately, the lack of information provided by the esteemed political reporter on the taxi companies, strip clubs, and a brothel called Sky Spa or Spa Sky closed by the attorney general for the District has led to unnecessary speculation that there may be some sort of vertical integration involving Asian immigrants working in the taxicab industry, nightclubs, and brothels, perhaps with ties to Asian organized crime groups. I was, however, unable to find any known mob ties to Jerry Schaeffer and his interests or any relationships to an outfit of loose associations such as that enjoyed by New York taxi king Gene Friedman, taxi medallion speculator Michael Cohen, limousine king William Fugazy, automobile executive Lee Iacocca, gambling casino entrepreneur Donald Trump and his lawyer Rudy Giuliani, and so on. Mr. Schaeffer was scandalized by the press for doing what kingpins normally do —put politicians in their pocket — when he unsuccessfully tried to get a medallion system of licensing legislated in free-wheeling Washington, but his reputation is not nearly as tarnished as members of the clan associated with today's legal outfit in the White House.

Ms. Miller told Mr. Schwartzman that protestors against her strip club were just saying what she expected 75-year-old white people to say after seeing black faces come out of the door manned by bouncers. He was evidently more than willing to play that race and age card. A Kalorama neighbor scoffed, in turn, at the notion that race was a factor in the objection to the strip club.

Prejudice is real and sells papers, but the facial protest of Assets was against the word "Assets" as advertising that would increase an already established public nuisance. That is, the protest was not against purported immorality but against the "secondary effects" of whatever was going on in and around the club. After all, the mores of a community, especially of a "swamp" occupied by so many transients, politicians, and lobbyists are subject to change as is more than evident in the current demoralization of America. Washington is said to be the U.S. capitol of corruption, but that does not preclude reform for better or worse depending on one's definition of progress, the current progress being relatively regressive as far as progressives are concerned.

What we have in this Washington Post report with its heading, 'A D.C. strip club had been there for years, but a new name is sparking protest,' is an occasion of something our nation's great leader would call "fake news," albeit unfairly, for something new is there but it is merely superficial. It is balanced in some respects, but seeks stereotypical answers to a very serious fault in our society. The article is composed in the style of the New York papers Mr. Schwartzman served well, the Daily News and Post, to please a populist base with foreshortened brains further shrunk by the rise of the internet and small screens

Washington does not have the population of New York but it has Mr. Bezos, who saved its Post from folding. Mr. Bezos, by the way, has been quoted by Motley Fool, much to the dismay of Amazon investors who observed him unloading stock, as saying his innovative Amazonian enterprise will be out-innovated and bankrupted someday due to rapidly advancing technology. We may suppose that, instead of thinking, people will be thought by the Supermachine. The President will no longer have to mechanically cite his speeches from a monitor because his unstable mind cannot grasp long reads. His addresses will be broadcast directly to the monitodal devices implanted in brains shortly after birth.

Although Mr. Bezos saved the Washington Post and proceeded to build an "embassy" in liberal Kalorama, it is difficult to divine just what his “ideology” is from his donations, unless we define 'ideology' according to its original meaning, scientific thinking, which we know is objective as it observes bits and pieces of nature. One might expect a wealthy businessman to contribute to the two ideological sides just in case, as if there are only two sides although they reverse themselves every so often, yet thus far his most noted contributions have been somewhat neutral and rather paltry in comparison to his vast fortune. For instance, he contributed to an apparently non-partisan committee advancing the causes of veterans. That naturally drew criticism because its contributors are allegedly gun happy. He has also contributed to education, anti-homelessness, and journalism programs. He has *not* bragged about giving by taking the Giving Pledge. Instead, he has asked for ideas on what to do with his amassed fortune.

Mr. Bezos would be wise to stick with scientific endeavors helpful to humanity regardless of the "ideological" prejudices of its constituents. After all, he is a technocrat in the Comptean sense, that of Auguste Compte, a "positive" or scientific thinker who foresaw human progress achieved by technical collaboration and cooperation of all sorts of workers in contradistinction to uncooperative, parasitic individuals. Most of our developed economy is devoted to the production of wants and not needs, a process fraught with the destruction of the very nature we need for life. Even then, there is no good reason for unemployment for everyone who would participate, and now that we have a relatively free virtual world to participate in, there is no limit to what artful people can do without polluting the physical world given friendly energy to power the grid.

Compte's sociology, as Mr. Bezos must know, was influenced by Henri de Saint-Simon, a French businessman and veteran of the American Revolution who envisioned society led to utopia by an industrial elite. Science is not, however, the highest good without motivation. Comte fell madly in unconsummated love with one Clotilde de Vaux, a married Catholic woman, and subverted his rational system into a humanist religion after she died. He was assisted in that project by John Stuart Mill, the practical philosopher who thought men and women could resolve their sexual differences and be united in loving friendship, enjoyed a purportedly sexless marriage with Mrs. Harriet Taylor after her husband died. The new "science of ideas" and social sciences evolving from the physical sciences was elaborated as "Ideologie" by Pierre Cabanis and adopted by Thomas Jefferson at his university, replacing theology —John Adams referred to ideology as "idiotology." The political bias of this line of positive thinking was generally republican-democratic, 'republican' being a political state led by highly qualified individuals, 'democratic' meaning the best among the highly qualified are elected by its liberated citizens. The conceptual regime was conserved with constitutions written and unwritten as verbal bulwarks against the tyranny of vain, egotistical despots.

Setting that digression aside, our long journalism having lost almost all our readers by now, we or our computers know the racial divide in the area ran deep even before rented slaves helped build the White House, and much can be said about the difference between the sexes and generations. So Mr. Schwartzman was right to quote what the young black lady said to about white fear of black faces of the salt-and-pepper clientele at the Assets strip club. The reader should still know, however, regardless of his or her gender, age, and income, that, generally speaking, strip clubs are unwelcome near any residential neighborhood, despite what a student may say in her thesis for a university degree or the attempt of jurists to split pubic hairs. The combination of alcohol and public displays of genitalia in strip clubs, absent relaxing orgies, fuels violence, prostitution, drugs, and racketeering in same, not to mention traffic and parking issues, and the usual nightclub racket that keeps working folk up at night.

Mr. Schwartzman did not have time or space to disclose that, among taxi king Schaeffer's real estate holdings was a property nearby, at 1215 Connecticut Avenue, N.W., scandalized by allegations that it was being used by an Asian massage parlor tenant, S&S LLC dba Spa Sky, presided over by Hak Jae Lee of Flushing, New York, a person previously arrested for provision of illegal sexual services. The facility was owned by Sun Hwa-Lee Lim of Falls Church, Virginia, was suspected of trafficking in immigrant girls, and allegedly operated as a house of prostitution employing unlicensed massage therapists offering services not permitted in the District of Columbia.

The District has a long reputation for prostitution: in 2005, more than 40 Asian massage parlors operated as fronts for brothels, claimed Derek Ellerman, co-executive director of the Polaris Project.

Each earned an average of $1.2 million a year, he said. At Spa Sky or Sky Spa, undercover police officers arrested prostitutes providing the well-advertised "Perfect Hot and Beautiful Massage." The attorney general of the District filed civil suit 0001450-11 on 24 February 2011 against the operators and Mr. Schaeffer's real estate company, and the operation, whatever it was, shut down. According to Ms. Drissel, it was only after a vigorous clamor from neighbors that decisive action was taken against the health spa.

Mr. Schwartzman also failed to solicit and include in his article the opinion of Mr. Bezos on the club despite the fact that he is one of the wealthiest men in the world even after his divorce, a prominent member of the neighborhood, and the savior of the newspaper the political journalist writes for. Furthermore, Mr. Bezos, like Ms. Calomiris, is celebrated for having a raucous laugh, the vestige of the ancient Greek roar or howling laughter of relief from tyranny after democracy was invented. That is perhaps one of the several reasons President Donald Trump, 73, who loves strippers and prefers caustic humor, hates Mr. Bezos. Mr. Bezos laughs raucously all the way to the bank, and his wad is evidently larger than the President's, at least according to stripper Stormy Daniels.

Washingtonian insiders are disinclined to warmly embrace outsiders, but the affluent residents of Kalorama, the District's knobbiest neighborhood, are glad Mr. Bezos is making the old Textile Museum into a 27,000 square-foot home with 25 bathrooms and 11 bedrooms, thus saving them from the horror of conversion of the structures into carpetbagger apartments. Speaking of George Washington, it is to the internet prophet's credit that his primary home is in a state named after George Washington, in the city of Medina, so named after the holy city on the Arabian Peninsula where Mohammad changed the direction of prayer towards Mecca.

Mr. Schwartzman sniffed around the group of protesters and kept coming back to Ms. Calomiris, dogging her for information including her telephone number. She happens to be an attractive and gregarious blonde, something she has in common with Ms. Drissel, accustomed to being the cynosure of gentlemen's attention at social functions where she has had occasion as guest speaker to raise funds to help abused women and children. She told the newshound that she believed in profitable free trade after he prompted her to do so when he discovered she was somebody, but she added that the sort of trade that Assets engaged in belonged in Las Vegas and not in Kalorama because the times had changed with #Metoo and Jeffrey Epstein.

She made the mistake of responding with persiflage as the reporter persisted with his flirtations, coming back around to her time and again, yet not inviting her to Assets for a drink. She is old school, hailing back to the days when the likes of Marilyn Monroe knew that they could joke around without editors using every detail volunteered, like what she said to a reporter when she dismounted from an airplane to marry Joe DiMaggio in 1954, so she did not expect every scintilla of her banter to be used as if it were news by the prestigious Washington Post, particularly her shameless brag, followed by a "raucous laugh," that she has a young Brazilian boyfriend in Miami.

The "flurry of personal details" Ms. Calomiris "volunteered" included the fact she is a member of a prominent Washington family, had never demonstrated before, had attended finishing school in the '60s, had never smoked, and had been married "several" times. The last, unnecessarily reported detail was perhaps printed to imply that women who protest strip clubs and have been married more than twice but not many times are hypocritical strippers themselves. That being said, it is true that Elizabeth Calomiris, nee Betty Jane Houser, is the matriarch of the Calomiris family, landholding Washingtonians of Greek heritage. She brought to the Greeks her noble German heritage. Her own forbears settled in Tennessee, where her grandmother was the land purchasing agent for the Tennessee Valley Authority. Her late father served the nation as a nuclear warfare intelligence consultant.

If the biased political reporter had been more interested in people instead of the sensationalist angle on his story, that rich old white residents were making a fuss in front of a strip club owner's house in their neighborhood, he would have questioned Ms. Calomiris properly and discovered that, after attending finishing school, which comes highly recommended for good girls along with ballet or gymnastics, she served National Geographic as an illustrator. Not only does she not smoke, the mere scent of marijuana tempts her to call the police, and, she is responsible for the conviction and rehabilitation of a former husband, a major stock swindler, in Clinton prison, notorious among cons for its tight security although several people then escaped with the help of a guard, a married woman enamored by a prisoner. Although she refuses to speak of politics in polite society, she is a staunch conservative who goes to work rather than protest on the street as liberals are wont to do.

A precise division into conservative or liberal is a false dichotomy depending on what some people want to preserve and from what they would be liberated. Many women who believe they are conservative do not know that they are conserving themselves as wage slaves and sex slaves who dare not protest patriarchy. The subordination of females is prehistoric despite the rumors of a matriarchal society. Women had to succumb to the stronger sex in order to survive, and suicide ran rife in some cultures. Their complaints were necessarily limited to pouting and sulking, as described in the Vedas. And upon the death of their husbands they were considered worthless and were thrown onto the funeral pyre and burned with their husbands. Fathers loved their daughters but moaned their birth, for they were treated like cattle, and even of late are raped and butchered. The only cultured and sophisticated women in the "good old days" some conservatives would conserve were concubines and prostitutes in harems. That is why historians have said the progress of civilization may be measured by the way women are treated. And that includes the manner in which they are respected, and that does not mean being placed romantically upon a pedestal and idolized and then taken down and debased including put in showers nude and be ogled at pruriently as so much brainlessly wiggling meat.

Despite her conservative tendency, Ms. Calomiris is no prude. She knows what all too many females have suffered in order to survive since time immemorial. Yet here, in the Washington Post Political section, politics being about who has power and why, including in the great battle between men and men and women in general, she was cast as one of twenty wealthy old white prudes making a big deal about a sign that might as well have been a pornographic illustration of a giant derriere for all they were concerned by the vision of ASSETS. If he had conducted a thorough investigation, he would know that young people have protested the renewal of the license because of disturbances of the peace and parking issues, and they have made videos of noisy incidents.

I suggested that, if the neighbors are interested in making a case against the renewal of Assets' liquor license, they should call the police about every disturbance and make sure their complaints become reported by the police department for future reference. And they should obtain the police record of complaints over the last ten years and examine the possibility that there is some concealed connection between the old and new operations of the club.

It seems that only one serious police incident so far at the newly named club, which got its certificate of occupancy in June 2019 and applied to renew the license that Mr. Schaeffer's limited liability front, Voyager 888 LLC, had obtained thanks to the real estate deal.

The nightclub was investigated in December by George M. Garcia of the Alcoholic Beverage Regulation Administration (ABRA), Investigation Number 19-251-00157, Case Report signed 4 December 2019.

A complaint of Robbery and Assault at Assets was made to the police department on 19 October 2019 by a man who had fled the scene to a place nearby to call the police. The victim of the alleged assault and robbery was accused of stealing money from the strippers. He was evicted from the club, beaten up, knocked down and kicked until he bled on the ground, by four of seven security guards present at the club after he tried to retrieve seized property he had taken from his person and placed on the hood of a vehicle to be searched.

A member of the security staff said the victim hit him in the face and grabbed his necklace when he tried to return the phone the man had dropped. A security guard said the man had tried to enter the club with a knife on him, but was then allowed to enter after he hid the knife at the Rite Aid across the street.

Jeffrey Schaeffer was identified as the owner and interviewed by the ABRA investigator. He was found to have scant knowledge of proper security procedures. He was not present at the time of the incident and was unaware that the club's surveillance cameras were inadequate. None of the guards were employed by Assets, Mr. Schaeffer said. They were employed by "American Protection Professional."

The victim was arrested later on in an unrelated matter yet was not available for an interview. Curiously, neither was the policeman who responded to the complaint at the club.

Mr. Garcia found no violation of the 2001 Settlement Agreement, but he concluded that the club was in violation of their approved Security Plan because the manager was not notified of the incident immediately; the violence was not immediately reported to the police department; several surveillance cameras were inoperable; the incident involving injury was not logged into an Incident Report Log along with contact information of the persons involved; and no such log was being kept in the office as required. Furthermore, an investigator determined that security staff lied about details of the event.

The ABRA report appears deficient enough to call for a further investigation into the possibility of a most troubling violation of the section of the District of Columbia Official Code, requiring the licensee or a manager licensed by ABRA to be present and responsible at the establishment during the hours liquor is being served. The outside security company was apparently running the club, so it should be thoroughly investigated.

Mr. Schaeffer was not present when the incident occurred 19 October, and, when interviewed on 17 November, he was found ignorant of the details of what had happened. The report does not include an interview with a licensed manager. A form dated 2 November requesting the surveillance camera record names one Tracy Kirby, ABRA License #115580, Exp. 28 January 2020, as the licensed manager, yet that name does not appear on the original police report nor was she interviewed by ABRA although a licensed manager is required by law to have been present in the absence of Mr. Schaeffer. The signature on that form is redacted, blacked out, leaving only two high loops in the hand of the person that signed. Those loops suggest that Mr. Schaeffer, who was not present on that date, but was interviewed on a later date, may have signed the form on the later date, rather than Tracy Kirby. If that is the case, it would arouse suspicion of impropriety.

Ms. Miller, when interviewed by the Washington Post, claimed to be the wife of the owner and the "proprietor" of the establishment, according to the reporter, and for all intents and purposes, the manager, yet her name does not appear as a licensed manager or owner. Neither was she reportedly interviewed by the police or the ABRA investigator, so it is fair to conclude that she was not present at the event either. All that if true would be cause to suspend or revoke the establishment's license.

The District Code provides a procedure for parties to protest liquor licenses. A protest dated 24 November was made by St. Margaret's Episcopal Church, which is located across the street from the strip club. Conceived in 1892 in what was then an affluent suburb, the church's patron is Saint Margaret of Wessex (1045-1093), an English princess and a queen of Scotland known for bringing the practices of the Scottish church in line with those in Rome and on the Continent. She was canonized in 1250 by Pope Innocent IV for her piety, charitable projects, and ministry to disadvantaged people. St. Margaret's and its Priest-in-Charge, Rev. Weinberg, who is fluent in Spanish and has served God in Costa Rica and El Salvador, are well regarded for ministering to Hispanic immigrants, the homeless, the poor, LGBTQ, and other underprivileged persons in accordance with Christian precepts and their fundamental mission, to realize the full potential of humans as beings created in God's image.

Rev. Weinberg opined in his protest letter that stripping does not support "vibrant all-inclusive family friendly worship." He said the church's opposition started in 1986, when a former rector of St. Margaret's voiced formal opposition to the Royal Palace operating there since 1975, presenting evidence to the liquor control board that parishioners and staff had been attacked by drunken clients of the strip club and the church property had been littered. Considerable expenditures were made since to improve the church property, he said, and damage to the property was feared.

"Now we are confronted with the name of the operation changed from an innocuous name—the Royal Palace—to a signage in pink and purple with the name Assets. We believe this is sexually suggestive and not in keeping with the residential character of our changed neighborhood." At least the name should be changed, he wrote, and hours of operation limited.

I thought confession booths, an important element of the Catholic Church, should be recommended for Assets' customers, but confession of sins to priests is not practiced in the Episcopal Church.

The protest from the church was dismissed by the Board because a representative did not appear for the hearing and because a non-profit church does not have legal standing before the Board. Official neighborhood councils do have standing, and other protests against the renewal of the license are scheduled to be heard in March and April of 2020.

A protest to ABRA was also made by Mr. Friedman, president of the Sheridan-Kalorama Neighborhood Council. He is a prominent Washington litigator who in his 43-years of practice thus far has litigated almost every kind of commercial dispute. He happens to also be a pilot, someone very interested in getting to a destination as directly and quickly as possible. He advocated efficient case management for early dispute resolution long before arbitration and mediation became the ethical thing for lawyers to do instead of fighting for the sake of fighting to run up fees. Given his penchant for mediation, he may attempt to arrive at some sort of settlement agreement with the club, whereas Ms. Drissel wants it gone.

Assets disturbs the peace, Mr. Friedman wrote, interfering with the residents' quiet enjoyment of their neighborhood with noise, litter, and at least one instance of violence thus far. It has an adverse impact on the parking needs in the area, interferes with traffic flow including access by emergency vehicles, has only two parking spots on Florida Avenue, and the sidewalk in front of the club is inadequate for the crowds attracted, endangering pedestrians and persons getting in and out of cars. Nude dancing "is like to depress property values" in the area. Finally, the sign "Assets" does not comply with applicable laws and the settlement agreement because the word "Assets," according to the Urban Dictionary, denotes "boobs, bett, hips" and the root word of the noun is "ass." So the neighborhood looks forward to settlement discussions on the issues with Assets, and a hearing of their protest if settlement is not obtained.

The actual root words involved are the Latin 'ad satis' or 'to enough,' in French 'asez' or 'enough', meaning asset, sufficient estate to allow for the discharge of a will. That was done in England, as Mr. Friedman would know, in a session of a law court called an assize where cases are assessed and settled. Neither of the terms are directly related to our 'ass', derived from the Latin asinus, in Old English 'assen' or 'she-ass', meaning, first of all, a horse-like animal, applied to a stupid person often said to be a horse's ass, and, more vulgarly, the buttocks, or the ass-end of anything.

An ass is an ass is an ass by no other name. Ms. Miller said that the name "Assets" could be changed to "church" and the stodgy white people would still complain.

Obviously the sign is not the main issue nor is it race. The problem seems to be the unwanted crowd public nudity attracts. The advertisement is protested because it might add to that crowd, all to the detriment of the neighborhood. As for the District itself, there is a moratorium on establishments which permit nude dancing. A licensee who regularly provided entertainment by nude dancers before December 15, 1993, may continue to do so at its establishment. Nine of twelve transferable licenses are presently in use, and here are zoning limitations to transferability. Since nobody wants strip clubs in or near their neighborhood except a limited number of clientele, perhaps the majority of them transient, it may behoove the government to zone them out without grandfathering any of the existing clubs.

Several cities have banned nude exhibitions in public places from city precincts altogether or have exiled them to boondocks on the city limits.

In 1976, Detroit became one of the first cities in the US to introduce zoning laws that were designed to counter the clustering together of adult businesses into a red light district. The law banned strip clubs from locating within 1,000 feet of any two existing adult businesses or within 500 feet of any residential area. Eagerness to follow the Detroit zoning method quickly spread to other cities.

New York City's former Mayor Rudy Giuliani famously abhorred New York City's adult establishments, calling them a "corrosive institution." It was during his reign in 1995 that New York City Council amended certain zoning laws to ban adult entertainment in commercial districts like Times Square and barred them from operating within 500 feet of residences, schools, or places of worship. These restrictive zoning laws are what forced strip clubs to sprout in neighborhoods on the peripheries of the outer boroughs, like the South Bronx, an industrial zone.

In 2015 an effort was made to wipe out strip clubs in the Bronx. Politicians led what was called a "witch hunt" in the Hunts Point neighborhood to shut down the clubs by revoking their liquor licenses. A club called Platinum Pleasures was closed down in the South Bronx during the crackdown. Their tactic was been simple and effective, particularly in the Hunts Point neighborhood of the South Bronx: Instead of going after the clubs themselves, they went after their liquor licenses, considered to be a faulty approach by defensive lawyers.

In 2017 the Reno City Council voted to require adult businesses like strip clubs to move out of the downtown area to industrial zones closer to the edges of town. Indeed, that approach, to put their adult uses in industrial zones and not in urban mixed-use residential and commercial zoning districts, is typical. Votes as well as money counts, and politicians are wont to heed bigger numbers of both. Wealthier neighborhood lead the way, so perhaps politicians and the residents and attorneys for the Sheridan-Kalorama neighborhood will expand their crusade to the entire district, doing away with the moratorium on new licenses as well as getting rid of existing licenses.

Specific city ordinances funnel strip clubs and sex shops into specific areas downtown, virtually spot zoning those areas. Perhaps the District of Columbia will keep them of Connecticut running northwest from Dupont Circle.

As of 2018 in Minneapolis it was legal to open a strip club downtown as long as it was not within 500 feet of a church or within 1,000 feet of a residential zone, or on Nicollet Mall, or if another strip club is already on the same side of the block. I visited a museum converted into a strip club in Minneapolis, at the turn of the century when I was a jazz dancer. I liked the bartender, a young lady studying to become a mortician. I was not interested in strip dancing unless it was artfully choreographed, so I offered some choreographic advice along the lines of striptease dancing.

Back in New York, a federal judge in 2019 blocked the city from enforcing the controversial strip club rules. The case worked its way through the courts for 17 years while the clubs remained open. Judge Pauley ruled that the city's zoning regulations infringed on freedom of speech rights and left them without viable alternatives, that is, places where they could move their business to comply with zoning law.

In another 2019 case, two strip clubs will keep operating in downtown Augusta while they challenge the city's zoning laws. The Augusta Chronicle reported that the heirs of James "Whitey" Lester sued the city in May of that year, saying city zoning laws violate constitutional guarantees of free speech and equal protection. A 1997 city ordinance had decreed that businesses in heavy industrial zones could host nude dancing or serve alcohol, but not do both.

While four other strip bars closed, Lester's two businesses were grandfathered and continued to operate. Earlier in 2019, Lester, Augusta commissioners denied his request to allow him to transfer licenses to operate the Discotheque Lounge and Joker's Lounge to a relative.

The constitutional right to free speech is not a right to inflict harm on the public, and the constituted police power including the courts have an immediate governmental interest in protecting the public from harmful behavior. There is, for instance, no absolute right to incite riots or advocate the violent overthrow of the government. In the case of Assets the jurists would consider the a city's substantial interest in protecting the public from the so-called negative secondary effects of strip clubs: an atmosphere conducive to violence, sexual harassment, public intoxication, prostitution, human trafficking, the spread of sexually transmitted diseases and other deleterious effects such as the demoralization of children.

The Assets nightclub might prevail in court given the current demoralization of the nation and the stacking of the court with justices favored by a President fond of strippers. The U.S. Supreme Court has not been enthusiastic about banning strip clubs on the basis of nudity. Challenges have indeed reached the U.S. Supreme Court, where the usual hairsplitting was conducted in accordance with the inherently irrational casuistry or case-by-case law typical of the Anglo-American judicial system, which supports the political-economic dominance of the legal profession over all walks of life via the speciously divided three branches of government. So we have "the O'Brien test" for evaluating restrictions on symbolic speech; to wit, the government generally has a freer hand in restricting expressive conduct than it has in restricting the written or spoken word. We should not be surprised, however, if so-called pussy-whistling is considered to be free speech; there was a popular place on Oahu frequently by men and women to get a laugh, and a free drink if they retrieved a flashing dildo a woman on a swing emitted from between her legs, and then she played the first four notes of Beethoven's Fifth.

The decisions made in a particular case are not, on the one hand, supposed to apply to all similar cases because each case is unique, yet, on the other hand, the rationalizations arrived at in a "leading" case may be used as doctrine to guide to decisions in other cases. The casuistry may become so obviously absurd from time to time that precedents must be overturned and new ones fabricated. Judges, despite their dissents, which are supposed to be ignored after rendered, prefer to remain steadfast in their biases for long enough to give their interpretative law a semblance of permanence or legitimacy. Yet there is almost inevitably a time for the overturning of everything man made, including leading cases, maxims, and doctrines, given the presumed moral progress of the race.

In the end, the people rule, if need be, by revolution: the judges will be hanged if they do not abide with the Rousseauian "general will."

In any case, if Assets winds up in the courts, we cannot be certain of the outcome except that that it may have no assets left after payment of the legal fees. I have suggested that the wealthy residents of Kalorama arrange for the purchase of the property to put it to what they perceive to be its highest and best use instead of wasting time and money on protesting its present use and trying to get its license revoked. After all, $10 million is chump change to the likes of Bezos. Or they could prevail on their neighbor to please not only the neighbors but other tenants to convert the usage of the corner to something decent, like a Turkish restaurant with belly dancing and a dance school upstairs, and to enforce residential parking with immediate towing and $1,000 fines.

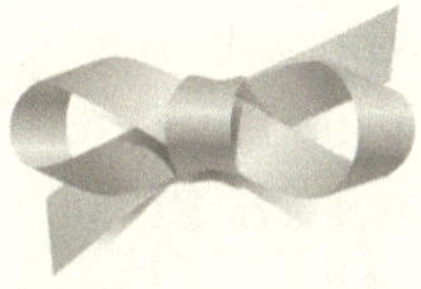

The Club Madonna Bamboozle

The Hoodwinking of Leroy Griffith

August 12, 2013. Word was out on South Beach's Washington Avenue this Spring that Leroy Griffith, owner of the totally nude strip joint, Club Madonna, was about to bring a fraud suit against the City of Miami Beach, City Attorney Jose Smith, former Mayor David Dermer, former Commissioners Simon Cruz and Saul Gross, and former city attorneys Gary Held and Murray Dubbin. Furthermore, it was joyfully proclaimed, Griffith planned to expose Mayor Matti Bower and Commissioner Deede Weithorn for promising they would help him get a liquor license in return for $4,000 in campaign contributions.

Most people are surprised and patrons of the naked arts disappointed that Club Madonna cannot sell liquor simply because its entertainers appear totally nude, although alcohol may be served in partially nude clubs where private parts are left to an imagination that can be more provocative than the real thing.

Recall that the great burlesque dancer Sally Rand was arrested multiple times for indecent exposure although her nudity was only imagined; a San Francisco judge who viewed her performance said that anyone who thought it was lewd had a perverse notion of morals.

Nude clubs elsewhere can sell liquor, so what in the world is wrong with the City of Miami Beach? Meyer Lansky must be spinning in the grave at the sight of the sunny city exercising a legalized monopoly on pursuits better left to illegally organized crime!

Maybe not: Griffith reportedly sued Charlotte, North Carolina, television station WBTV and Fayetteville police Capt. William Johnson for damages in excess of $10,000 for calling him a "Meyer Lansky man" and "one of Meyer Lansky's boys" during an April 1984 broadcast, in which the program said Griffith's Astor Theatre in Charlotte was the only theatre in town that showed only X-rated homosexual movies. According to a *Fayetteville Observer* report dated Dec. 4, 1984, Capt. Johnson was referring to a 1982 New York Select Committee on Crime report that said, "Leroy Griffith, a former Meyer Lansky man, is alleged to be the adult movie king in Miami." Griffith complained that Johnson's statements were false and malicious, and that he had never been associated in any way with organized crime. The disposition of that federal case is unknown at deadline. Sadly, the allegedly false and malicious allegation was reiterated in Appendix Five to Part 4: Chapter Four, entitled "Organized Crime," of the 1986 Attorney General's Commission on Pornography, wherein operations in various states including Florida were described based on investigators' reports.

Describing Florida, the pornography report implied that Griffith was guilty by leasing, a kind of guilt by association: "Benjamin Sigelbaum is a former banking official who has been known to set up Swiss bank accounts for organized crime figures. He also acts as an international courier of monies for organized crime figures. It is believed that he is the financial backer of Bernard Rose's pornographic enterprises. Rose owns the controlling interest in three X-rated movie theaters in Dade County which are leased to firms that actually operate them. He owns approximately 600 theaters in the United States. Rose is alleged to front investments for Meyer Lansky in Esquire Theaters. Benjamin Sigelbaum is also an associate of Meyer Lansky. Leroy Griffin (sic), a former Meyer Lansky man, is alleged to be the adult movie king in Miami. He owns and operates several adult theaters the Roxy Theater, Pussycat Theater, Paramount

Theater, and the Gaiety Theater, all in Dade County. It was recently reported that he is now leasing the 79th Street Theater and the King-Rex Theater from Bernard Rose."

We are still left wondering why the gentleman, ostensibly defamed by associational allegations, could not serve liquor in his licensed nude establish in Miami Beach thirty years later. "That's what they do, put information out there to ruin people," said a security worker who spoke under condition of anonymity, saying that mere association with the strip club industry had ruined the life of a friend of his, who eventually committed suicide.

"That information you're talking about is probably from the F.B.I. It is supposed to be provided to the government in secret, but then the committee report or the court report is released with all that crap in it. And the Internet is seeded with it now. What kind of privacy is that?

"I've worked for strip clubs in Atlanta, Vegàs, and Miami," he said, "and I worked for Leroy too. I remember when Leroy wanted to buy a club in Miami. People looked on the Internet, and decided not to even to talk to him because he was made out to look like a racketeer on the Internet. Strip clubs were called a racket in the Florida law books, so anyone who had an interest in them was called a racketeer."

"He's no hood, no Mafia man. I know Mafia. He's just a businessman. He runs a clean business. I worked security for a competitor of his on the beach just a few months ago, and everything was exposed inside, all kinds of sex acts going on too, that's nothing new, but they won't let Leroy have a license because he's Irish and up against the Jews and Cubans. As long as they run the beach, he's never getting a license. Miami is different."

In Atlanta, an anti-Semitic motive was asserted for the 1999 prosecution of Steven Kaplan, owner of the Gold Club. Wherever behavior is criminalized the crime is likely to become organized or attract organized crime families if the crime is highly profitable. Kaplan was indicted on federal racketeering charges including credit-card fraud, prostitution, money laundering, police corruption, and involvement with organized crime. The trial drew national attention from sports fans because some of his customers were famous athletes. Small-time hoodlums alleged Kaplan was paying for Mafia protection provided by the Gambino crime family. Defense attorney Steve Sadow said that prosecutors "recruited every scoundrel, every scumbag, every criminal that they could possibly get and have offered them their freedom and money for their testimony." Former beef smuggler Jack Galardi, a subject of the F.B.I. Operation G-string probe in Las Vegas also operated strip joints in Atlanta, Florida and San Diego. He was allegedly making huge payments under the table to several Las Vegas officials. Prosecutors there were accused of being on a fishing expedition.

It seems like the political assembly governing the City of Miami Beach is running a legalized protection racket. Griffith over the years has complained of selective enforcement, a common refrain on the lips of residents in regards to code enforcement in general. It is usually random enforcement due to bureaucratic laziness and gross negligence, or moral corruption, but there is plenty of room for criminal corruption, and every so often the F.B.I. moves in for the kill. The regime is so unaccountable, given the absolute discretion of officials to do what they like, that City Attorney Jose Smith has called a proposal to account for some of it "moronic," stating that all officials have to do is "follow the law," which is to do as they like.

"Leroy is good man but he is stubborn, his own worst enemy," said local hotel and restaurant association president David Kelsey, familiar with the Miami Beach political scene for decades, when I asked him why Griffith does not simply convert his club to a burlesque entertainment theatre, having his girls don pasties and thongs so he can get a license.

Another local businessman, a political insider, practically echoed Kelsey's viewpoint. "Leroy is his own worst enemy. I told him how to get a license, but he wants to fight city hall for his civil rights. He has integrity, but he will never get a license now that he has sued commissioners and one of their wives."

Kelsey declared at public hearing on the issue in March 2004 that the irrational liquor ban on total nudity was drafted for graft. That makes sense: Legendary theatre entrepreneur Griffith has been trying to get a liquor license for over a decade and has plenty of money, making him the politicians' favorite chump for their liquor license con game. He has long complained that his competitors over the years have been allowed to serve liquor with nudity in violation of the law enforced against him alone because he actually applied for a liquor license. The mutual tattle-tale game between clubs was almost as bad as the current war between Las Vegas wedding chapels. The corruption allegations even included peeks and blowjobs to induce the policing power to look the other way.

Griffith believes he has a natural constitutional right to provide the sight of genitalia onstage to his customers if not during lap dancing, and he was not deterred by unconstitutional hindrances. In 1970 he and his performers were charged in the Municipal Court of the City of Miami Beach with producing, presenting, directing or participating in obscene performances at the Roxy Theatre (now Club Madonna) in regards to the performance of the play 'Fear of Love.' Further, he was himself accused of violating the ordinance against operating a house of ill-repute just for showing the play. The ladies were prosecuted for lewdness, that is, for being found nude. The State of Florida came after him too, but the case was thrown out on the basis that it subjected the convicted defendants to double jeopardy.

In 1971, his burlesque business was evicted from the New York City Century Paramount Hill for violating a clause in the underlying lease prohibiting the exhibition of burlesque shows or adult or sex exploitation films.

Proceedings were instituted against Griffith in 1973 for showing porno-chic 'Deep Throat,' a 1972 comedy with a budget of $30,000, starring Harry Reems and Linda Lovelace, who said she was paid only $1,250 for her supporting role in the film, which grossed an estimated $45,000,000. She claimed her fee was confiscated by her husband whom she said had beaten and imprisoned her, forcing her into pornography and prostitution at gunpoint. The comedic plot involved the discovery by a doctor that the protagonist had a clitoris in her throat. Somehow the female on the receiving end whose only function was to please males became a champion of sexual liberation. The film elicited the ire of feminists, President Nixon and the Christian right; judicial proceedings were instituted throughout the country.

Griffith was eventually sentenced to $3,000 and five days in jail in lieu of payment, later reduced to $500, for contempt of court for violating an injunction as to the advertising of a revised version of the film in which the most explicit scenes were edited out. He would go on to sue Linda Lovelace over a contract he made with her to perform live for $15,000 a week in a Las Vegas type show replete with a band and comedians at his Paramount Theatre. She said she was supposed to sing and dance for Griffith, and that Sammy Davis, Jr. had promised to show her how to do that for $500. But she still did not show up. Griffith claimed he had shelled out $75,000. The judge ordered Lovelace to pay around $32,000. She appealed, saying she was "worthless" as a live entertainer, and that what she was expected to do was illegal, which Griffith denied. A Miami News article of May 5, 1975, reported that she claimed she had almost gotten an Academy Award that year, and that wives were asking for her autograph to give to their husbands. She eventually advocated against porn before Congress and elsewhere.

Furthermore, Griffith was prosecuted by the United States for interstate transportation of an allegedly obscene film entitled 'Illusions (or Hallucinations) of a Lady," observed in 1976 by a FBI special film investigator at the Sinerama Adult Theatre in New Orleans. The question at issue on appeal was whether the film was obscene. The court had no difficult determining that there was at least probable cause to believe it was indeed obscene after reading the investigator's first-hand, detailed account of various sexual acts, Obscene or not, we have no doubt that any pubescent child who can read plain language and possesses an illustrated anatomy text will find the court's decision stimulating, to say the least. Frankly speaking, the court document should be stamped "XXX-Rated.

That is not all, but suffice it to say that Griffith is conservative in that sense of free speech. After all, genitalia advertisements hail back to primitive humankind, and are still current in the worship of the lingam and yoni in India and their private counterparts in other parts of the world, not to mention the reddened displays of baboons and the exhibitions of other members of the Animal Kingdom. Griffith evaded the unconstitutional restriction for a while by keeping nudity behind a glass wall, but that just will not do now. Total nudity is a matter of principle for him no matter what, and he will be glad to contribute to your campaign if you promise to aid him in his righteous quest to strip his girls down to their birthday suits where liquor is served.

I had never met nor conversed with Leroy Griffith even though a rumor was spread that I was on his payroll, nor had I been inside a strip club since my stay in Alaska during the oil boom. Long before that, when I ran away from home to Chicago at age 13, my first love was a 17-year-old bisexual stripper for the Outfit in Cal City, yet I was never fond of strip dancing per se unless it was choreographed well and the dancers were genuinely sexy. Bump and Grind is boring. Muckraking is far more exciting. Having heard the glad tidings on

South Beach's seamy strip, that politicians and city lawyers were about to be sued for defrauding Griffith and the court, I rushed over to Club Madonna to get the sordid scoop.

Griffith did not know me from Adam. He kept security by my side during my visit. I introduced myself as the wildcard journalist who had reported at length on his March 3, 2011, bar complaint against Commissioner Michael Gongora, a likeable weathercock now running for mayor, regarding an alleged discussion held during at July 12, 2011, luncheon:

"Michael Gongora, Esq. ("Gongora"), City Commissioner, Miami Beach, conspired to extort me, Leroy Griffith, owner of Club Madonna, into hiring a well-known lobbyist in order to hear an issue Gongora had been promising me for seven months that he would present to the full City of Miami Beach commission. If I did not hire this lobbyist, Randy Milliard, Gongora would be effectively barring me from appearing before the commission to present a proposed amendment to an ordinance that has been the subject of controversy since 2004, when it passed by a 5-2 commission vote and was subsequently defeated upon its second reading 4-3 due to the interference and unethical behavior of Jane Gross, the wife of then-commissioner Saul Gross. At this time I believe Gongora is guilty of extreme misconduct as both an attorney and public official. I am alleging that Gongora engaged in behaviors that he knew were against the Florida Rules Regulating the Florida Bar, exhibiting dishonesty, deceit, misrepresentation, and fraud. He blatantly breached the public trust in the fair administration of justice through his attempted extortion efforts. As a lawyer who holds public office, he should be held to even higher standards I believe that he abused his public position for personal gain, which is in direct violation of the Rules of Professional Conduct."

Saul Gross, owner of Streamline Properties Inc., situated on Washington Avenue, is a wealthy real estate lawyer and entrepreneur whose biography states: "His experience as a real estate attorney in New York City with Morgan, Lewis & Bockius and as a Vice President with The Urban Group, a syndication company specializing in renovation of historic properties, set the stage for Saul's success in Miami Beach." Jane Gross, who recently listed her employment status as "homemaker," is a respected member of the community, nominated in January 2013 for reappointment to the Historic Preservation Board by Commissioner Jorge Exposito, Commissioner Deede Weithorn and Vice Mayor Michael Gongora. Her resume filed with the city touts her experience in construction, examining documents and bank statements, and her work as Assistant Controller of a corporation prior to moving to Miami Beach. It recounts how she, "liaison to all potential investors" in the Art Deco District, "assisted the New York owners who restored the Cinema Theater and created South Beach's first premiere nightclub, now after many incarnations, the "Mansion." The Mansion, an urban music nightclub, is on Washington Avenue, a block south of the elementary school.

Jane Gross was honored by the City of Miami Beach during Women's History Month 2006. "Dedication to our community and long hours of volunteer service is the reason we are honoring Jane Dee Gross as a Miami Beach "Woman Worth Knowing". Jane relocated to Miami Beach in the early - 80's after a successful Corporate Marketing Career in Connecticut; met and married not yet Commissioner Saul Gross in the late 80's and gave birth to Jonathan in 1990. Anonymous benefit projects have always been Jane's favorites however, she regularly volunteers for a wide variety of civic organizations; Temple Beth Shalom, Daily Bread Food Bank, Community Partnership for the Homeless, New Life Family Shelter, American Cancer Society, WLRN Radio Reading Services for the Blind, Miami Dade School System. She is a Board member of People Acting for Community Together (PACT), Miami Design

Preservation League and the Miami Beach Community Health Center. A favorite quote of Jane's is 'Life is what happens to you when you're busy making other plans' (John Lennon 1980)"

I asked a realtor who is intimate with the history of historic preservation in Miami Beach if the decisions of the Historic Preservation Board could be corrupted to profit realtors and developers. Speaking on the condition of remaining unnamed, the realtor, claiming to have no knowledge of corruption, said it would be difficult if not impossible to buy off the majority of the members of the Board. When asked if considerable influence for his or her own benefit could be exerted on the Board by a member of the real estate industry active in historic preservation, someone who may even have a family member on the Board, believing their notions of preservation are not only good for their business but for the community, the realtor said, "I know who you mean. I cannot speak to that right now as I am very busy, but I can say that there is no such thing as true historic preservation despite all the talk about it."

The Club Madonna led the restoration of its block. The deleterious "secondary effects" Jane Gross believes it causes pale in comparison to the incidents around the Mansion and nearby urban nightclubs, where in 2006 a much beloved bouncer who tried to break up a fight was stabbed and died in front of the Mansion. Another person was taken to the hospital in critical condition with a stab wound, while another had a severed finger. Three suspects were arrested. In 2008, eight bouncers were arrested for beating up three Delaware students because they repeatedly demanded to see a bill charging them $700 for a two hour stay. In August 2010, a tourist from Philadelphia was beaten to death at the Felt Club next door to Med Pizza as customers stood by, one of them videoing the event for posting on You Tube. That is not all for the Mansion and the area around to the Mansion, including across the street, where the Chalk, a huge nightclub with pool tables where Gongora threw his birthday fete, has opened in a space once occupied by an erotic toy store. In December of 2011, a police officer was forced to shoot dead a Washington Avenue regular who pulled a gun on him in front of now closed Med Pizza, just across the street from the Mansion, as the culmination of a fracas that ensued inside the pizzeria among individuals who had been clubbing and did not like what someone said to a girlfriend. An employee of Med Pizza, now closed, called the people in the area after 11 pm "BS people," and recounted how a pimp visited the pizzeria with his girls, one of them going down on him as he ate pizza in the store. Another employee recalled that a police officer was beaten unconscious with one of the stools from the place, and how a judge let a man off for urinating on the floor because, just before the case came up in court, the witnessing police officer was told to leave by the clerk.

Suffice it to say that nightclubs without even partial nudity but plenty of violence-celebrating urban music and gang bangers have long flooded Washington Avenue and adjacent areas with so-called secondary effects, e.g. fistfights, stabbings, rapes, murders, robbery, drug dealing, public drunkenness, panhandling, loitering and so on, and many of the incidents are never reported by the only daily newspaper. One that was covered: a policeman on overtime shot a man to death in front of the Twist, a gay nightclub across the street from the police station on Washington Avenue. Someone called in to say that the man, a tourist who was believed to be looking for someone who had challenged him for abusing his wife on the street, had a weapon, perhaps an assault weapon, concealed on him, but he turned out to be unarmed after he was shot, and it was believed that he may have been earlier carrying a wooden coat hanger taken from his room at Loews to pretend that he was armed.

In any event, residents have to deal with the detritus wandering their neighborhood and on the way to work as late at 7 am, including on the buses when the go to work over the causeway in Miami. Calls to shut down many or all the clubs have fallen on deaf political ears. Only an expensive campaign by the Miami Beach Police Department, more popular clubs in downtown Miami, and the Great Recession have served to ameliorate South Beach's urban nightclub plague, the plague known in courts everywhere as "secondary effects," which Club Madonna has nothing to do with.

Gongora tried to assist Griffith with the licensing issue at a Commission Retreat held at the Eden Roc Hotel on April 30 and May 1, 2010, with Matti Bower, Deede Weithorn, and Jose Smith attending among others. He asked if there were any interest in revisiting the Club Madonna issue, but there was no interest, not since Griffith sued the wife of a member of The Family, Jane Gross, the spouse of former Commissioner Saul Gross, for libel and slander. The Planning Board did take the question up again on September 28, 2010, and voted 5-2 to recommend the commission deny the proposal while recommending 7-1 that a citywide study Adult Entertainment Study be conducted. Whatever its recommendation might be, the meeting was an exercise in futility since the commission was not about to entertain an amendment.

Deede Weithorn also tried to assist, broaching the issue with a March 23, 2012, Memorandum urging that it be referred to the Land Use Commission for the consideration of a one-year trial period for serving liquor, but she withdrew her proposal at the April 11 Commission meeting.

As for Griffith's Bar 2011 complaint against Gongora, the lawyers circled their wagons around Gongora; the Florida Bar found no probable cause to doubt his integrity. After all, Gongora's inherently credible lawyer simply wrote a letter denying the charges that were made in two sworn witness statements and a Bar complaint signed under penalties of perjury, and refused to make further inquiries into the behavior of the lawyers. The Miami-Dade Ethics Commission kowtowed to the Florida Bar and refused to inquire into the matter and ask Gongora and Hilliard to sign denials under penalties of perjury. But the Ethics Commission had fined Gongora $2,000 in 2011 for failing to report $3,000 in contributions from Griffith in 2009. And, the Ethics Commission and the court on appeal ruled against Gongora and Becker & Poliakoff, the powerful law firm he works for, when they challenged the law prohibiting the law firm from representing its clients before the Miami Beach commission while Gongora sat on it. That cost Gongora the 2008 election when Ed Tobin ran against him and questioned his ethics. Gongora is an openly gay politician, a likeable man known for his carousing around town, over which he would now preside as its mayor. Becker & Poliakoff's lobbying arm has a reputation for a perfect record of obtaining its lobbying goals in Hollywood, Florida. In August 2013 a lobbyist with the firm was arrested in connection with the arrest of the Miami Lakes and Sweetwater mayors for bribery in an F.B.I. Sting.

When I visited Club Madonna I told Griffith that I had heard the word on the street that he was going after Smith and others, and I wanted the story. I jokingly said that I also wanted to collect my Club Madonna paycheck because, according to SunPost editor Kim Stark, Gongora or Hilliard had said I was only writing about Gongora's run-in with the Florida Bar because I was on Club Madonna's payroll. Griffith gave me a free pass to the club instead. I have not used it yet because I fear I might become addicted to female genitalia and shall have to get a good job or rob liquor stores to support habitual lechery.

Hilliard, who had been a SunPost political columnist for several years, is a feared operator whom politicians are reportedly fain to fund to keep them out of his crosshairs. He is currently known as Gongora's "political satan," so-called because he once called himself the Prince of Darkness. And he turned state's evidence on Key West familiars in a lucrative bribery scheme involving building permits. Of course that goes to an old meaning of the word 'satan,' i.e. one who performs the beneficial public service of informing on accomplices to imperious authorities.

My articles criticizing the Florida Bar, its "professional racism" being one of my pet peeves, were rejected by Stark. She had encouraged me to write the stories so she could see what I had shortly after I mentioned the possibility of illicit recordings of Gongora's meeting with Griffith to the Florida Bar and Ethics Commission. After she read them, she said she had made a deal with Gongora not to run anything reflecting negatively on him because one of her columnists had hurt his feelings and he was in tears. She eventually blackballed me at the behest of City Attorney Smith, whom she named SunPost *Best City Official 2013* although she wrote twice that she did not know him. Smith had defamed me and flattered her in public record email to her for the second time after I asked him to respond to criticism for the sake of journalist balance, and he told me twice that I would not be in the city for long. Smith now says he has hung the SunPost nomination on his wall along with his Florida Bar and F.B.I. credentials. He named me *Best Moronic Journalist 2013*, and I named him *Best Magic Eight Ball Lawyer 2013*.

Griffith at 86 is a likeable grandfather, a fast-talking yet soft-spoken, rather laid-back balding businessman with a broad smile, almost childlike or naïve, trusting whomever he encounters, but do not underestimate his craftiness and dogged persistence in getting his way. To understand him better, one must remember that as a young man he fell into his career of entertaining men with naked women, not an entirely unpleasant occupation for a fellow given the foundational preoccupation of straight gentlemen, and a quite remunerative profession at that.

Griffith started in the theater business when he left the sixth grade of school in 1949. He began as a projectionist, cashier and usher at the local theater in his hometown. A short time later he worked concessions for Oscar Markovich at the Grand Theater in St. Louis, Mo.

Markovich, according to a March 6, 1957, report in the *Toledo Blade*, started out selling candy in Toledo's burlesque theatres, wound up owning the concessions there and in the entire circuit besides before buying and presiding over the luxurious Lucerne Hotel in Miami Beach for $4 million. His concession company also operated on Miami Beach, handling concessions, most famously, for the 1964 Clay-Liston fight conducted illegally under the fiction that it was sponsored by a non-profit, the VFW. He testified the VFW had nothing to do with staging the fight wherein Clay knocked out Liston. Box-office receipts were a measly $225,000. The proceeds were fought over, and the court said a contract against public policy is void.

As for Griffith, he was drafted into the armed services in 1955. After his discharge he opened his first theater in Portland, the theater staying open a short time. After operating a Kansas City restaurant and working for Markovich again, he opened a theater in Detroit. Three or four years later, in 1962, he moved to South Florida, where he started a conglomerate of entities that owned and operated theatres and a film rental business. It is unknown how he managed to accumulate sufficient capital to acquire and operate what 1988 Tax Court Memorandum 1988-445 called an "enormous business" in Florida. He is known as a "savvy businessman." He got into a lucrative business at the right time. He was also involved with theatres in New York, North Carolina, and Louisiana, and perhaps in other states as well.

According to the 1988 Memorandum in the matter of Griffith v. Commissioner, Griffith liked to gamble for relaxation, going off to the Bahamas or Las Vegas from time to time. His pastime was playing cards with chums William Berger, Joe Savino and Hyman

Lazar in the old days: Nothing more than that was said about them in the Memorandum. Who were those guys, anyway? It looks like Guilt-by-Association is implied. I know nothing at this time about Berger and Savino. As for a Hyman or Hymie Lazar or Lazer, I found this: At a hearing held in Miami on October 24, 1978, by the U.S. Senate Permanent Subcommittee on Investigation of the Committee on governmental Affairs on Organized Criminal Activities, with Sam Nunn presiding, Hyman Lazar was identified as a junketeer who arranged junkets between Miami and the Riviera casino in Las Vegas, and who was observed by undercover agents at Florida racetracks, where packs of $100 bills were being exchanged without anyone going to the window, as part of an on-track betting operation allegedly conducted with the knowledge of racetrack owners and operators. He was also often observed meeting Lansky at Wolfe's Restaurant on 21st and Collins Avenue.

So Lazar played cards with Griffith. So what? I played pool with a couple of Capone's old soldiers when I was a kid in Chicago. I did not have the faintest idea who they had been or how they made a living nor did I care. I may have been seen talking to Sam in a Rush Street lounge one afternoon—he told me that I was a good boy and that I should stay away from both forms of organized crime, i.e. the government and the mob. So what? Does that make me a Giancana Man?

I loved to play pool but was no pool shark, and I do not believe that Griffith is a card shark. He certainly does not come off like a sharpie, but maybe he is sly as the devil and I am naïve. He was affable enough when I visited him at Club Madonna. He was blunt in his opinion of what happened to him at the hands of city officials whom he said he had "trusted to eventually do the right thing." I asked myself, "Is he kidding?" His beef: city officials had wrongly denied him his right to a liquor license for many years, and he was not going to let the matter rest until justice was done.

I offered my opinion that he would be better off if he would stop fighting city hall, have his girls put on fast-change costumes over pasties and thongs, convert his club into a sophisticated venue for great burlesque shows, replete with liquor license, a small band, a choreographer, and so on. After all, I said, burlesque is enjoying a comeback as young folks revert to the Dionysian traditions of their parents, like imbibing wine and watching bawdy spectacles.

Burlesque was always done in good fun, having originally been a joke for insiders educated in the classics lampooned but was converted into popular variety shows in democratic America, and eventually stripped down to strip shows. Alcohol enhances prurience hence Prohibition and its prudish majority dealt quite an inhibiting blow to the burlesque striptease industry, but it come back somewhat with the booze, and grew less evermore sleazy, devolving into down-and-dirty exhibitions without the *burla* (joke).

Indeed, Neo-burlesque was the way to go for Club Madonna, I told Griffith. That reminded him of the old saw about the father who told his son not to go into a certain place because bad things were happening in there. One day the son ventured therein, and the first person he saw was his dad.

Griffith, who directed the 1966 off-Broadway presentation, 'The Wonderful World of Burlesque,' and who is currently a member of The Golden Days of Burlesque Historical Society, has been there, seen and done that. He converted some of the movie theatres he bought into live burlesque clubs featuring such classic cabaret stars as Tempest Storm and Blaze Star. He ran adult films in others.

His theatres, some of them subjected to police raids during the Reagan years of moral righteousness, have included Gayety Burlesque, Pussycat, Kittycat, Cameo, Paramount, Carib, Paris Follies, Flamingo, Ritz, Roxy, Luv, Adam and Eve, and Navy Point theatres among many others. The old Roxy Theatre is presently his Club Madonna. His clubs have had competition from time to time, some serving alcohol with nude entertainment and rumored peeks and blow jobs for cops. Griffith frequently complained of selective enforcement of the ordinances.

Suffice it to say that Griffith has a prurient business as far as prudes are concerned, but business is business in every trade and he is willing to do what is necessary to get it in his. He handed me copies of four checks, for $500 each, to Commissioner Deede Weithorn, and four checks, also for $500 each, to Mayor Matti Bower, allegedly for their support in getting an ordinance approved for selling liquor around totally nude entertainers. Washington Avenue is awash in booze and other drugs, violent urban music in nightclubs, and several shootings have occurred of late, even one across the street from the police station, in front of the gay Twist Club, where Mayor Bower has been photographed supporting small business by stuffing money down the front of a male stripper's jock strap. However, as almost everyone knows, if proprietors are allowed to profit from selling liquor anywhere near totally naked people, especially if patrons are being sat on, they will attract patrons likely to commit lewd acts, engage in other unseemly behavior, including going berserk when lap dancers do not go all the way, and that will surely corrupt the morals of the surrounding neighborhood, even though people who can get drunk in dozens of places on the bawdy avenue cannot actually see what is going on inside unless the pay admission, and the theatre is closed during school hours.

Dividing the checks to Weithorn and Bower was an image of a woman with three breasts. I supposed the image was an Aryan version of Minakshi, the goddess with three breasts, one of which will disappear when she finds a husband. I recall she went through quite a few gods before she found the top one and duly married him.

Minakshi brings to mind H.L. Mencken's 'Recollection of Notable Cops' (1899): "The girls in the red-light district like to crochet neckties, socks, and pulse-warmers for (cops). It was not unheard of for a cop to get mashed on such a girl, rescue her from her life of shame. And set her up as more or less an honest woman. I knew of several cases in which holy matrimony followed. But the more ambitious girls, of course, looked higher, and some of them, in my time, made very good marriages. One actually married a banker, and another died only a few years ago as the faithful and much respected wife of a prominent physician."

Mencken said cops laugh when they hear that working girls always wind up in the gutter, for they know some respectable women who were once prostitutes. We know that prostitution is a degrading career that can have evil consequences although many of us do not seem to mind renting body and soul under a different name.

Campaign contributions, by the way, are supposedly limited to $500 per person unless a person has several entities write checks for $500, a practice called "bundling." Incidentally, a different form of bundling is the custom similar to lap dancing, of having sex fully dressed, as I experienced as teenager in Hollywood, Florida, under the watchful eye of a mother who picked up a few of us cadets from Riverside Military Academy in a Cadillac convertible and took us home to party with her daughters and their girlfriends. Ethics Commission Director and former public corruption prosecutor Joe Centorino aka "Sleeping Joe" did not respond to our inquiry about the propriety of the practice or how to do it properly so as not to flout the law.

"After I wrote Weithorn her checks," Griffith said, "Mayor Bower said, 'Hey, where's mine?' so I wrote her four checks too. They are dated a day apart because my secretary postdated a check she wrote for a delivery before she wrote Bower's checks. They were here together discussing the amendment for my liquor license."

"Isn't that a violation of the Sunshine law?"

"I think so."

"Heck, I should run for the commission," I said, "I'll register several companies, come by and get a few thousand dollars from you, throw some campaign parties, maybe hire some of your dancing girls."

When asked if officials had solicited bribes in exchange for action that would get him a liquor license, or if they had tried to extort money from him for the same reason, he produced the business cards of two FBI agents, and said that he had provided information to the State Attorney from time to time, but would not get into the details with me.

"Well, I heard you're going to sue Jose Smith." I told Griffith. "I'm not prejudiced, but it would tickle me pink if you have something on him. He has taught me to despise him. Whenever I present critical information for him to respond to in the interest of balanced reporting, he threatens me, implying he will sue me for defamation, and badmouths me to editors. As far as he is concerned, anything said criticizing him and his clique is baseless, frivolous and delusional."

"I know he has defamed you," said Griffith. "Now let me show you something."

Griffith turned to his Mac, fumbled around with his mouse, explaining he was not adept with computers. He finally showed me a video of a melodramatic CBS4 I-Team news feature, 'Sex, Money, Politics in Miami Beach' (July 4, 2008), recounting his "dime-story novel" feud with the city.

"I'm looking for an attorney to re-open a federal case against several officials who conspired to extort lawyer fees out of me. The court refused to dismiss the case. We settled it on the promise that I would get a public hearing of my proposed ordinance amendment, but I did not. The proposal was voted down on the first reading. I was cheated. The deal was a fraud."

"I think there is a time limitation, and it is really difficult to get cases re-opened," I said. "Final judgments are supposed to remain final. Was the settlement a fraud on the court?"

"Yes and on me. The city agreed to give me a public hearing of the proposed ordinance reading on the second reading, but I didn't get a public hearing. They came in and denied it on the first reading."

"So they pulled a fast one on you."

He did not respond. I bid him farewell after collecting a copy of the federal complaint and settlement, saying I would look into the matter. I thought he was a damn fool when I read certain parts of the settlement agreement, for it appeared that he and his lawyers had subjected him to the mercy of the very people he had sued, members of 'The City Family' who had an inherent conflict of interest, who hated him for suing Jane Gross, the wife of one of their own, Commissioner Saul Gross. The settlement did not give him what he wanted, a liquor license, but only an opportunity to beg for it and make further contributions to campaigns.

"The parties acknowledge that adoption will require two readings and a public hearing at the second reading, but that failure to obtain a majority vote at the first reading will mean no second reading and public hearing will be held.... Club Madonna agrees that Commissioner Saul Gross will decide for himself whether or not to abstain from discussion or vote on the Proposal. His participation in the Commission's disposition of the Proposal shall not constitute a breach of this Agreement and shall not be grounds for Club Madonna to make further attack on the City's Ordinances, or a collateral after-the-fact attack on the Commission vote provided for by this Agreement."

Ironically, I thought, here is a man of principle, the owner of a so-called sleazy business putting up the good fight against the sleazy maneuvers of self-righteous and unwittingly unprincipled politicians. Yes, I thought, Griffith is a frank businessman in a frankly salacious industry, but somewhat of a chump for knavish politicians to string along for cash from campaign to campaign. What else could he do in his business, I wondered, but to keep trying to buy them off? Set up a sting with the FBI?

Well, he sued the city in federal court for the violation of his right to show stark naked performers in his club while serving alcohol. Griffith is certainly not reluctant to use the courts, but he claims this suit was brought at the suggestion of City Manager Jorge Gonzalez after the City Commission voted down a proposed resolution that would have amended the ordinance prohibiting total nudity. A lawsuit would bring the issue into executive sessions to discuss the litigation in secret. The Commission was unlikely to revisit the issue hence this would provide Griffith with an opportunity to negotiate a backdoor deal. Part of any settlement, some of the conspirators in conventicle believed, would have to include a denial that the city itself suggested a suit be brought against it, for that might not be understood by the electorate. Gonzalez, at one of three midyear closed-door meetings held in 2005, said he did not remember suggesting any such thing, and City Attorney Gary Held said it might have been Commissioner Bower's idea, to which Mayor David Dermer commented, probably not, but he would not comment on it except for that comment.

In any case, the city commissioners and lawyers did not appear to be at all offended by the federal suit against the city. What got their gall was that Griffith had, subsequent to bring the action against the city, filed a libel and slander suit against Jane Gross, the wife of Commissioner Saul Gross, for orchestrating an alleged smear campaign against him.

On May 7, 2004, Griffith's attorney, Pablo Perez, demanded that Mr. and Mrs. Gross retract slanderous and libelous statements to the effect that Griffith and Club Madonna were promoting prostitution and other criminal activities, including failing to pay certain amounts and failure to accurately report income. Mr. Gross would be dropped from the suit because as an official he was absolutely privileged to speak his mind freely on public issues without retaliation.

"She was saying I was a tax cheat, that I caused prostitution" Griffith would later tell CBS4 Investigates. (CBS Miami, July 4, 2008)

Richard J. Ovelmen, Esq. responding for Jane Gross, said that legally actionable defamatory statements had not been made inasmuch as Mrs. Gross was exercising her right to speak of the "secondary effects" effects that strip clubs are said to have, citing the opinion of various court cases. She did not speak at the first and second readings of the proposed ordinance amendment in 2004. At this time we have not ascertained precisely what she did say in her so-called smear campaign via email or in person, which would of course have a bearing on whether or not her statements would be actionable. Griffith declined to turn over email he said he had in his possession that constituted defamatory statements, because of impending litigation.

If Jane Gross had said, for example, "Establishments that serve alcohol with totally nude entertainment including lap dancing have secondary effects, that is, they contribute to crime in their areas," that would probably not be actionable, and a libel suit brought against her on that basis would be groundless and frivolous. But if she had said, "Griffith is running a prostitution ring and drug business out of Club Madonna," that would probably be actionable.

For the tax issue 5to be actionable, we would be looking for some such definite statements as, "Griffith and his club cheats on taxes, pockets cash from the box office or gives out bonuses that he does not pay employment taxes or sales taxes on, and he evades federal income taxes."

This is exactly what Jane Gross said in her April 8, 2004, widely circulated letter to the City Manager and Commission:

April 8, 2004 City Manager and Elected Officials:

In the wake of your wise decision not to adopt an ordinance for the benefit of one man to sell alcohol in his (and thankfully our city's only) all nude establishment, I'd like to take the opportunity to thank you for keeping this Pandora's box closed. I am told that local bars were watching to be sure there would be no monopoly granted that would deprive them of fair and equitable treatment by the City, should Club Madonna compete with their liquor sales, but be the only full liquor establishment with full nudity

In addition, it has come to my attention that Mr. Griffith, while being touted by some as a good, honest businessman was in fact, found to have under-reported his taxes by approximately $2,000,000. That's a lot of income to hide when your taxes come to $2,000,000. In addition, the court found that 30 days after this judgment against him, Mr. Griffith tried to evade payment of his taxes (and here the term "fraudulent" was used in the court transcript) transferring all his assets to his then new wife and declaring bankruptcy. He tried to fold the $2,000,000 in taxes due into the dischargeable debts in his bankruptcy, He lost, then appealed, and he lost again. The cases are public information and are easily accessible on the Internet. His appeal was denied March 4, 2000 by the United States Court of Appeals – Eleventh Circuit (No 97-4845). I am not sure how he can be the owner of Club Madonna under these circumstances, let alone qualify for a liquor license.

How fortunate that Miami Beach officials did not change its laws to benefit such a litigious, tax-evading citizen (although he does not even reside in our city). That would have been particularly embarrassing considering how hard the city administration and commissions strove to maintain such a fine ethical stance to the public. Many citizens that I have never met have approached me in my daily errands around town to thank me for standing up on this issue. When it comes to the quality of life here in Miami Beach, "sometimes the needs (and the wants) of the many outweigh the needs (and wants) of the few," as Dr. Spock once said. Mayor Dermer in his deciding vote, put it appropriately when he said, "When push comes to shove go with the residents."

I hope we (and many staff personnel) don't need to waste any more time and energy on this issue. Mr. Griffith has been afforded a full and fair process and his request was respectfully denied. Thank you again for maintaining the high standards we expect from our elected officials.

Sincerely,

Jane Gross

Interestingly, she kowtows to Mayor Dermer for casting the deciding vote, when Jose Smith had also changed his vote. In any event, she is saying something like, once a fraudster always a fraudster. That is, if he ever were a fraudster. Never mind that the court at one time said not. That is not how equity works in America. After studying the same documents on the Internet available to her, we can understand why Griffith would take offense at that letter alone, regardless of what she might have otherwise said, and sue her for libel. Her attorney said Mrs. Gross was merely paraphrasing or quoting judicial reports in tax cases, which would probably not be actionable if not maliciously made to imply that Griffith was a criminal. The tax cases involving Griffith readily found on the Internet are archaic but do provide insight into his business operations.

"The case lasted forty years and went to the Supreme Court, and I had to pay $700,000 in the end," said Griffith when I called and asked him about the taxes. "My accountant did my taxes. There was a problem with depreciation, and the IRS said I took more out than

I put in. There is no way I made enough profit to owe two-million dollars."

The confusion that led to the tax assessments beginning around 1969 with a stated deficiency of $60 and mounting to a high of $148,000 in 1975, was by no means unusual for small business owners who set up multiple legal entities to shield the owner while protecting each one against the liabilities of the other entities so they are not all brought down at once, and then wind up transferring money around the various entities to meet cash contingencies, some of the cash coming into and out of the personal accounts of the owner, worsening the confusion caused by comingling of funds. When the owner and his employees keep inadequate records, accountants are especially hard pressed to properly allocate the cash being sloshed around every which way. Griffith's records happened to be in shambles at the time, something accountants are all too familiar with and are happy to deal with for a fee.

Griffith used the popular Subchapter S corporate form for some of his entities, allowing him to shield himself from liability while having the gains flow through to him directly without being first taxed as dividends as in a regular corporation. He would have been allowed to take losses up to the amount of his contributions to the entity; anything in excess of that had to be held over pending accumulation of adequate profits, or further contributions from him. If he withdrew more money than he put into a specific S-corporation, it would be taxable income.

Griffith's tax situation was further complicated by certain payments to the order of "cash" and by his keeping of a bank account called "My Third Wife, George," which he used in part for his personal gambling pursuits; by depreciation and maintenance deductions; by carrying backwards and forwards certain tax credits; and there was the matter of deducting expenses for a house which he lived in and was owned by his corporation—that proved no fraud, said the court. His accountant, by the way, was not a certified public accountant or an enrolled agent, yet Griffith gave him an unlimited power of attorney on tax Form 2848 to represent Griffith in all matters before the IRS for the years 1970-1979, although that form is valid only for persons eligible to practice before the IRS, a distinction raised by the tax court in respect to the validity of a consent the accountant signed to extend the statute of limitations.

Among various court filings, which Jane Gross apparently noticed, may be found references to a tax liability of $2 million. We would expect her to carefully read the documents from her perspective as a former corporate controller with bookkeeping experience.

The tax court's Memorandum on Griffith's 1988 appeal (TC1988-445) found a $620,000 tax deficiency due from Griffith for the years 1968-1978, and another $103,000 due from a regular corporation. To those deficiencies were added a 50% fraud penalty per Section of 6653(b) of the Internal Revenue Code. His personal income as a single individual for those years would have been about $1 million at the marginal tax rates prevailing, which in some years ran as high as 70% for income $100,000 or more.

After considering Griffith's various entities, their expenses and other deductions, the court found no clear and convincing proof of fraud: "After having viewed the witnesses at trial and taking note of petitioner's level of formal education, we do not believe he intended to evade taxes he knew were owing. Petitioner is an astute businessman and has hired accountants to do his tax planning. No evidence presented at trial convinced us that petitioner conveyed an intent to carry out fraudulent schemes with his accountants, nor were we convinced he tried to evade taxes without his accountants' knowledge. Additionally, we do not find fraud in 1969, 1970, 1972 or 1973, the years before us solely by reason of respondent's disallowance of net operating loss carrybacks and investment tax credit carrybacks and carryforwards."

If Jane Gross had relied on this particular aspect of Griffith's tax woes to allege to others that Griffith was a tax cheat, her allegation would probably be defamatory.

The IRS noted that Griffith had the aid of key employees in running his enormous business, so his personal responsibility, if there had been any hanky-panky by underlings, would be doubtful to a jury.

Interestingly, Jane Gross was herself subject to allegations of irresponsible financial oversight in a 2012 scandal over alleged embezzlement and unauthorized compensation of over $7 million by Kathryn Abbate, CEO of the Miami Beach Community Health Center Inc., a non-profit health facility funded in part by the public and is well known for its treatment of relatively poor people and AIDS patients. Outsiders were astonished at how obvious the malefactions should have been to overseers. Jane Gross was Chairman of the corporation at the time. The corporation is blaming its accountants for inadequate oversight.

But that was not the end of Griffith's tax ordeal. On October 10, 1988, less than a month after the 1988 decision absolving him from fraud penalties, a corporation called NuWave was formed with his girlfriend Linda owning all the stock. Nine months later, on June 8, 1989, they married, and, pursuant to an prenuptial agreement, three Griffith corporations and $300,000 in notes were transferred to them as tenants by the entirety, and assets from another of his corporations was transferred to NuWave, Inc. The IRS made a fresh total assessment against Griffith in September 28, 1989, amounting to $2 million. The transfers to himself and wife as tenants, and to his wife alone, appeared to be a classic "badge of fraud" or indication of fraudulent transfer to evade the debt of the transferor, Griffith. 1989.

However, explained the appellate Circuit Court, the Tax Court believed the United States could not claw back the assets: "The assets transferred pursuant to the antenuptial agreement were insulated from being levied upon because assets held by tenants in the entirety cannot be levied upon without a judgment against both owners. Additionally, Griffith no longer had any ownership interest in those assets transferred to NuWave, Inc."

The lower court apparently ignored the basic principles expressed in Queen Elizabeth I's 1570 "Act Against Fraudulent Deeds, Gifts, Alienations, &c." and Her Majesty's 1585 "Act Against Covenous and Fraudulent Conveyances. For example, the 1570 Act was "For the Avoiding and Abolishing of feigned, covinous and fraudulent Feoffments, Gifts, Grants, Alienations, Conveyances, Bonds, Suits, Judgments and Executions, as well of Lands and Tenements as of Goods and Chattels, more commonly used and practice in these Days than hath been seen or heard heretofore: which Feoffments, Gifts, Grants, Alienations, Conveyances, Bonds, Suits, Judgments and Executions, have been and are devised and contrived of Malice, Fraud, Covin, Collusion or Guile, to the End, Purpose and Intent, to delay, hinder, or defraud Creditors and others of their just and lawful Actions, Suits, Debts, Accounts, Damages, Penalties, Forfeitures, Heriots, Mortuaries, and Reliefs, not only to the Let or Hinderance of the due Course and Execution of Law and Justice, but also to the Overthrow of all true and plain Dealing, Bargaining and Chevisance between Man and Man, without which no Commonwealth or civil Society can be maintained or continued."

On January 15, 1993, Griffith filed for bankruptcy and tried to get his tax debt discharged. The government objected and the Bankruptcy Court agreed: "Although there was no evasion with respect to the assessment of the tax," stated the Circuit Court, "the bankruptcy court, looking to the 'badges of fraud,' found that Griffith's conduct occurring after the Tax Court issued its decision amounted to a willful attempt to evade or defeat the payment of the tax debt." The applicable statute spoke about evading or defeating assessments but did not use the word 'payment,' as it did in other statutes, wherefore the pettifoggers proceeded to quibble over results found in a previous case, where the taxpayer had paid some legitimate obligations and was thus left bereft of funds to pay a tax assessment, that a taxpayer may not deliberately evade or defeat an assessment, but may legally avoid paying the tax assessed. We notice that several vendors supplying the Gayety Theatre brought suits against it during those years, leading us to believe Griffith was hard pressed for cash for some reason, that the squeeze was being put on him, perhaps for his gambling debts.

Ah, but this case was presumably different, reasoned the casuists, demonstrating that common law reasoning on statutes is irrational inasmuch as its principles and therefore the written codes interpreted are not set in stone because standards must be flexible enough to allow judges to make novel or equitable decisions to suit exceptional cases, thus fictitiously upholding their previous decisions.

"The bankruptcy court's finding," held the appellate court, "that Griffith's transfer of property to Linda implicated several badges of fraud, including being 'an exchange to a family member, during a period of serious financial difficulty, for inadequate consideration,' is not clearly erroneous. These findings are sufficient to justify a finding of fraud and, thus, to support the finding that Griffith's conduct was willful. See Sternberg, 229 B.R. at 246 ('While a single badge of fraud may amount to only a suspicious circumstance, a combination of them will justify a finding of fraud.'). III. Conclusion We AFFIRM the district court's order affirming the bankruptcy court's determination that Griffith's tax debts are non-dischargeable under 523(a)(1)(C)." See: in Re: Leroy Charles Griffith, Debtor. Leroy

Charles Griffith, Plaintiff-Appellant, v. United States of America, Defendant-Appellee., 206 F.3d 1389 (11th Cir. 2000)

The decision was explained in the Treasury Department's General Litigation Bulletin 475 of June 30, 2000. The Circuit Court initially thought that Congress had deliberately avoided the phrase 'in payment thereof' from the statute because in other statutes it usually used the language "willfully attempts to evade or defeat any such tax or the payment thereof" because that would give bankrupts a "fresh start," and held that Griffith was relieved of liability. However, on rehearing the case, the Circuit court found its interpretation of Congressional intent too broad: "Applying this new interpretation to the facts of the case, the Eleventh Circuit found that mere nonpayment would exclude a debtor from liability, but upheld the lower court's determination, that the debtor Griffith committed fraud in his transfer of property not clearly erroneous. According to the court, Griffith (1) had a duty under the law to pay taxes; (2) knew he had that duty and (3) voluntarily and intentionally violated that duty. Therefore, the debtor's tax debts were non-dischargeable."

So there was no fraud as to the assessment of the tax, but civil not criminal fraud was found as to the payment of taxes assessed. The U.S. Supreme Court refused to hear Griffith's appeal. He wound up paying $700,000, he says, not $2 million. Would it them be actionable defamation for Jane Gross to say, based on this tax squabble with the United States in which the courts waffled from no fraud to fraud and back, that Griffith, despite the arguments of his lawyers to the contrary, was a tax cheat, that he tried to cheat the government out of $2 million? A statement that Griffith had a propensity to cheat or evade taxes based on this case would be inadmissible as evidence in a court of law.

Let those without sin subject volunteer for a thorough audit of their returns over the last 40 years and cast the first stone, and ask if she cast hers maliciously. Griffith might say that it is the duty of every citizen to avoid taxes to restrain the government from tyranny, and that he had no fraudulent intention to evade taxes. No less than Justice Learned Hand famously said, in Commissioner of Internal Revenue v. Newman (1947), "Over and over again courts have said that there is nothing sinister in so arranging one's affairs as to keep taxes as low as possible. Everybody does so, rich or poor; and all do right, for nobody owes any public duty to pay more than the law demands: taxes are enforced exactions, not voluntary contributions. To demand more in the name of morals is mere cant." The Newman case involved the use of a trust by a family to reallocate income to avoid taxes, and not simply to provide security for its children. The commissioner presumed the trust agreement, the intent of which the lawyers quibbled over, was a fraudulent scheme to evade taxes on an independently wealth wife's income.

The line between avoidance and evasion is thin and goes to unseen intentions presumed though fallible inductive reasoning upon the observation of limited facts.

In any case, the intention of Jane Gross appears to have been to assert that Griffith was, at the time she made her statement, a “tax-evading citizen” hence someone currently cheating on his taxes, a conclusion unsupported by fact and based on a spurious interpretation of events thirty years prior.

When the Eleventh Circuit Court of Miami-Dade County dismissed Griffith's complaint against Jane Gross on September 28, 2004, the court declared that it had analyzed the tax and bankruptcy proceedings and determined that her statements reflected true or accurate republications of judicial opinions and were therefore not legally actionable. The court's finding on that point was based on misunderstanding and false analysis, and it ignored the fact that Jane Gross misrepresented the dated judicial opinions so as to cast Griffith in a bad current light in order to defame him as a chronic tax cheat or evader. It should appear to a reasonable judge unprejudiced by the sight of pornographic pictures presented to him, which were not even taken from the rather tame Club Madonna website, that the defendant's statement was reckless in the sense that, if she were not motivated by self-righteous, Puritanical ill will or malice, she would have known it was probably untrue.

Jane Gross' legal fees to defend against Griffith's libel and slander suit already ran an a phenomenal $30,000 by the time the city's commissioners and lawyers met in closed executive sessions to discuss settling the federal suit against the city. The libel suit had been dismissed but Griffith had moved for a rehearing, and another $100,000 in fees was expected, which would of course come out of the pocket of Commissioner Gross. As a result the secret sessions took on the shady aura of crime family meetings. Griffith, it was pronounced, had gotten "personal." A suit against a commissioner's wife constituted an attack on their "family." Griffith must drop both the federal suit and the defamation suit, and pay the private party's fees of $30,000, or he would get no deal at all. And the transcripts even as redacted make it clear that whatever the deal was, he was bound to ultimately lose for his insult to The Family, which it construed as "blackmail." That is, any settlement with a blackmailer would definitely not be made in good faith.

On the other hand, Griffith construed the condition that he pay Jane Gross' $30,000 fee as "extortion" or bribery, and his attorney reported the "linkage" of personal and official business to the State Attorney. State Attorney Joe Centorino handed it off to the Ethics Commission, which he now directs.

City attorneys like to say that disagreeable suits against the city and its ruling "family" are baseless and frivolous. Was Griffith's suit against the commissioner's wife groundless, merely a blackmail attempt answered by an extortionate demand, or extortion compounded? Exactly what had Jane Gross said or done to draw a libel suit, and was her so-called defamation legally actionable? Perhaps the complaint was specific about what was said orally and by email, but the case was marked for destruction in 2009. Griffith has declined to provide the information pending the renewal of the lawsuit. Other sources are being queried as we speak.

Jane Gross, who claimed she is not a prude, and said she had a business on historically seamy Washington Avenue, was dead set against mixing total nudity and alcohol on her avenue. That avenue included alcohol related businesses her husband had a financial interest in via a partnership, as disclosed in his 2005 campaign finance filing, including MB Two Liquor Store, and Club B.E.D. During the composition of this research report, I asked Saul Gross to comment on whether or not his investments in competing alcohol-related businesses while voting to withhold a liquor license from Club Madonna constituted an unethical conflict of interest. His wife, in her widely circulated letter to the City Manager and Commissioners of April 8, 2004, stated that, ".... I am told that local bars were watching to be sure there would be no monopoly granted that would deprive them of fair and equitable treatment by the City, should Club Madonna compete with their liquor sales..."

Although Saul Gross is no longer a commissioner, City Attorney Jose Smith, apparently acting as his attorney, interceded on August 14, 2013, denouncing me as "demented," relating me to a despised Internet character he calls "The Count," some fictitious character who apparently said Smith is intellectually challenged. He advised Gross not to answer my question. Smith characteristically denigrates and defames interlocutors who beg askance of him and his colleagues, and any complaint he does not agree with is naturally "baseless and frivolous." "Delusional" is one of his favorite terms. His assertion that critics of his power clique are mentally diseased reminds one of how Soviet psychiatrists diagnosed and committed dissidents to gulags for being afflicted with "sluggish schizophrenia," the failure to recognize that their government was the best of all possible governments.

A proposed amendment was in the works since 2003 to change the City of Miami Beach's antiquated ordinance sections 6-40 and 6-41, prohibiting total nudity and sexual conduct where alcoholic beverages were being served, to allow alcoholic beverage establishments to offer both partial nudity and totally nude adult entertainment. The contemplated amendment would have allowed total nudity only on stage, and lap dancing too, but would have prohibited private booths. Total nudity by definition is not limited to exposed genitals: a bared nipple suffices.

Jane Gross claimed to have the interests of children at a nearby school at heart in her adamant opposition to the amendment, although the club agreed not to operate during school hours, and few people knew it did not serve liquor. Generally speaking, first readings are not public hearings; however, the mayor who chairs the commission may allow members of the public to be heard and, according to the Citizens Bill of Rights, they have a right to be heard. Jane Gross did not testify at the January 14, 2004, first reading of the proposed ordinance amendment. Only one member of the public, Dr. Morris Sunshine, a sociologist, did so, to say that proliferation could be thwarted by prohibiting both lap dancing and private rooms. Commissioner Gross then worried about the proliferation of bawdy houses, but Planning Director Jorge Gomez said that distance regulations and state statutes would limit the spread. Indeed, there were objections all along that Club Madonna would in effect have a monopoly on the trade; on the other hand, that might not be such a bad thing since there would be no proliferation. Besides, Club Madonna was well kept, large investment property on an otherwise decrepit block. The resolution passed 5-2, with Dermer, Smith, Cruz, Garcia, and Steinberg in favor, and Bower and Gross opposed, therefore the issue would have a second, public reading.

All hell broke loose on Griffith's head at the second reading held on March 17, 2004. That hell was, he insists, "orchestrated" by Jane Gross, whom he said launched an email campaign against him, falsely accusing him of being a tax cheat and spawning prostitution among other things. He declined to provide us with a copy of the email because his attorneys are contemplating renewed litigation.

As a result of the alleged "smear campaign" of Jane Gross, the proposed resolution was greeted by a column of opponents at the second reading, creating the impression that the public was overwhelmingly against such an inherently immoral proposal.

Helen Stank (?), representing PACT (People Acting For People Together) introduced the opposition at the school. She said her organization represented 50,000 people among whom were parents with children attending the meeting for the purpose. The City Manager translated into English the testimony of Patricia Ramirez, representing the PTA. She complained about the television screen depicting nude dancing on the front of Club Madonna, remarking that it was just a few steps from the school. Her 9-year old daughter said kids passed by the club and saw screens of naked ladies when they passed by the place, and talked about it at school: "It is not right." Olga Figueras, principal of Feinberg/Fisher Elementary School, situated a block from Club Madonna, complained that society was too permissive, and was teaching children to murder and sexually violate one another, and that prostitution and drug abuse were normal. A statement was read, written by a woman who was taken to hospital because her legs fell asleep sitting on the auditorium chair: We must help save the children from the half-clad woman sitting on the big chair outside the theatre in the early evenings. Carmen Ojeda, a parent, complained that the proponents for the ordinance amendment were only interested in money when they should be considering the concerns of residents. Timothy Sally, a teacher at the school for 24 years, said we need to help our children because they are in trouble, that children are our future, so we must teach them well, let them lead the way, showing all the beauty they have inside, reminding us how we used to be, and give them a sense of pride to make that easier.

And there were others opposed, including Dr. Morris Sunshine, who elaborated on his notion that the real issue was not nudity but lap dancing resulting in sexual arousal enhanced by the consumption of alcohol, which was bound to result in the release onto the streets gangs of intoxicated young men in a state of arousal, ready for anything, and would hugely boost the prostitution market. He said a lap dancing advertisement, "Friction and Full Release," shown to the Planning Board was a big reason why the Board voted against the ordinance 6-0. He cited two dozen arrests at the Pink Pussycat on the mainland, for exposure of genitals and prostitution and so on, and said the community cannot expect any higher moral behavior at Club Madonna even though no record of immoral behavior was presented. He said he had received no email whatsoever from parents wishing that their daughters could be strippers, and when that time came, he would move to Siberia.

Erika Brigham, a local resident who used to have a business around the corner from Club Madonna, said that serving liquor at the club would result in the degradation of women and Washington Avenue, that kids on their way to school would be confronted by customers hanging out after the club closed in the early morning, and that having horny, drunken men wandering around the streets would not be in the best interests of the community. Conventioneers, she said, could go over to the mainland if they wanted to drink and consort with naked women at clubs.

Atlanta had nearly 41 strip clubs back in 2000. An economist asserted in Atlanta Magazine that nudie bars generate more economic impact than the Braves, Falcons, and Hawks sports teams combined. Conventioneers swarm there to honor the combination of nudity and alcohol.

David Kelsey, president of the local hotel and restaurant club testified that conventioneers do expect adult entertainment and they should have it. As for prostitution, he said it is centered on Loews Hotel over on Collins Avenue, not near Club Madonna, where nude entertainment was offered for eight years without adverse incidents.

Jane Gross was evidently behind the campaign. Commissioner Cruz said he had respect for her but differed from her opinion. He said there was no data supporting her notion that prostitution had risen because of the presence of Club Madonna, and that large events such as the Boat Show drew prostitutes, mainly to the large hotels, not to Club Madonna, so Club Madonna was not the problem. Commissioner Garcia stated that he did not see a big deal on the issue, that there was more violence and nudity on television than can ever be seen in Club Madonna.

Commissioner Jose Smith observed that total nudity was a constitutional right, yet inquired about the constitutionality of the combination of nudity and alcohol. City Attorney Gary Held said there is no constitutional right to enjoy alcohol while viewing nude dancing. The issue depends on community preference.

Mayor Dermer waffled for a moment, and asked City Manager Jorge Gonzalez for his recommendation. Gonzalez said the amendment should be denied because there would be few positive benefits if it were approved. Dermer, not wanting to take personal responsibility for his hypocrisy on the issue, said Gonzalez was a wise, good, and decent manager, so he would rely on his opinion, and that of the Planning Board.

Griffith had clearly been broadsided. Still the vote against his desired objective was close, 4-3, with Dermer, Gross, Bower, and Smith against the Club Madonna proposal, and Cruz, Garcia and Steinberg in favor. Both Dermer and Smith had changed their position from positive on Club Madonna to negative. It was rumored that Smith began to align himself with Dermer on issues, agreeing not to run against him for mayor in exchange for appointment to the lucrative city attorney position. Smith, subsequent to his appointment to that job in 2006, has vehemently denied that rumor in insulting terms.

At a 2005 closed door conventicle discussing a possible settlement, Smith said. "I feel even uncomfortable sending him the message that we are even going to be speaking to him, because from everything that we've heard – and I've listened to a lot of the Planning Board discussion on this and how we were trying to accommodate, how we were going to do this so that it wouldn't have an effect and impact in the surrounding area – but when those school kids came in and the parents and the teachers and everything else, even though I was open-minded originally and thought maybe we could come up with an ordinance, I just don't see how, personally, I can support what he is asking for under any circumstances, whether he dismisses Saul, whether he pays attorney fees. I just don't see him – I don't see myself agreeing to any alcohol and nudity at that location.

So Griffith, not about to give up his cause, had brought the federal suit that resulted in the closed door meetings, and then the suit against Jane Gross. The federal suit was dropped, and a settlement was reached in the suit against Jane Gross wherein Griffith promised to cause his suit to be dismissed with prejudice, meaning the decision was final, and not to pursue his appeal of the dismissal of that case, and Ms. Gross agreed not to file a motion for attorney fees or sue for malicious prosecution. Both parties generally released the other from all claims arising from the incidents mentioned in the complaint, without admission of wrongdoing. But The Family wanted her attorney fees paid to save her husband the expense, or else there would be no legislative access, or so it was alleged.

According to a CBS4 Investigates report on Independence Day 2008, former Commissioner Luis Garcia Jr. admitted that the city would not consider Griffith's petition after he dropped his suit against the city in consideration of getting that consideration unless he paid Jane Gross' expenses. CBS managed to chase Saul Gross down. He denied he had linked the payment of his wife's legal fees to Griffith's access to the legislative process. City Attorney Jose Smith, when questioned, blamed Griffith for the linkage. But Griffith was blunt: "It is extortion, I mean, if somebody tells you that they're not going to hear city business unless I'm paying 35 thousand (or) 30 thousand dollars, that's extortion," he reportedly told the I-team.

Leroy Griffith was reportedly "blunt" when asked what he thought the bottom line to all this was: "It is extortion. I mean, if somebody tells you that they're [not] going to hear city business unless I'm paying 35 thousand (or) 30 thousand dollars, that's extortion," he told the CBS Investigative Team.

He said a city attorney had approached him and said he would not get any consideration if he did not pay Jane Gross' $30,000 in legal fees. She was a private person, not a public official, and the city had no business paying her fees simply because she was the wife of a commissioner. Therefore Griffith reported the solicitation of the bribe to the State attorney. As far as he was concerned, they were obviously committing the crime of extortion and should be prosecuted.

Joe Centorino, a public corruption prosecutor for the State Attorney office who has since been appointed to the position of Director of the Miami-Dade County Commission on Ethics and Public Trust, a sort of retirement farm for old prosecutors, washed his hands of Griffith's complaint, dumping it onto the relatively toothless Ethics Commission.

The Ethics Commission has such limited jurisdiction and incapacity to seriously punish infractions that it is considered virtually useless except as a publicity or educational device to teach ignorant officials the difference between good and evil, one main evil being the use of public office for private gain, which is a rather common practice since time immemorial. There is a good reason, for example, for requiring all campaign contributions be reported. Jimmy Morales, the Harvard law school grad and former Miami-Dade Commissioner who was appointed City Manager for the City of Miami Beach to replace involuntarily retired Jorge Gonzalez, advertises that he had a hand in creating the Ethics Commission, but he does not advertise that subsequently pled no contest to an ethics charge brought against him for not providing documentation for $580,081 in campaign expenditures, and agreed to pay a stunning $250 fine. As we have seen, Gongora was not as fortunate as the county bureaucrat: He paid a fine of $2,000 for a mere $3,000 in unreported contributions.

Ethics Commission Advocate Michael Murawski, although impeded by conflicting statements from city attorneys and by reluctance to disclose evidence, concluded that, "it appears very likely that Commissioner Gross, along with other City Commissioners, engaged in wholly inappropriate behavior by linking and conditioning the payment of Mrs. Gross's legal fees to the settlement negotiations between Griffith and the City. It would be no less inapt but is extremely doubtful, that the City would have attempted to secure payment of legal fees for any other citizen victim of a SLAPP suit being sued by an individual who was also suing the City. The evidence suggests that the City Attorney allowed the City Commission to push their collegial bonds over the ethical line."

Murawski used the term SLAPP loosely. Under the Florida law entitled Citizen Participation in Government Act, Strategic Lawsuits Against Public Participation (SLAPP) brought to shut people up with the threat of expensive lawsuits are disallowed only when filed by "governmental entities" against private persons, and not by private persons such as Griffith against other private persons or public officials. However, that Murawski's analogy was loose is beside the point, the point being the apparent "extortion" of money to pay a private individual's legal fees in return for favorable government action.

Why State Attorney Joe Centorino did not prefer criminal charges, and instead referred the matter to the Ethics Commission, remains a mystery at press time. Extortion is generally defined as the unlawful taking by any officer, by color of his office, of any money or thing of value that is not due to him, or more than is due, or before it is due, while bribery is generally defined as the receiving or offering any undue reward by or to any person whomsoever, whose ordinary profession or business relates to the administration of public justice, in order to influence his behavior in office, and to incline him to act contrary to his duty and the known rules of honesty and integrity. Who knows what Centorino was thinking given his experience with positive Florida law?

Advocate Murawski had a troubling aspect to consider howsoever defined: "The troubling aspect of this case is whether the City inappropriately attempted to wrest payment of Mrs. Gross's legal fees from Griffith by conditioning their payment on resolving the lawsuit between Griffith and the City. Since the City knew, through Ms. Olin's research and opinion that the City could not simply outright pay Mrs. Gross's legal fees, it seems all most certain that the City raised the idea with Griffith."

Nonetheless, Murawski, despite behavior that smacked of extortion, and although he averred that, "Undoubtedly some City of Miami Beach officials improperly intertwined City business with the personal lawsuit pending against Commissioner Gross's wife and may have improperly 'participated' in Commission discussions when they stood to be enhanced by the action of the board," he decided to dismiss the matter, first of all, because "the officials acted with apparent full knowledge, advice and approval of the City Attorney's office and we have generally declined to file complaints in the past in such situations."

That is, the Ethics Commission has a tradition of not prosecuting officials who act under advice of city attorneys. City attorneys who engage in unethical behavior are also immune from action by the Ethics Commission, but let them be advised against similar appearances of impropriety. There were howls of derision from activists inasmuch as everyone accused of wrongdoing in the case except wealthy banker Saul Gross was an attorney, so there were city attorneys advising attorneys on the commission to engage in unethical behavior; they like everyone else are presumed to know the difference between right and wrong may do wrong with immunity. Perhaps they have been doing wrong so long that wrong seems right.

At an Ethics Commission meeting with bloggers on March 7, 2012, I spoke on the subject of legal professionalism as a form of "racism." I voiced the historic concern that lawyers are becoming more and more of a scourge on society, and observed that the Ethics Commission itself is dominated by lawyers at the behest of a legislature dominated by lawyers. I mentioned the Griffith case, and how the advocate had determined that a matter would not be prosecuted because the unethical conduct was a tradition and had been condoned by legal counsel. The advocate asked if I would think it was all right to do something if an attorney said it was legal, to which I replied, "No, not unless I were morally and mentally incompetent." I mentioned that the advocate had implied in one of his Instructions that one does not have to be a lawyer or expert to know the difference between right and wrong:

"We define ethics as knowing the difference between what you have a right to do and what is the right thing to do. In our opinion, ethical behavior is quite simply the doing of what is right, what is good. In the realm of public governance that generally means doing what is in the best interests of the citizenry. This should be a simple task. It should not require the burdensome interpretation of legalese or engaging in lengthy analysis in order to discern what is being done for the 'public' good or what might be being done for a personal or private good."

I noted the classical definition of sophists, from Socrates on down. Once a case gets into the hands of the casuists, the difference between right and wrong becomes confused and principles are lost in the shuffle. Lawyers are likely to favor their own kind in ethical disputes, as can be seen in the hoary history of the bar.

The Ethics Commission took the Advocate's report in the Club Madonna case to heart, and sat on fence with a 2-2 vote, but the ethics commissioners were unanimous in their January 29, 2009, decision to have him issue a Letter of Instruction cautioning county officials against like appearances of impropriety in the future: "We hope this Letter of Instruction impresses upon the City of Miami Beach as well as all governments subject to our jurisdiction, that they must be mindful that their own best interests and those of their citizens are best served by open, honest and transparent governance regardless of whether it is 'legally' or 'ethically' required."

Griffith rejoiced at the unanimity, but it was of little or no consequence to his cause.

Now Griffith had already dropped his first federal suit, without prejudice so he could renew it, and his suit against Jane Gross, with prejudice, so it would be final, with the understanding that Jane Gross would pay her own fees. Consideration: the commission would discuss his proposal. But that is all the commissioners did on December 7, 2005, discuss it.

Simon Cruz, whose attractive wife Mariana was identified by the scandal-mongering Miami New Times as a former sexy film actress whose dog bit a postal worker delivering mail at her mansion, said the issue had been clouded by personal concerns, that there was a pink elephant in the room that prevented revisiting Griffith's cause until he resolved the personal matter.

Of course that would be the $30,000 in fees that Commissioner Gross had to pay for his wife, for no one would give a hoot if the fees had accrued to some Jane Doe unrelated to the commissioners. City Attorney Murray Dubbin reminded the commissioners that there were no long any outstanding suits in the matter, and that the Griffith should be treated as anybody making an application for an ordinance change, referring the matter to the appropriate committee. Nevertheless, said Cruz, there was that personal matter. Hence the discussion was dropped because here was no sentiment to continue.

Griffith steamed in his juices for some time while his efforts to get his cause reconsidered were in vain. So the pink elephant, appalled at the continuing attempt to get him to pay Jane Gross' attorney fees, which was not only, as he saw it, extortion and bribery, but was contrary to the settlement agreement he had made with her, brought another civil suit, on December 16, 2008, in federal court against the conspirators. Saul Gross, Simon Cruz, Jose Smith, Gary Held, Murray Dubbin and David Dermer, Club Madonna alleged, had conspired to deprive and actually deprived it of access to the city's legislative process. Furthermore, the city's ordinances are unconstitutional to begin with. The alleged extortionate behavior of the commissioners and city attorneys was referred to.

Griffith's 2008 complaint filed in federal court alleged that Assistant City Attorney Jean Olin, who handles ethical issues for the city, advised officials that the city must not pay a private citizen's legal fees. "On June 8, 2005, July 6, 2005 and July 27, 2005, the City Commission met in closed-door, executive session meetings to discuss Club Madonna. According to the Miami-Dade County

Ethics Report, despite having been informed that the issue of Mrs. Gross' legal fees was not City business, "[t]here is little doubt that the issue of having Griffith pay Mrs. Gross' attorney's fees was discussed at least some of the executive sessions in question. The City admits as much."

The conclusion of the Ethics Report was quoted in the federal complaint: "In conclusion, it appears very likely that Commissioner Gross, along with other City Commissioners, engaged in wholly inappropriate behavior by linking and conditioning the payment of Mrs. Gross's legal fees to the settlement negotiations between Griffith and the City."

Again we are astonished that Griffith, after the abuse he had suffered at The Family's hands, would trustingly relegate the fate of his quest into their hands again, agreeing to dismiss the suit against the alleged conspirators with prejudice, expecting that they, after one of their own wives was personally insulted with a lawsuit, would give him a fair hearing. Talk about an inherent conflict of interest! But that is what he did. Unsurprisingly, the September 9. 2009, first reading was a charade with a foregone conclusion, the unanimous rejection of his proposed ordinance for a liquor license. Of course the ordinance was rejected without prejudice, meaning that he could start all over in a lower committee that was dead set against the idea. Good luck with that, Larry, you balmy fool.

Again, the settlement of the federal suit was clearly worded: "The parties acknowledge that adoption will require two readings and a public hearing at the second reading, but that failure to obtain a majority vote at the first reading will mean no second reading and public hearing will be held.... Club Madonna agrees that Commissioner Saul Gross will decide for himself whether or not to abstain from discussion or vote on the Proposal. His participation in the Commission's disposition of the Proposal shall not constitute a breach of this Agreement and shall not be grounds for Club

Madonna to make further attack on the City's Ordinances, or a collateral after-the-fact attack on the Commission vote provided for by this Agreement."

Griffith had evidently put himself at the mercy of the very people he had sued, people who had the power to make sure he did not get what he wanted. Accordingly, Griffith is now looking for gunslingers willing to make a collateral attack because he thinks both he and the court were defrauded. He has a good point inasmuch as he says he was led to believe the first reading would not be a public hearing, and that the proposal would pass, perhaps after being referred for redrafting if there were any technical objections from commissioners, then he would have a full-on public hearing at the second reading, which he would prepare for by rallying support. He informed me that there was some back and forth between the attorneys over the technical details, and that he and his attorney were willing to make modifications, but the city attorneys insisted on none.

Indeed, it looks like he was set up for a fall on the first reading on September 9, 2009, and one wonders over the comment of the tax court during his tax travails that he is a savvy businessman, leaving grammar school to launch his career, and the observation that he played cards with so-and-so—he must have been their favorite pigeon. Yes, he is a likeable fellow, no doubt about it!

City Clerk Robert Parcher was careful to announce at the outset of the first reading: "This is not a public hearing." Later on, Mayor Bower would repeat, "This is not a public hearing." And then Jose Smith, now City Attorney, just as the discussion was closing, asked if there were any public comment, prompting Jane Gross to speak. She spoke of the "secondary effects" all over again, the danger to the school, and warned against giving Club Madonna a monopoly or opening the "Pandora's Box, of nudity with alcohol, with no mention of Griffith's tax issues. The City of Miami allows nudity with alcohol, but the City of New York and Las Vegas do not. Remember, she said, that Griffith does not even live or vote here. So just say no.

Since the first reading was not to be a public hearing, there was no crowd present to speak, but Dr. Sunshine, identifying himself as a sociologist, was there as usual to warn against the commission about lap dancing under the influence of alcohol. David Kelsey repeated that it would be foolish to deny Griffith to serve a drink inasmuch as strip clubs have been popular among conventioneers for decades and Miami Beach should have one or they will go elsewhere. Donna Zemo said she had been in tourism for 29 years, and not once has there been a request for a topless dancer, so do not open up a can of worms. Bill Farkas said he had been around for 77 years and had never heard of anyone recommending nudity for historical preservation of the structures of buildings or beautification of the community. Frank Del Vecchio, a former jet fighter pilot and retired attorney, gave legal advice against the adoption of the amended ordinance. Dr. Barry Ragone expressed reservations against the commission regulating morality. Everybody knows about nude clubs, he said, and interested people normally do not go around ask tourist information desks where they are. If the city were to ignore the needs of businesses whose owners do not live in the city, which is true of many businesses, then businesses would have no business being here.

Tammy Talbots said customers are already drunk when they go to Club Madonna. And it is silly to regulate live nudity and not still-life nudity or artistic nudity and performance art at Art Basel, where alcohol is being sold. Is this class discrimination, that we feel people can handle high-class nudity but not low class nudity?

Finally, Griffith introduced himself as the owner of Club Madonna, as someone who has in fact owned a home on Miami Beach, several penthouses, an apartment building, and a number of theatres over the years, but then moved to the mainland because it was more convenient location for him to travel to the airport and his businesses.

He then asked Commissioner Gross what he had against him to try to extort money from him. Jose Smith, now City Attorney, advised Gross not to answer the question. Griffith continued that line of questioning, saying that he had wanted to come to the meeting and make a fresh start, but Jane Gross wheeled in to attack him again so he had to respond to that. Mayor Bower, acting as chair, understood, but did not want him to continue. "What is he afraid of?" Griffith persisted, saying that the city would not even talk to him unless he paid $30,000. "Is that the way you run your city here on Miami Beach?"

Smith, visibly irritated, pronounced him out of order with a wave of his hand. Griffith posed the embarrassing question about extortion again. Mayor Bower pleaded with him to talk about the proposal and to stop accusing people. Finally silenced by disgust, he walked away.

Griffith's attorney, Daniel Aaronson, a former public defender and criminal defense attorney well known for obtaining acquittals in felony cases including two murders, has specialized in adult entertainment and First Amendment cases. He was instrumental in efforts to have Florida's criminal lewdness laws declared unconstitutional. He had lewdness stricken from the state's racketeering law, and established that misdemeanor lewdness requires the presence of one or more offended persons, none of whom may be police officers. Consequently, the Florida legislature amended the laws. He and his partner, James Benjamin, successfully established what evidence cannot be seized by warranted government agencies when searching for evidence of criminal lewdness.

Aaronson told the commission that Griffith is a man of integrity, not an evil ogre intending to attack the city commission. Griffith, he declared, truly believed he had been defamed by Jane Gross, and the very idea that he had sued her to gain advantage in his cause with her husband was patently absurd because the commissioner would naturally be offended. After he took the case, he said, he was told by First Assistant City Attorney Held that the matter of her $30,000 in legal fee had to be resolved before the commission would proceed. But that ran against his grain as a criminal attorney, for he knew the $30,000 would be a bribe. They had a good case in federal court in terms of current law, he said, and the court refused to dismiss it, but Griffith in good faith had agreed to voluntarily dismiss it to obtain the settlement agreement. So here they were, and here he was after having attended many meetings where he was not even allowed to speak.

First Assistant Gary Held said the suit was both against Mr. and Mrs. Gross for libel to begin with, and was an effort to manipulate the city into approving of an ordinance amendment, which the city could not allow anyone to get away with.

Hashing over the history leading up to the settlement agreement was to no avail, impertinent to whether or not the city should amend its ordinance. It would be wrong to say that the commission would be alienated by the current discussion, for they were already alienated by the past, and the 7-0 conclusion they would arrive at on September 9, 2009 was foregone. It was as if to say, "If you want to slap someone with a law suit when you feel wronged, you go right ahead as long as it is not a member of our family. If you do so and cost any one of us money, you will never get what you want." Mind you, the family members, if their hate-Griffith-based self-love was true, would have shared paying the $30,000 legal fee. And if the wealthy Gross' loved the school so much, they might have told Griffith that, if he bore the legal expense they would match it with a contribution of $30,000 to the school.

The first hearing was a charade. No, morals were not being regulated. No mention was made of the Pink Elephant this time. No, the issue was lost on a technicality. You see, the draft of the ordinance had technical faults. There has been a back and forth between Griffith's lawyers and the city attorneys over the wording, but nothing definite was concluded. Aaronson begged the commission to approve of the amendment on the first reading to give him a chance to work things out with the city attorneys. Too bad, too late, technical knockout, you're done, return to Go and start all over again, and lots of luck to you, pal.

So Griffith got his hearing and the decision was unanimous, but he believes he and the court were defrauded. To prove his point he would have to prove he was a fool bamboozled by city officials. It is high unlikely he will get his federal case reopened or a fraud suit tried unless he comes up with a great deal of new evidence.

All he seems to have is his claim that he was supposed to get a public hearing, and that a first hearing is not a public hearing. I contacted City Clerk Rafael Granado and inquired into the general hearing process.

"When the Clerk announces to Commission at beginning of a hearing THIS NOT A PUBLIC HEARING, what does that mean, i.e. what are the ramifications? What then if the chair allows members of the public to speak on the subject; is that proper procedure?"

"It means the Mayor is not required to take public comment/input; but may (and she usually does) - if someone wishes to speak."

"Is the public noticed in advance that the hearing on the agenda item will NOT be a public hearing?" I asked.

"First readings of ordinances are not public hearings," said Granado. "Second readings of ordinances are public hearings. Which are advertised and the public is noticed of same."

"Then would it be improper to vote down ordinance on first reading, especially since public pro and con may not show up and parties might be prejudiced by that lack of input?"

"Please note that all items in the City Commission Agenda, including backup materials, are posted on the City's website. For more information on the legally required public notices you may wish to consult the Office of the City Attorney. I have confirmed with the Office of the City Attorney that Florida Statute 166.041 (3) as well as City Charter Section 2.05 do not require (nor prohibit) a public hearing on a first reading of an ordinance. Thus, City Attorney's Office states that there is no 'impropriety' if an ordinance is voted down on first reading without a public hearing.

"Thank you. Please email me a copy of that statement. The City Clerk at one hearing opened it with THIS IS NOT A PUBLIC HEARING. The parties were informed in advance that it would not be public therefore were not prepared for it."

"I apologize, but I do not understand your question..."

"I reiterate my request here because you may have misunderstood it: Please email me a copy of that statement.... The statement I am referring to is the one made by the city attorney that the described procedure is proper...."

City Attorney Jose Smith interposed himself in the conversation at this juncture, and in his characteristic fashion.

"Why don't you ask your question in simple English so that you can be understood? We do not understand gibberish."

"The Clerk announces to the City Commission at beginning of a hearing on the first reading of an ordinance, THIS NOT A PUBLIC HEARING. The interested party was not prepared for a public hearing, being informed that the public hearing will be at the second reading. The chair allows members of the public to speak on the subject. The city attorney has an interest in the subject matter, and advises that the ordinance should be voted down. The commission votes down the ordinance. Is that proper procedure? You are still talking gibberish. The City Attorney does not 'advise' commissioners on how to vote on an ordinance. The City Attorney's ONLY "interest" is the best interest of the city. The City Attorney would recuse himself on ANY matter affecting his private interests. You, sir, are delusional!"

Again, "delusional" is just a hackneyed term Smith applies to denigrate or defame someone who questions his opinions as to how the world works. To be fair, the settlement agreement made with Smith and the others did not prohibit a down vote at the first reading, and did not call for anyone sued to recuse themselves because of personal interest in the matter. They were simply required to give Griffith a hearing. That it was an unfair hearing is Griffith's mistake or that of his attorneys for allowing him to naively get into such an absurd situation contrary to his best interest. Further, citizens have a right to be heard by commissions, committees, agencies, and the like if being heard does not interfere with the process.

Still, Smith's statement does not make sense. First of all, his duties under Sec. 3.01 of the Charter of Miami Beach, which he does not seem to fully understand after serving as same since 2006, include "(d) to attend all meetings of the City Commission, and (e) he/she shall recommend to the City Commission for adoption, such measures as he/she may deem necessary or expedient." A "recommendation" from the city attorney very well might be considered as his "advice."

Now, then, on the one hand, he claims he does not advise commissioners; on the other hand, he says he would have to recuse himself instead of advising them on matters affecting his interest.

We notice that, at the September 9, 2009, first hearing, Smith advised Commissioner Saul Gross not to answer Griffith's question as to what he had against him that would cause him and his family of commissioners to extort $30,000 from him just to get a hearing of his cause. We notice that Smith tacitly advised the chair, at the last moment, to hear members of the public, starting with Jane Gross, who was standing eagerly by for that purpose.

Anyone of average intelligence would not be surprised that a so-called impartial opinion from the City Attorney Office, which is led by Jose Smith, on the technical aspects of a proposed ordinance, as well as the handling of negotiations with its advocates, would have some influence on the commissioners' votes, and that the opinion and the process leading up to it could be wittingly or unwittingly prejudiced. And the commissioners most likely heard Smith's televised statements, to the effect that Griffith's suit against Jane Gross was an attempt to blackmail the commission into getting him a liquor license.

Indeed, given my personal experience with Smith's penchant or propensity for outraged personal attacks on anyone who questions him and his associates, "The Family" whomsoever it comprises, about allegations of misconduct, even when the questions are put for sake of journalistic balance, I believe that he is their perfect representative and perhaps even their mastermind. After all, we hear no objections from the city commission or other city officials when he bitterly maligns anyone who dares to criticize members of The City Family. Why should they? Are not such attorneys in demand? Do not attorneys have a license to extort, at least in a court of law, and even to advertise themselves as pit bulls? Would the Gotti syndicate have reprimanded or fired Bruce Cutler for defaming their prosecutors?

"We hear these extortion threats all the time in litigation," pronounced Commissioner Smith in a 2005 secret session. "There isn't a lawsuit that doesn't sound like extortion, so I'm not worried about that. If that's what he (Griffith) wants to do, let him have a good time."

It appears to laymen from the evidence including witness statements that city officials did try to extort $30,000 from Griffith, and of course they may be mystified as to why State Attorney Joe Centorino did not bring criminal charges against one or more of the conspirators. It is fair to suspect that he would bring a charge against you and me if we did what they did. Discretion is a key word here, and sovereigns enjoy more of it than anyone else despite the blather that justice is blind.

Two wrongs do not make a right, but the consequences may be mitigated. The Family would not have minded if you or I were sued for defamation for what we said at their hearing, but they felt that Griffith initiated the "blackmail" or extortion process with a suit against one of their own. We understand why Griffith was deeply offended by the "smear campaign" of Jane Gross when he thought he had a lock on a liquor license. But was what she said legally actionable? If it were not, why would Griffith's attorney bring the lawsuit? And is Griffith not as naïve as we think? Well, we would like to have all the facts, ma'am, so we can know exactly what Jane Gross said, and that is why they are being requested at this time.

Griffith declined to turn over the allegedly defamatory email to me because of impending litigation. I informed him that I had been researching his 81-year personal history, and that, in my opinion, he is far more interesting than his lawsuit.

"No, no, this is not about me!" he said on the telephone. "It is about the liquor license, what the city did to me."

"You are a little known South Beach treasure. I would like to compose a biographical sketch in popular style for a national publication."

"Call me in a couple of weeks. I'm going on a cruise," he said impatiently, and hung up.

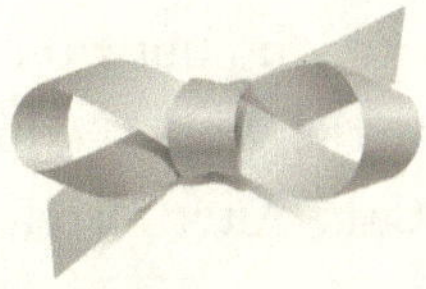

The Lucky Break I Direly Need

I knew that I was avoiding my fate, a few years back, that I was not doing what I was cut out to do, therefore I resigned from the best job I had ever had, and plunged my life savings into the realization of this command:

Be one of the greatest authors the world will ever or never know.

I did not say *writer*: I said *author*. There is a big difference between the two as far as I'm concerned: the writer is a craftsman, perhaps a master craftsman, while the author is an artist, perchance a creative genius. Of course one may become the other, or the two may happily meet in one person.

I inserted the *or* in my command because Success in this world can be a real bitch no matter what one does. With that *or*, my life might end blamelessly, with either success *or* failure. Either one of two essays would then suit the occasion: *How to Succeed*, *or*, *How to Fail*. Both might be put to good use by aspiring writers who want both sides of the story. No doubt Perfectionists would argue that, since no author is perfect, every success constitutes a failure; wherefore history, no matter how it is written, is always a mistake. But never mind, for it behooves us to stick with Either/Or in order to get something done.

As for worldly success, I followed the good advice I received. At least everybody said it was good advice in those days. First of all, they said, be yourself and do what you were cut out to do. That is, do what you love to do most of all, follow your core passion.

I had always fancied myself as a great author. I wrote a cool story in the second grade, about me saving the world. I scrawled out quite a bit between marriages and jobs, but wrote nothing of great note. I was not fully committed to the Work yet; my hand was not set firmly and consistently to the task. After all, there are many ways for a dreamer to avoid reality in between marriages and jobs. Nonetheless, quite a few of my little articles were published in the local papers. More than one substantial person said:

"Never stop writing."

Not only did I stop writing, I stopped reading everything except financial statements and reports. Nor did I watch television or listen to the radio, hence I knew little about what was going on in the world. "Why do the black people look so mad today?" I asked. "Didn't you see the papers? Because the Italian gang beat one of them to death with baseball bats last night." "Oh, I'm sorry to hear that."

What did I do instead of write? I worked and saved. I danced modern, ballet, jazz, and Afro. I acted Method and I sang Blues. I quit smoking everything and I drank lots of Bass Ale to make up for it - I eventually kissed the ale goodbye. That's about it, until 1997, when I quit my job, turned down an even better job, sold my stocks at 5% of what they would be in two years, and fled to paradise to pursue the real love of my life.

"Never stop writing."

I wrote and wrote and wrote, I wrote so much that my worst critic called me "an infernal writing machine." I don't know how much inventory I have saved up, but I think it is quite a lot. When I was not writing, I was in the library stacks, sitting on the cold, tile floors in the aisles, studying, studying, and studying, for years. After all, I was determined to be more than a writer, more than a craftsman who can succeed with superficial thinking and writing. Again, I was to be an *author.* Wherefore I needed to figure things out, deepen my thinking, study the greatest literature ever written, absorb the thoughts of geniuses, and so on. That is what I had literally dreamed of doing one night; the dream included a voice that said, "This is what you must do." I showed up as instructed the next day - at the Hamilton Library in Honolulu.

Sometimes I resorted to magic; I stood in my favorite sections of the library and intuited the contents all at once. Eventually, things started coming to me, out of the deep so to speak. The voices of the masters silently spoke. I was haunted. I was beside myself. I was I and not-I at once. Writing became an interpretive meditation and an addiction. I had been a dancer for several years, in fine shape: and now I was wasting away physically. I no longer "lived here." That 'here', Hawaii, was an earthly paradise that I barely noticed.

Never stop writing, indeed! Writer's block was unknown to me. After all, what else was there to do at the time but write? Nothing, so I had to sit down and do it or go absolutely mad! And here is my beloved work, the product of my core passion and the advice I took from you and you and you, for what it's worth.

What? What credentials? Tear sheets? What tear sheets? The editor wants my credentials and tear sheets, he says, to prove that I can write well, to prove that I know something about my favorite subjects, before he will even read my work, let alone accept it for his publication. That is, the editor is not qualified to judge the quality and substance of my work. I don't understand. My works are my credentials and tear sheets.

Before all, I was told, be original! That was the easiest advice to follow, for I have always been a bit rebellious. As my father puts it, I have a "conflict with authority." Most of us do, and I would capitalize on mine since I have managed to survive authority somehow. Think outside of the box? Hell, I have never been in that box. No, I did not play the ropes, I did not mount the slippery rungs of the ladder to success: I just read some of the best thinkers in the world, wracked my brains for my own positions, and I wrote and wrote, I strove to become my own author and authority, my own man, something more people should do instead of relying on the authorities - believe me, their works should be subjected to a thorough investigation.

Another piece of good advice: If at first you do not succeed, try and try and try and try again ad infinitum. Now I have done very well at whatever I set out to do, even though the work I took up ran against the grain according to occupational preference inventories and the like.

"David does a great job as the company's accountant, but he's not an accountant," said the accountants. In fact, according to the tests, that was the last occupation I should have taken up, but I was hungry one day and the bookkeeping job was immediately available instead of a job as an author, professor, public relations director, interior decorator, hairdresser. I was very good at a lot of other things: dancing, singing, acting, playing instruments, making love and so on, not to mention a few business arts. But just as I was on the verge of completing something, I dropped it and went on to something else.

A ballet teacher once screamed at me: "David, you've got to finish things! Don't fly across the stage, then slump down as you get near the curtains, and slouch into the wings! The audience must believe that you are going somewhere, that your performance has a purpose."

Yes, finish things. Good advice. Perhaps not the best advice for all aspiring writers and authors, however, given the odds against getting accepted by publishers. Finishing things can be a prescription to write oneself to death, to commit suicide by writing. According to the television show about cold cases, it might be a prescription to become a lonely serial killer living in a crummy room papered with rejection slips. But here I am. The ground is coming up fast, for I also took the advice to be courageous, to risk everything for what I love to do most, which is being and becoming myself as one of the greatest authors the world will ever or never know. To wit: I jumped without a parachute, and I need a lucky break, not a crushing blow, so we'll see.

An anecdote: One day I heard Luigi, the jazz-dance master, ask a dance student how he made his living. "Waiting on tables," said the young fellow. "Are you a dancer or a waiter?" Luigi asked. "Uh, a dancer," he replied shamefacedly. "Then dance, don't wait on tables. Dance! Get a job dancing!" exclaimed the master. The last I heard, the young man was studying to be a Jungian psychologist.

Ballet provides a different anecdote: a famous ballet master I know approached a persistent ballet student who believed she would become a professional ballerina. He walked her over to the window of the studio, pointed at the bus stop, and said, "You are not going to succeed at ballet. Take the bus home. Find something else to do." She left in tears.

Here is more good advice for those who aspire to succeed in any walk of life: Be generous with yourself. You must give first, then you will get. If you are generous, your generosity will be returned several fold - or at least with a ten-percent profit margin.

Given my incorrigible vanity, being generous with my work came easily for me. I went to considerable expense photocopying and mailing my brilliant pieces to friends, politicians, activists and editors. But I practically gave up on editors when the Internet was made available. Most publications did not accept online submissions, and one could always publish one's own work on open publishing sites - how convenient! Renting computer time is an expense I can hardly afford any more, but I still am quite generous with my work, posting it here and there. My rule, however, is to hold back 90% of my inventory for commercial use. Even so, one critic told me that I am giving myself away, wasting myself, pissing into infinity - he said that since my work is consistently good, that I should get off the Internet and do some marketing.

Market? Grub for dollars? Who, me, one of the greatest authors the world will ever or never know?

Money isn't everything. Of course writers make money. Great authors must be independent, must they not? What they need is to be discovered, to be adopted by understanding patrons, publishers, editors. What they need is a break! I am getting very lonely for dollars: I want to invite my leggy neighbor from France to dine with me at one of those sidewalk cafe's on Lincoln Mall - by means of a note under the door, she suggested that we do so, but I must beg off with a lie because I do not want to tell her I am presently married to Lady Poverty and simply cannot afford $50 for dinner.

No, of course not, money is not everything. The best things in life, like free lunches, are free. Thousands of people have read my work on the Internet since 1997. I even have fans. I enjoy the comments people make - I have learned to feel sorry for the nasty commentators too. But I would not mind getting my money back. All told, my investment in becoming one of the greatest authors the world will ever or never know is about $100,000. At the very least, I suppose I should receive $100,000 in return for being so generous with my money and self.

Thus far I have received $600. Perhaps the best is to come. I certainly hope so. Now it is too late to start all over again and do it right, play the ropes, climb the slippery slope to success. Just for beginners, I would be long dead before I saved up enough tuition to buy a degree.

I am in dire need of a lucky break.

Don't miss out!

Visit the website below and you can sign up to receive emails whenever David Arthur Walters publishes a new book. There's no charge and no obligation.

https://books2read.com/r/B-A-VVMQ-ZCAUB

BOOKS 2 READ

Connecting independent readers to independent writers.

Also by David Arthur Walters

The Seed That Fell On Rocky Ground
South Beach Florida Coronavirus Panic 2020
The Yellow Vest Movement
Signs of Madness
The Compassionate Heart of America
My Hawaii Nei
The Amazing South Beach HDD Sewer Project
Tracey's Secret
The Amazing Kansas City Library
The Helgalian Chronicles
The Espanola Way of Doing Business
Katherine Sergava
No Hard Feelings - A Dancer's Reflections
Sovereign Immunity - The Debasement of the United States
Helene and Paul - A Characterological Romance
Anarkhia
Random Ramblings
Melange
Ideology aka Idiotology
Accounts Payable - My Life Past Due
The Sly Way Gurdjieff & Ouspensky
Groundhog Days - Timely Intercourse
The Black VIrgin
APXH - Wicked Political Musings
Open Publishing

My Hand

www.ingramcontent.com/pod-product-compliance
Lightning Source LLC
LaVergne TN
LVHW041016150826
845672LV00001B/113

* 9 7 9 8 2 3 0 8 2 3 2 9 2 *